Praise for

THE NEW EDUCATION

Winner of the Association of American Colleges and Universities
2019 Frederic W. Ness Book Award

"*The New Education* is an inspiring, well-researched, and compellingly written manifesto for a revolution in learning and teaching. It is a book for everyone who wants to understand why and how universities need to be reimagined for the twenty-first century—those who have been 'educated' and those who aspire to be. It is the most important book I have read in many years."
—Tony Wagner, Harvard University i-lab expert in residence
and author of *The Global Achievement Gap*

"Davidson is one of the most thoughtful voices from within academia calling for a more student-centered university. *The New Education* is a welcome collection of stories detailing how professors, administrators, and students are designing paths through higher education that are relevant to our changing culture and society. At her best, Davidson writes in the tradition of Du Bois and Dewey, a pragmatist tradition that puts inquiry first and sees learning through the potential of the full, complex human beings students can become."
—*Washington Post*

"Davidson argues persuasively that student-centered, active learning can transform classrooms and even online courses. [Her] enthusiasm and her examples should inspire creativity from a lot more college teachers."
—*New York Times Book Review*

"An engaging, anecdotal, wide-ranging look at educational innovation. A persuasive plea for creative learning."
—*Kirkus Reviews*

"The fact that Davidson is able to bridge her narrative on the history and future of higher education across a popular and academic audience is a testimony to her skills as a scholar, an educator, and a writer. Davidson knows her stuff, has something to say, and has clearly worked very hard in crafting a book that should be discussed by everyone who cares about higher education. Powerfully argued, beautifully written, and doggedly grounded in research and examples."   —*Technology & Learning*, Inside Higher Education

"*The New Education* compels us to equip our students with creative new tactics for navigating the volatile present. Grounded in a deep understanding of both historical and current crises in education, Davidson challenges us to reinvigorate and reconsider our approach to reform."

—Danah Boyd, author of *It's Complicated: The Social Lives of Networked Teens*

"*The New Education* takes a good hard look at the old education, and finds it sorely wanting. Are colleges and universities failing an entire generation of young people? Yes, argues Cathy N. Davidson, a renowned literary scholar and a leader in higher education reform. This is an important and illuminating book whose argument is driven by a deep knowledge of the past and an even deeper commitment to the future."

—Jill Lepore, David Woods Kemper '42 Professor of American History, Harvard University

"*The New Education* offers valuable reflections on ways educators can reexamine approaches to preparing young women and men for a rapidly evolving modern world. Grounded in decades of classroom experience and scholarly inquiry, Cathy N. Davidson makes a compelling case for educators to interrogate traditional structures in higher education, and help students seek, in her words, 'a sustained and productive life.'"

—John J. DeGioia, president, Georgetown University

"Cathy N. Davidson offers us an inspiring and lucid explanation of how we got the educational system we have and how to build the one our students and our country needs and deserves. A must-read for those interested in higher education."

—Diana Taylor, president, Modern Language Association, and university professor, New York University

"A visionary book."   —*Critical Inquiry*

THE NEW
EDUCATION

Also by Cathy N. Davidson

*Now You See It: How the Brain Science of Attention
Will Transform the Way We Live, Work, and Learn*

The Future of Thinking: Learning Institutions in a Digital Age
(with David Theo Goldberg)

*No More Separate Spheres!
A Next Wave American Studies Reader* (co-editor)

Closing: The Life and Death of an American Factory
(with photographer Bill Bamberger)

*The Oxford Companion to Women's Writing
in the United States* (co-editor)

*Subjects and Citizens: Nation, Race, and Gender
from Oroonoko to Anita Hill* (co-editor)

36 Views of Mount Fuji: On Finding Myself in Japan

Reading in America: Literature and Social History (editor)

Revolution and the Word: The Rise of the Novel in America

Ideology and Genre: The Rise of the Novel in America

*The Experimental Fictions of Ambrose Bierce:
Structuring the Ineffable*

THE NEW EDUCATION

How to Revolutionize the University to
Prepare Students for a World in Flux

CATHY N. DAVIDSON

BASIC BOOKS

NEW YORK

Basic Books
Hachette Book Group
1290 Avenue of the Americas, New York, NY 10104
www.basicbooks.com

Printed in the United States of America
Originally published in hardcover and ebook by Basic Books in September
2017.
First Trade Paperback Edition: May 2022

Published by Basic Books, an imprint of Perseus Books, LLC, a subsidiary
of Hachette Book Group, Inc.

The Hachette Speakers Bureau provides a wide range of authors for speaking events. To find out more, go to www.hachettespeakersbureau.com or
call (866) 376-6591.

The publisher is not responsible for websites (or their content) that are not
owned by the publisher.

Print book interior design by Linda Mark

The Library of Congress has cataloged the hardcover edition as follows:
Names: Davidson, Cathy N., 1949– author.
Title: The new education : how to revolutionize the university to prepare
    students for a world in flux / Cathy N. Davidson.
Description: First edition. | New York : Basic Books, [2017] | Includes
    bibliographical references and index.
Identifiers: LCCN 2017008496 (print) | LCCN 2017032975 (ebook) |
    ISBN 9780465093182 (ebook) | ISBN 9780465079728 (hardcover)
Subjects: LCSH: Education, Higher—Aims and objectives. | Educational
    change.
Classification: LCC LB2322.2 (ebook) | LCC LB2322.2 .D39 2017 (print) |
    DDC 378—dc23
LC record available at https://lccn.loc.gov/2017008496

ISBNs: 9780465079728 (hardcover); 9780465093182 (ebook);
9781541601277 (paperback)

LSC-C

Printing 1, 2022

This book is dedicated to all students. You deserve a great education to prepare you for your future.

And to parents, professors, pundits, policy makers, and presidents who can work to change higher education now.

It requires courage to quit the beaten paths in which the great majority of well-educated men have walked and still walk. . . . Conservatism is never more respectable than in education, for nowhere are the risks of change greater.

—CHARLES W. ELIOT, "The New Education," *The Atlantic,* February 1869

CONTENTS

PREFACE TO THE 2022 EDITION

IN THE FIVE YEARS SINCE THE ORIGINAL 2017 PUBLICATION OF *THE New Education*, everything changed in higher education—and not nearly enough.

Remember how we used to think academe was hidebound, overly bureaucratic, stuck in its ways, and incapable of transformation or even modest change? Then the COVID-19 crisis happened. Faculty, staff, administrators, students, and students' families turned everything upside down and inside out in a matter of weeks. We moved online, changed how we taught, altered academic calendars, shortened or extended term lengths and seat-time requirements, invented new kinds of assignments, and experimented with different grading methods. In an emergency, we did all that and more.

Now the question is, how much of what we changed will remain? How much should? What did we learn that was beneficial? What revealed, even more harshly, the glaring inequities of higher education? And what did we learn about ourselves and our own capacity for change? In an emergency, we had to review everything—process and product, successes and failures, humane responses and persistent inequality. How can we use what we learned to truly revolutionize the university to prepare our students for a world that's more in flux than we even knew?

As we see throughout *The New Education*, successful models are crucial in academe. They help us see past inherited structures, legacies, and our own training to imagine what we did not think was possible. Because we are so connected, one institution to another, when one institution makes a successful change, it can impact others. Take the quick action of President Ana Mari Cauce of the University of Washington during the pandemic. After consulting with health policy advisers and faculty leadership, she made the bold, early decision to close the entire University of Washington campus on March 7, 2020, sending more than fifty thousand students into remote learning. She set an example: in the United States, within weeks of the University of Washington closure, over eleven hundred other colleges and universities followed suit, putting over fifteen million students online.

Lives were saved. The vast majority of students managed to stay in school even as everything was upended by a horrific financial and health catastrophe. Faculty learned how to teach online using equipment and tools not designed for that purpose even as they, too, may have lost family members or experienced medical, financial, or psychological crises. Administrators, IT staff, and others worked day and night to keep higher education functioning remotely. They had to address the stark reality of the inequality of staff, students, and faculty. Gender inequality was especially obvious, and it mirrored patterns in the nation as a whole. With children sent home from school and social distancing impossible for childcare workers, women disproportionately shouldered family responsibilities. By some accounts, the employment rate of women in the US labor market plummeted to 57.0 percent by winter of 2021, a low not seen since 1988.

Technology also became an issue of inequality. Who lacked laptops and bandwidth? How could those problems be addressed rapidly? Many universities, faced with the reality of student food and housing insecurity, kept food pantries open even when the rest of campus closed. Realizing that some students, both domestic and international, faced housing insecurity, some administrators found ways to create safe housing spaces for students. Many institutions understood that they could not simply think about students in school but also had to think about students' full, complicated, and often imperiled lives outside of school.

Only a small proportion of those instructors who began emergency remote instruction had ever taught online before or knew anything about what does or does not contribute to effective distance learning. Teaching and Learning Centers got to work sharing resources, offering one-on-one consultation with faculty, and sharing resources through social media. All across the country, everyone responded to emergency conditions in real time.

In the years since the original publication of this book, I have spoken to thousands of educators, students, and private citizens about transforming higher education for today's students. I've conducted workshops at colleges and universities and worked with committees, commissions, and communities. We have discussed together all the different areas of higher education I address in the pages of *The New Education*: semester schedules, student workload, grades, grading systems, standardized testing, the uniform credit hour and "seat-time" requirements, closed-book exams, the lack of cooperation across institutions, tenure clocks, and our faculty reward systems. Ironically, now, when I ask audiences what changed during the pandemic, all of these seemingly intractable issues are the ones that were somehow, magically, altered during the crisis.

As we think about redesigning a better system of higher education—creating "the new education"—the best evidence we have that change is possible is our very own experience. With the benefit of the pandemic months behind us, we can use the knowledge we gained but without the exigency of a global health emergency. To every naysayer who insists "higher education will never change," we now have an answer. During the pandemic, we changed. We must not forget that. *We changed when we had to.* We can change again.

At my own massive, public, urban institution, the City University of New York, Chancellor Félix V. Matos Rodriguez provided another great model of change when he announced a comprehensive emergency grading policy. In the earliest months of the pandemic, New York City was hit harder than any other city in the country. During April 2020 alone, there were approximately twenty-nine thousand more deaths than in the same month in 2019. New York simultaneously became a ghost town and a disaster area. Health disparities reflected and magnified the city's income and racial inequalities.

Many of CUNY's working-class students or their family members work in health care and other forms of work deemed "essential" to keeping the city functioning during the health crisis. One student in our program was delivering goods and supplies on his bike until two in the morning, and then showing up for Zoom class at nine a.m. Recognizing these hardships, Chancellor Rodriguez put into place an emergency grading system, which gave students ten days after receiving their final course grade to decide whether they wished to keep the letter grade they earned or to have it changed to Credit/No Credit. Students could simply request the grade change from their campus registrar; they did not need to petition their instructor or state a reason for the change request. This policy allowed students to make decisions on the basis of their own situation (and the many, varied regulations for state and federal scholarships, international students, plans for graduate and professional school, and beyond).

Many of us asked: Why don't we *always* give students this opportunity? Aren't there always unavoidable emergencies in life? We have extensive research on how unreliable a grade is as a "proxy" for student learning. Why should a grade during a time of crisis be part of a student's permanent record? Is our job to grade? Or to teach? In a pandemic, we asked these foundational questions and gave ourselves a blueprint of care and the power to change.

Other universities made different revolutionary changes. At some, entire schedules were changed (starting a new term early, ending before the fall break, condensing fifteen-week semesters into twelve, and so forth). Even required contact hours (seat time) were changed. Astonishing! The Carnegie credit hour has been a sacred cow of academe ever since the 1910 "Academic and Industrial Efficiency" study commissioned by Harvard president Charles Eliot pushed to better align higher education with the Fordist model of standardized assembly-line industrial production. Suddenly, in the pandemic, people were thinking, *If we can change the Carnegie hour, we can change everything!*

As we see in *The New Education*, for all our pride in higher education as an engine of social mobility—and it is that, to be sure, at many of our institutions—it is also one of our society's most effective means of perpetuating inequality. Here, too, the pandemic exposed rampant inequality in the starkest terms. In higher education, inequality is meted out through what Harvard law professor Lani Guinier has called the "tyranny of meritocracy." The term refers to the full array of testing, selectivity, school district modification, tax regulations, and other forms of seemingly neutral accounting and subsidizing that contribute to social, income, and racial disparities. We act as if we are selecting "the best" students for college, but we are really adding up what philosopher Sylvia Wynter calls the "mathematics of inequality."

A 2017 study by the team of economists led by Professor Raj Chetty of Harvard found that thirty-eight of the nation's elite private universities have more students whose families come from the top 1 percent of the income scale than from the entire bottom 60 percent. One contributor to the disparity is the seemingly "objective" measure provided by standardized testing. The "mathematics of inequality" is simple: if intelligence and academic achievement are what school really measures, these should not correlate with wealth. Yet, as we see in *The New Education*, a map showing the distribution of SAT scores, for example, is almost identical to one showing income level by school district. It's not subtle. Students from families with higher incomes have higher test scores. Period.

When the COVID-19 crisis virtually halted SAT testing in the spring of 2020, the number of applications to college soared, especially among students of color and students from working-class backgrounds. Middle-class families routinely hire expensive SAT coaches to teach children how to improve their test scores. These coaches show students how to "game" a standardized test, down to using statistical analyses of the best way to guess at an answer they don't know. The suspension of SAT testing and the relaxation of SAT scores as an admission requirement increased the income and racial diversity of college applicants. Something parallel happened with the suspension of Graduate Record Exam (GRE) scores for graduate school application. Yet admissions officers insisted that the actual rigor and overall quality of the applications did not drop; they improved. The revelation during the pandemic about standardized testing is a lesson we should take with us into the future. And, indeed, that's happening. Many colleges and universities are now adopting or contemplating "test optional" applications.

The pandemic highlighted other forms of educational inequality, too. The college dropout rate during the crisis correlated strongly with family income. Students from low-income backgrounds were more likely to leave higher education than were wealthy ones. Community colleges and public, regional universities saw a more significant drop in enrollment than private and four-year flagship institutions. Although dropping standardized testing requirements meant more students without funds for test fees could apply to college, at the same time those students from the most financially stressed families were no longer able to afford college at all. The pandemic exacerbated income inequality, and college applications followed the same economic pattern. As the numbers of applications to the nation's community colleges dropped, applications to elite universities soared, as did applications for graduate school.

As you read this book, keep in mind all we accomplished in higher education with our schools during a global health emergency. At the same time, think about where we have resisted change. We didn't all behave perfectly in the pandemic, of course: some institutions and individuals seemed preoccupied with "grade inflation," "relaxed requirements," "ensuring rigor," and "observing established practices" at any cost. Most, however, made sound and even bold decisions that took into account the reality of their students' lives.

The New Education shows that most of the principles and practices of higher education were designed in a specific historical moment and context. I discuss how nineteenth-century higher education was modernized to address the needs and the assumptions of the Taylorist workforce and the hierarchical model of management of the new, powerful corporations. The era of mass industrialization, globalization, automation, and standardization inspired an educational revolution that turned the Puritan college into the modern research university.

Our students face a very different world. Standardization and hierarchy look different in a world driven by artificial intelligence and mass, interconnected social networks run by the biggest monopolies in human history—Facebook, Google, Microsoft, Amazon, and beyond. Students live in a time when anyone can propagate misinformation while obtaining (and exploiting) our most private personal data. Our students must contend with the gig economy, precarious jobs without benefits. They also contend with soaring tuition debt and hear over and over from pundits who insist "college isn't worth it" (even as those same pundits often send their own children to elite private universities). *The New Education* asks which of our inherited practices serve students now, which can be changed, and which need to be relegated (finally!) to the dustbin of history.

Since the publication of *The New Education*, I have continued to research the eugenic philosophy underpinning the design of the modern university to further understand the roots of inequality and why it is perpetuated year after year, despite our best efforts. Belief in eugenics (the advocacy of controlled selective breeding based on an idea that some human populations are superior to others) was prevalent among intellectuals and educators in the nineteenth century and early twentieth century, and persists in different forms and sometimes with different names, in the present. Charles Eliot, who was chosen as Harvard's president in 1869, for example, was also a committed eugenicist. He had a tremendous impact on all of higher education, and on K–12, during his forty-year reign at Harvard. He believed that one function of higher education was to improve the quality of the human race by selectively educating the elite, upper class. After retiring from his Harvard presidency, Eliot worked on America's first sterilization law, passed in Indiana in 1907, and authored the essay "The Suppression of Moral Defectives." As vice president of the First International Eugenics Congress, he decried "racial suicide" among Anglo-Saxon Europeans who intermarried with Catholics and southern Europeans and, in 1914, he helped organize the First National Conference on Race Betterment in Battle Creek, Michigan.

We live and work at a great distance from Eliot's time, yet the architecture of those late-nineteenth-century systems remain. Racism, exclusion, and structural inequality are among the legacies built into our elite, selective educational apparatus. Is that the inheritance we want?

A second problematic legacy handed down to us from Eliot's day is pedagogical. Most of us who teach college don't know very much about teaching. This, too, is a structural issue and an inheritance; when Eliot created the first professional school to train teachers, the Harvard Graduate School of Education, he intended it only to train future elementary and secondary school teachers. He decried the poor preparation teachers received at the nation's "normal schools." Future college teachers were excluded from the first "ed school" because Eliot didn't believe that college professors needed to teach well. To this day, this segregation persists. One receives a Doctor of Education (EdD or DEd), not a PhD, from a school of education. Most doctoral students, even now, take at most one course (usually not-for-credit) in pedagogical theory and practice. Few college profs have ever been exposed to the extensive research on what makes for effective learning.

Most college instructors remain wedded to the lecture model of instruction or, in smaller classes, to what I call the "distributed lecture" (basically, the typical "raise your hand if you know the answer" format of most seminar discussions). Not only does this method leave out the majority of students, but it also typically favors the small percentage of students in a class who most resemble the gender, racial, social, economic, and educational background of the professor. One recent study of over seven thousand professors across all fields at PhD-granting departments in the United States found that faculty are from more affluent backgrounds than their students and are twenty-five times more likely than the general US population to have a parent with a PhD. This also contributes to certain fields, such as computer science or nursing, being dominated by one gender. It also perpetuates racial inequality. The percentage of students of color in our nation's universities is now about twice as high as the percentage of faculty of color.

Few college instructors have been exposed to alternatives to traditional teaching methods, even though we've now had over a thousand studies showing that active, participatory learning is the most effective and equitable way to teach. All students—from the least to the most academically well prepared—learn more through engaged, student-centered, active learning methods. A great lecture inspires us, but it is very poor for actual learning (as we all know from common sense when we ever set about to master something new). As noted by Carl Wieman, the 2011 Nobel Laureate in Physics (and a professor in both the Stanford Physics Department and the School of Education), our current archaic forms of one-way education (with information flowing from the instructor to the student) are an ineffective way of enabling students to master complex ideas, from physics to philosophy. In a 2014 "metastudy" in the *Publications of the National Academy of Science*, researchers examined over 225 separate, rigorous studies of effective learning. By any measure, active, engaged learning proved to be superior. In fact, the authors of the metastudy concluded that if this had been a pharmaceutical study, traditional education would be taken off the market.

In *The New Education*, I discuss our norms for credentialing, accrediting, and counting student learning outcomes and faculty research outputs. These come down to us via the archaic Taylorist theory of scientific labor management, developed at the turn of the twentieth century. Certifying expertise and standardizing knowledge acquisition became the higher ed ideal in the age of automation. Once the beacon of progress, those values became anachronistic in 1992, the year that the Mosaic 1.0 browser was released for free to the public, which ushered in the contemporary Internet era. Now, anyone who has an Internet connection can communicate anything to anyone. Anyone can be an "influencer." Information is everywhere. Yet we remain wedded to an idea that knowledge is a "thing" you receive from one prof, in one class, as documented by your score on a final exam. We prize a mode of learning known as "sequestered problem solving" (focusing on students' ability to solve problems unaided) even as we live in a world rife with information and roiled by deliberate, dangerous misinformation.

Three decades after the debut of Mosaic 1.0, most of us still teach as if the Internet does not exist, or as if it should be banned from our school rooms. Universities spend millions of dollars every year on questionable, invasive surveillance systems designed to "proctor" exams and "detect" plagiarism and cheating. For online exams during the COVID-19 crisis, many universities even bought expensive products such as Proctorio, Respondus, and other commercial systems that prohibit students from using their other devices to search for information and that even track students' facial, body, or eye movements to "flag" potential cheaters. Yet, as architecture professor William Littman asks pointedly, "If the answer can, and will, be easily found using online sources, why are we asking these kinds of questions in the first place?" Shouldn't we be asking exam questions that challenge students to use every kind of information available and then to evaluate and apply what they find wisely and well to the problem at hand?

All of these issues of equality and efficacy are part of the lesson plan laid out in *The New Education*. As we shall see, Charles Eliot wrote "The New Education," his manifesto for educational reform, in 1869, in the wake of the Civil War and a series of financial catastrophes. He and his colleagues revolutionized American higher education in response to the social, economic, and technological urgencies of their day. We are now in a similar liminal moment, in the midst of crisis and on a cusp. Virtually every issue discussed in these pages has been amplified by the pandemic and extreme social divisiveness. Our historical moment requires us to envision similarly expansive transformations.

In a beautiful essay written in May 2020, looking back at the Columbia University course in African American literature she had moved online during the pandemic, the renowned literary scholar Farah Jasmine Griffin quoted from novelist Arundhati Roy's essay "The Pandemic as Portal": "Historically, pandemics have forced humans to break with the past and imagine their world anew. This one is no different. . . . We can choose to walk through it, dragging the carcasses of our prejudice and hatred, our avarice, our data banks and dead ideas, our dead rivers and smoky skies behind us. Or we can walk through lightly, with little luggage, ready to imagine another world. And ready to fight for it."

In this spirit, Griffin asked her students to think about what they wanted to take with them as they passed through this portal:

1. What one book from class would you want to take with you?
2. What, if anything, from your old life do you want to leave behind?
3. What do you appreciate that you would like to take with you?
4. What change, if any, would you like to see, and commit to bring about, on the other side?

What do we want to take with us? What have we learned that we want to keep? What does it mean that we now know universities can change, that *we* can change? How does this new knowledge about ourselves, our students, and our institutions change the prospects for revolutionizing higher education and realizing the vision of equitable, effective learning set forth here? If we can turn everything we do upside down and inside out in a global pandemic, we can do this transformative, revolutionary thinking to address all the crises higher ed and our students face today.

In these pages, I hope you find inspiration to rethink the systems that keep higher education from being as relevant, urgent, and significant as it should be. I hope the inequality laid bare by the pandemic also helps all of us consider the high cost to society of our five decades of defunding higher education. Tuition costs have risen not simply out of whimsy or caprice. Only one or two states in the United States have even returned support for their universities to the pre-2008 (pre-crash) funding levels. When we pass those costs to students as tuition, we contribute to income and social inequality.

When faced with a pandemic, higher ed responded at a scale literally no one would have imagined possible. *No one.* If we could change in the face of a health crisis, we can change in the face of the educational crisis we now confront. How do we prepare students to think for themselves while working with others who contribute different insights, information, and perspective? How do we teach them to seek new kinds of solutions, to test those under the most exacting conditions? How do we give them the confidence to break new paths, for themselves and others, and to become leaders who lead wisely, fairly, and well? Learning how to learn means knowing how to sort and understand information, how to communicate with those who know both more and less than you. It means being able to analyze and critique as the beginning (not the end) of a process whose ultimate goal is designing and implementing something that works better than it did before.

I hope the pages that follow offer inspiration, models, guidance, and a lesson plan for change. The original edition of *The New Education* ends with two appendices. "Ten Tips for Getting the Most Out of Your College Experience" is designed for students. "Ten Tips for Transforming Any Classroom for Active, Student-Centered Learning" is designed for instructors. For this 2022 edition, I have added a third appendix: "Ten Tips for Transforming Your Institution." This appendix is designed for higher education leaders, administrators, and faculty dedicated to institutional change—and for all of us (including students and parents) to think about together.

From constant, daily interaction with students, faculty, staff, and administrators since the original publication of *The New Education*, I know there's a will to change, there's an inspiration to change, there's an imperative to change, and, perhaps most importantly, there's experience that shows us, unmistakably, that we have what it takes to change.

We can do this. No one can stop us now.

INTRODUCTION

IN EVERY MYTH, THERE'S A DOORWAY, A PORTAL, A RIVER, A LADDER, a mountain, a pathway. There is a threshold and, if you are the hero, your journey requires you to cross over: you start on one side, and the challenge is to reach the other. There are obstacles—gorges, rapids, bandits, hunger, temptations, cowardice, despair. There are also guides along the way, some wise, some not. How can you tell? It's tricky. As ancient maps portend: "*Here be dragons.*"

In modern life, the threshold that looms largest, defining almost all that follows, is the age of majority. One day you are the legal responsibility of a parent or a guardian, the next you are on your own, responsible for making your own way, treading the cliff's edge.

When you are 17 years and 364 days old, your parents can tell you what to do. When you wake up the next morning, 18, they, legally, cannot.

You have crossed over. Before and after.

In individual and social terms, the consequences of that crossing are so vast that they are constantly debated. How old do you have to be to drink? To be tried and executed as an adult? To go to war? To vote? Sometimes it is eighteen, sometimes twenty-one, and there are arguments about which age is more just. Because it matters. And not only to you, the individual, but also to your society.

Your rite of passage represents all of the life-and-death issues that we grapple with together in democracies. We argue over when childhood ends, when adult responsibility begins, when the torch should be passed. Your journey is our journey, your future is ours. How you are prepared to join and perhaps lead a community, a generation, a world, matters to those who have gone before you and those who will come after. The consequences have weight and heft, the journey, peril and promise.

You are crossing from definition by others to self-definition, from dependence on others to legal independence. You are moving from control by others to self-control, from ideas shaped by others to your own ideas, from received opinions to your own ability to determine where you are going next, to discern, evaluate, make judgments, and then to act.

It is a pivotal moment. Existential. You are on your own. This is the stuff of mythology, from the *Epic of Gilgamesh* forward.

In America, we call it college.

I HAVE WITNESSED THIS TRANSFORMATION THOUSANDS OF TIMES over my long career as a college professor. It doesn't happen for every student in the same way or at the same age, but it is apparent enough that you can drop an academic into any random classroom and we can tell immediately whether we are meeting first-year students or those who have been in college a year or more.

Parents witness the transformation, too. The child who goes off in September is not the adult who returns over Thanksgiving break. "Who is this?" many a parent has asked about the stranger knocking about their child's old room. It's not just their age that changes but their way of being in the world.

College makes this happen—and not only for the young. Depending on how you count, between 40 percent and 70 percent of current students are so-called nontraditional students. Like the eighteen- to twenty-two-year-olds who go away to college and live in dorms, these adult, commuter students are on a journey, making sacrifices of time, money, and attention to strive for a significant change in their lives. The lackadaisical high school graduate who has no idea what to do next, the sixty-two-year-old insurance executive taking night classes to fulfill a lifelong goal of earning a college degree, the student returning from a gap year to enter the flagship state university, the twenty-something Somalian refugee working multiple minimum-wage jobs while taking English as a second language at a community college, and the eighteen-year-old private school graduate with perfect SAT scores on her way to Stanford with an eye on a future career in Silicon Valley—like the rest of the nation's college students—are all volunteers. They voluntarily choose to make college part of their journey toward an adulthood they can live as independently, responsibly, and with as much satisfaction as they are able to achieve.

This book is for all of them, the 21 million students in college today, and for all those students who are on their way to college, wondering whether it is worth it, trying to figure out how to gain the best education possible. It is also for recent graduates, the much-maligned Millennials who have been through college in the last fifteen years.

I believe they've been given a raw deal.

Why? Because the schooling they received was developed in the late nineteenth and early twentieth centuries to train farmers and shopkeepers to be factory workers and office managers. At the height of the momentous changes to life, work, and society driven by industrialization and the accompanying urbanization, America's elite Puritan colleges went through a massive redesign, shifting away from their founding mission to train ministers toward the selection, preparation, and credentialing of future leaders of new professions, new institutions, and new companies. Such prescriptive, disciplinary, and specialized training worked well for most of the twentieth century. But it makes a lot less sense for our postindustrial and post-Internet world, in which the boundaries between work and home are far less distinct, work itself is more precarious, wages are largely stagnant, automation is expanding and becoming more sophisticated, democratic institutions are failing, professions are disappearing, and the next shock to the economy is on the horizon, even if we can't see it yet.

Our institutions of higher education are helping young people transform themselves, as they always have, helping them move from dependence to independence, from childhood to adulthood. College is *good* at that. Yet college is no longer good at equipping graduates to succeed in an ever more complex and bewildering world.

People who say "higher education hasn't changed since Socrates' Academy two thousand years ago" have it wrong. The modern American university is only about 150 years old. Basically, the infrastructure, curriculums, and assessment methods we have now were developed between 1860 and 1925. An ambitious cadre of educators led by Charles Eliot, the energetic and forward-thinking young president of Harvard in the late 1800s, redesigned the Puritan college for an unfolding age of industrialization and urbanization that required managers, not ministers.

Eliot and his peers from the nation's most distinguished institutions set about modernizing the university in every way. To support a newly differentiated labor market, they defined academic disciplines, fortifying and separating departments and divisions, majors and minors. They regulated the curriculum down to the credit hour and segregated general education and the liberal arts from the new, specialized, high-prestige research enterprises of graduate schools and professional schools designed to certify the expertise of an emerging professional-managerial class. They founded ranking and accreditation organizations that systematized and enshrined their values. Even without a unified system of higher education, every institution was ranked (explicitly and implicitly) against others. Smaller liberal arts colleges and the proliferating public universities were judged according to benchmarks established by the most elite, well-funded institutions in the country.

Educators of the late nineteenth and early twentieth centuries also developed the educational measurements we use today. Grades, statistics, standard deviation, regression from the mean, bell curves, IQ tests, admissions exams, and timed and standardized multiple-choice tests were all new ways of assessing academic inputs and outputs, of distinguishing what kinds of intelligence, aptitude, and achievement counted and what kinds did not. The revolution in higher education was partly inspired by management theorists of the day who were gauging the productivity of factories smelting pig iron and assembly lines turning out Model Ts. In essence, all of these features of higher education add up to the university that exists today.

Yet it's been a full generation since April 22, 1993, when a new world was born. That's the day scientists at the National Center for Supercomputing Applications announced that the Mosaic 1.0 web browser was available to the public. There were fewer than twenty websites in existence at the time; by the end of the year, there were more than ten thousand, and Internet use that year alone increased by over 2,000 percent. Overnight, anyone with access to an Internet connection could communicate anything to anyone else in the world who had access to an Internet connection. This is an almost unimaginable extension of the human reach.

As was the age of industrialization, the Internet era has been marked by complex and far-reaching social, political, and economic changes wrought not by steam power and assembly-line mechanization but by digitization and algorithm-based global redistribution of ideas, capital, goods, labor, and services. Modern networked computing has changed everyday life and work, and these changes accelerate each year. Even our ideas about what it means to be human and social—a "self" and a "society"—fail to encompass the close ties of people who never physically meet, who can interact virtually—as friends, lovers, or trolls—and who may not even be who they say they are. Suddenly, we spend more time online than off, interacting in a world with no centralized publisher, no editor, no broadcaster controlling, filtering, or verifying content; all of our vast power to access and communicate anything at all is available without a pause or a retract button. Everyone has a platform. No professional-managerial class is in charge. *No degree required.*

This is not just new technology but a new way of being that has so fully transformed the world that it is hard to grasp how much we have changed. Yet, for our students, those born after 1993, there is no "before" and "after." It's difficult, cognitively, for them to even comprehend what came before this technological age. In *Between the World and Me,* Ta-Nehisi Coates tries to explain to his fifteen-year-old son how it was to live, think, and learn before the Internet: "For all of your life, whenever you've had a question you have been able to type that question out on a keyboard, watch it appear in a rectangular space bordered by a corporate logo, and within seconds revel in the flood of potential answers. But I still remember when typewriters were useful, the dawn of the Commodore 64, and days when a song you loved would have its moment on the radio and then disappear into the nothing. . . . For a young man like me, the invention of the Internet was the invention of space travel."

Space travel. The metaphor is evocative, and useful. There has been a before and after that most of my students today don't comprehend, which also means they don't fully grasp how unprepared the outmoded educational systems have left them in this world. Those of us who are old enough to recognize that we are living in new ways, as if on a new planet, must take responsibility and begin to think seriously about how to remake the university to equip students to thrive in this murky and often polluted new atmosphere that we now all breathe. In a world of such complexity—no human or collection of humans can begin to predict or parse the data our devices generate in a nanosecond—we're still going to school the way we did in 1993, which is to say, pretty much as we did in 1893.

What would it mean to redesign higher education for the intellectual space travel students need to thrive in the world we live in now? What would it mean to reorient educational paradigms that, at present, overly standardize, test, diagnose (from disability to giftedness and all points in between), specialize, and discipline students in one-way-transmission models inspired by the hierarchy of the factory and the assembly line, not the interactive Internet? What would it take to really educate students who do not know how, a full generation ago, a new technology changed everything and yet who must contend with, be prepared for, and find a way to prosper among these vast changes?

That's the challenge, as daunting as it seems. History is our friend here, because the difficulties we face in remaking higher education now are no greater than the ones Eliot and his peers faced little more than a century ago when they designed the modern US research university. They succeeded in an age as stressed and chaotic as our own. If they did it, why can't we?

In 1869, Charles Eliot wrote "The New Education," a stirring critique of existing forms of higher education in America and a manifesto for the higher education revolution he would go on to lead in his forty-year reign as president of Harvard. Published in two parts in *The Atlantic Monthly*, Eliot's essay begins with the provocative question asked by a father pondering his child's higher education: "What can I do with my boy?" The father says his son is not cut out for the careers the elite colleges prepared students for, namely, to be a "preacher or a learned man." Eliot acknowledges those colleges had become obsolete. "Here is a real need and a serious problem," he writes, before cataloguing the three kinds of education available and why they need to be revolutionized, top to bottom. He wrote this piece a few years after the Civil War and after a series of financial catastrophes had left the future in question. "The American people are fighting the wilderness, physical and moral, on the one hand, and on the other are struggling to work out the awful problem of self-government. For this fight they must be trained and armed." He then describes, in considerable detail, his vision for revolutionizing the university to prepare students for careers while educating them deeply enough to assume important roles in a fragile democracy.

Eliot and his colleagues succeeded in realizing that vision. And today, we find ourselves at a similar tipping point. So dramatically has society changed since Eliot's day, and especially in the last twenty years or so, that we need a "New Education" for our own time. Again we are confronting antiquated institutions that don't prepare students for the world beyond the academy. Again there is desperate need for education in active participation in what Eliot calls enlightened self-government.

Just as Eliot and others wholly remade the Puritan college, so too do we need to redesign higher education systemically and systematically, from the classroom to the board of trustees, from the fundamentals of how we teach and learn to how we measure outcomes, select, credential, and accredit in this hyperconnected, precarious time. Students today need so-called soft skills, including strategies, methods, and tactics for successful communication and collaboration. These are necessary to navigate a world in flux, where they cannot count on continuing for any length of time in the job or even the field for which they were originally trained.

Students need new ways of integrating knowledge, including through reflection on why and what they are learning. They don't need more "teaching to the test." They need to be offered challenges that promote their success after graduation, when all the educational testing has stopped. This is an engaged form of student-centered pedagogy known as "active learning." Students are encouraged to create new knowledge from the information around them and to use it to make a public, professional, or experiential contribution that has impact beyond the classroom. Students don't just master what an expert sets out for them but, rather, learn how to become experts themselves. It's a survival skill for the journey that is their lives.

Right now, our educational system focuses on tests and outputs, standards and institutional requirements. Redesigning higher education demands institutional restructuring, a revolution in every classroom, curriculum, and assessment system. It means refocusing away from the passive student to the whole person learning new ways of thinking through problems with no easy solutions. It shifts the goal of college from fulfilling course and graduation requirements to learning for success in the world after college. It means testing learning in serious and thoughtful ways, so that students take charge of what and how they know, how they collaborate, how they respond to feedback, and how they grow. It teaches them how to understand and lead productively in the changing world in which they live.

IT WILL NOT BE EASY TO TRANSFORM THE UNIVERSITY FROM THE inside. Many academics are traditionalists, and many institutions revere their traditions and are rewarded for them. They often reject innovation simply because it represents a departure from how things are done. Perhaps they too subscribe to the notion that higher education hasn't changed since the time of Socrates and aren't aware of how much of what they think of as traditional was devised for a very particular historical moment that no longer exists.

There are other challenges to higher education transformation that come from outside the academy. Two recent reform movements have promised to bring about sweeping change but in fact offer nothing of the sort. One is the educational technology movement, often championed by businesspeople and pundits who campaign for "modernizing" higher education and who advocate for the "end of college," with professors and classrooms replaced by new forms of technology. Whether from a misguided sense of what constitutes the right preparation for a precarious job market, an inadequate understanding of what technology can and cannot do, or vested commercial interests in high-cost technologies, many supposed innovators ignore how learning actually happens. Dumping iPads into conventional classrooms without changing teaching or assessment methods and putting traditional lecture courses online and grading them by automated multiple-choice testing systems simply digitizes nineteenth-century assumptions about standardized learning, narrow specialization, and passive pedagogy. Yet too often we glibly praise these attempts as not only visionary but also necessary to disrupt the hidebound, tweedy university.

Efforts of a second group of reformers overlap with those of the first. These politicians and critics call for more "skills training" to make students "workforce ready." They assume that humanities departments and programs such as women's and gender studies are a waste of time and money. They typically argue that only skills in STEM—science, technology, engineering, and mathematics—lead to good jobs and economic growth. At the level of state and federal legislatures, they justify the radical defunding of public higher education on the grounds that we should be cutting away the "frills" outside of narrow job training. This is a disaster for youth in the new economy. Specific skills-defined jobs are doomed to obsolescence fast, through outsourcing and automation. IBM is convinced use of its robots, driven by artificial general intelligence, will eliminate whole swaths of middle-class employment in the next two decades, especially in the STEM sector. Anyone who claims to know which specific skills will protect students in the future is misinformed.

Some reformers have good intentions. Others are motivated by greed or ideology or both. Whatever their motives, their diagnosis that college is out-of-date is partially correct, but their prescriptions fail.

THESE REFORM MOVEMENTS STEM, ONE WAY OR ANOTHER, FROM A deeper problem: we're living at a moment of low support for higher education, even as the need and the demand for college are higher than ever. The loss of faith in higher education as a public good deforms everything associated with it today. We know from numerous studies that the expansion of college beyond educating the elites has provided a pathway to the middle class and has been crucial to democracy. That was the finding of the Truman Commission during the early implementation of the GI Bill (the Servicemen's Readjustment Act of 1944) in the wake of World War II. The Golden Age of American higher education spanned roughly from the GI Bill to the Great Society under President Lyndon Baines Johnson. In President Johnson's terms, the passage of the Higher Education Act of 1965 increased higher education funding, in particular, financial aid. When Ronald Reagan became governor of California, through the time when he was president of the United States, support for higher education turned in the opposite direction, with cutting of per capita funding. This downward trajectory has continued to the present.

Today, conservative forces, from the Tea Party to the US Department of Education under the Trump administration, wage the assault on higher education at the state and federal levels. In most states, the extreme cutbacks in higher education that resulted from the financial crisis of 2008 have not been reversed, even in states where other social goods and services have been returned to their pre-2008 levels. The war on higher education in some states has had devastating effects on students' lives and student debt. It has resulted in higher tuition, fewer course options and advising services, and exploited faculty. At universities, now nearly half of all courses are taught by adjunct, part-time laborers, some of whom effectively make less than the minimum wage.

This is terrible for students, for faculty, and for institutional change. The cuts in higher education that have damaged our public universities over the last decades make many faculty suspicious of change. With reason. In some states—notably, North Carolina and Iowa—governors or regents have intruded into faculty and administrative governance at the highest levels, replacing good leaders with political and ideological insiders and justifying the changes as part of "modernizing" strategies.

In the last decade, it has become fashionable to say higher education would be more efficient and modern if it were run as a business, treating students as "customers." This notion could not be more wrongheaded—wrong as a business model and wrong as a mission. It turns the massive investment we must make in the next generation's future into a cash cow for the handful of people producing whatever can be sold to educational institutions. The goal of helping young people transform themselves into adults who can thrive in tough times is subverted, turned into someone else's financial opportunity. A deep conflict of interest turns educational institutions into intermediaries in an operation whose primary goal is to report financial growth to shareholders while secondarily selling services and goods to students. Learning doesn't seem part of the business plan.

Traditional-age college students who were born after the invention of the Internet have spent their entire lives in an ecology of a disappearing, disrupted, distributed, disturbed, and disturbing economy. They have watched entire industries and professions change, shrink, or disappear: the music business, journalism, banking, law practice, entertainment, retail, college teaching. For the Uber generation, which has been called "Generation Flux," the new normal is contingent, on-demand, part-time labor. Many students expect to have jobs with no benefits, no insurance, no assurances, to pay expenses out of pocket, to have no promise of advancement or futurity. They see this diminished form of work in the adjunct professors they encounter: students are guided through their college journey by professors who have no job security; likely, neither will the students when they graduate.

MY STUDENTS WHO COME FROM THE MOST PRECARIOUS PERSONAL backgrounds have had and lost jobs and have witnessed their parents find and lose jobs. As they make their way through college, they want something more: a career, a vocation, a life path, a way to contribute, a way to make themselves and their families proud and their communities strong. They don't just want a skill for a changing world. They want to be changemakers. They don't just want to understand technology. They want to design technologies that serve society. That's what I want, too, from the future generation that will be leading the world even as their parents and grandparents prepare to retire from it.

At Duke University, where I spent most of my career as both a faculty member and an administrator charged with innovation, and now at the City University of New York, which I joined in July 2014 to create and direct the Futures Initiative, I have encountered thousands of students who are engaged, aware of the problems they have inherited, and determined to gain the skills necessary to address serious social ills. Pundits are just plain wrong about this Millennial generation. Google hasn't made them stupid; their iPhones don't make them lonely; college hasn't made them dumb and passive. They want to learn enough about the world to lead it. They want to do a better job addressing major world problems than their elders, frankly, have done.

Do they want jobs? Of course. But they don't want *only* jobs. They are too realistic to believe training for a job guarantees they'll get one. They are too idealistic to settle for an entry-level job when there is a chance they can build a pathway to a meaningful career. How can they accomplish their goals? How can we train them to succeed in a world that changes so fast that no one can predict what will happen next?

The college education we need today must prepare our students for their epic journey, the mountain and the cliff's edge. It should give them agency, arm them to take on a difficult world, to push back and not merely adapt to it.

If that sounds like a formidable challenge, there's good news ahead. On almost every college and university campus right now, smart educators—sometimes a handful of visionaries, sometimes a substantial cohort—are working on new models for higher education. This is happening at community colleges, liberal arts colleges, regional public universities, and massive state universities. If you are a parent or a prospective student, it's important to consider these institutions. One might be a better match for your child's or your goals than a more expensive, high-prestige university. In our most exclusive educational enclaves, too, innovative faculty members and programs are trying to make change. We don't often hear about them, but they are there. *The New Education* is also for them, with the hope that the models explored here will inspire others to strike out on their own way forward. To revolutionize the university, we don't just need a model. We need a movement.

On an institutional level, this movement seeks to redesign the university beyond the inherited disciplines, departments, and silos by redefining the traditional boundaries of knowledge and providing an array of intellectual forums, experiences, programs, and projects that push students to use a variety of methods to discover comprehensive and original answers. What shapes belief? How do we change minds? Typically, bold and relevant programs already exist at our institutions. Often they are interdisciplinary programs, with uncertain funding and no faculty hiring power, and yet they are better suited to solving the problems students will face in the real world. They cover the range of complex skills employers routinely ask for. These programs often span undergraduate and professional education. An interdisciplinary program in environmental solutions, for example, requires understanding the science of ecology plus knowledge in the fields of law, engineering, computation, policy, regulation, and business. It requires some statistics, data science, and a rigorous, practical logic course in how to evaluate evidence. If the program's goal is to educate students in how to actually implement solutions (not just study them), then it must require human and social science disciplines so that students understand culture, politics, ideology, economic theory, and the dynamics of power—all of the social factors that can promote or impede progress toward resolving a chronic problem.

Programs like environmental solutions often exist as boutique or even student-designed majors that the most talented and ambitious students can pursue. Often they operate outside and across the core departments and disciplines by which institutions are ranked and professors recognized. The new twenty-first-century education makes the academic periphery the core, emphasizing not requirements to be checked off on the way to a major and a degree (the Eliot legacy) but an intellectual toolkit of ideas and tactics that are as interactive and dexterous as our post-Internet world demands.

If we can revolutionize our colleges and universities so that we do not teach to the test but rather challenge and empower students, we will do the best possible job helping them to succeed in an uncertain world. This necessitates a new kind of teaching, one that focuses on learning how to learn—the single most important skill anyone can master. Learning how to learn equips students to become independent and demanding researchers who can use an array of creative, critical, and computational methods to solve problems, wherever they face them.

The goal of higher education is greater than workforce readiness. It's *world* readiness. No road map shows what lies ahead in the time after college, when there are no more grades and requirements, theses and dissertations, professors and advisers. *Here be dragons.* The new education prepares students for a journey where anything might happen, the journey that is about to begin.

1   QUARTER-LIFE CRISIS

CHARLES WATCHED IN HORROR AS ONE FINANCIAL INSTITUTION after another collapsed, first in the United States, then in Europe, then in emerging markets worldwide. A recent Harvard graduate, with honors in theoretical chemistry, he was fortunate to be able to live off his family inheritance and pursue research in pure science, the kind of occupation that may not be remunerative or even practical but that had the potential to lead to a breakthrough that might one day change the world.

Not anymore. With his father's portfolio in shambles, Charles faced the same challenge to make a living as his classmates. Time to recalibrate. In addition to pure science, his training was mostly in the traditional liberal arts. What kind of job was this elite education suited for? More and more experts were insisting that a traditional college education was useless in the modern high-tech, globally connected world. Would his be the first generation in America to be less prosperous than the one that came before? Had his Harvard education trained him for his future or for the past?

My students call this a "quarter-life crisis." Instead of celebrations of youthful optimism at the beginning of bright careers, they throw twenty-fifth birthday parties to commemorate their collective indecision and existential sense of uselessness: degrees in hand, perfect grades, excellent credentials, top honors, few job prospects. Even the ones who graduate in fields that supposedly make them "workforce ready"—computer scientists, mathematicians, engineers—wonder whether they need further education to be a better match for jobs that compensate them well enough to pay off student loans and survive outside their parents' basements, to be productive members of society, to compete with the robots that everyone says are coming.

Like Charles, my students express real fears with their sardonic celebrations of quarter-life crises. There is one crucial difference though. Charles was no anxious Millennial but was, of course, Charles William Eliot, the person most decisively responsible for designing the modern American research university. Born in 1834 and graduating from Harvard in 1853, Eliot wasn't concerned about whether his job prospects would vanish as a result of the gig economy driven by artificial intelligence, but he was just as worried as students today about the role of technology in his future. He agonized over changes brought about by the second phase of the Industrial Revolution, the era of the telegraph, electricity, railroads, mass printing methods, steel manufacturing, commercial oil drilling, urbanization, and the assembly line. Scion of one of America's most illustrious families, Charles Eliot was inspired to become a reformer of higher education because he believed the outdated Puritan college in which he had been trained and in which he taught was inadequate to the task of preparing future managers and leaders of America's new technology-driven industrial age.

The Panic of 1857 rocked Eliot's world, as it rocked the entire world. The first worldwide financial crisis was exacerbated by the new technology of telegraphy. Morse code communicated financial disasters faster than they could be contained, spreading the panic.

The failure of the Ohio Life Insurance and Trust Company created a domino effect of collapsing credit and creditors in securities markets and banks, first in the United States and then abroad. When the S.S. *Central America*, carrying a shipload of gold to stabilize the New York markets, sank unexpectedly in September 1857, so did hopes for mitigating economic disaster. The entire world economy was damaged. The United States did not fully recover from the collapse until the Civil War.

Eliot understood the causes of the financial meltdown and shared the widespread opinion that the single biggest contributor to the financial panic was American grandiosity and naiveté. If only there had been greater oversight and regulation of the banks; if only greedy creditors weren't so overextended on risky loans without sufficient collateral to back them; if only Congress had been paying attention to the worrisome signs of mounting debt instead of being gridlocked by partisanship, this disaster might have been prevented.

The Panic of 1857 dimmed the reputation of the United States as a bright, emerging superpower. Other nations—especially those in Europe—pointed to America's lack of a sophisticated, fully realized higher education system that could prepare its elites to handle the nation's increasing prominence in world affairs. They blamed the bursting of the economic bubble on American provincialism. Americans were inventors and innovators, but Europeans believed that Americans placed blind faith in technology, that Americans had not fully grasped the social or economic implications, for example, of rapid communication.

In 1857, Eliot was a tutor in chemical mathematics at Harvard. He could see that the university had changed little from the Puritan school founded in 1636 to train ministers. When he had entered Harvard at age fifteen in 1849, directly from Boston Public Latin School, the college had had no real admissions requirements, although he did sit for an entrance exam. Here is a typical exam question from that time: "Translate into Latin: *'Who more illustrious in Greece than Themistocles? Who when he had been driven into exile*

did not do harm to his thankless country, but did the same that Corio-
lanus had done twenty years before?'"

This kind of exam may have been useful in 1636 for assessing ministers trained in the classics, but it was hard to see what Themistocles had to say to the 90 percent of Harvard students who, in Eliot's day, had no interest in a career at the pulpit and who, like many people around the world, were facing a world full of the greatest technological and social changes yet in human history. What good was the Latin dative case in the age of the telegraph?

In any event, how well Eliot did on the exam mattered little given that his real entrée to Harvard was the fact that his father had attended Harvard. His grandfather Samuel Eliot had been the president of the Massachusetts Bank and had endowed the Eliot Chair of Greek Literature at Harvard. On his mother's side, his ancestry ran directly back to Edmund Rice, one of the founders of the Massachusetts Bay Colony. His lineage was the price of admission into America's oldest university.

The curriculum Eliot encountered at Harvard was no more relevant than its entrance exam. It too had been in place since Harvard's beginning. Students were to master a restrictive sequence of required courses primarily in three subject areas: Latin, Greek, and mathematics. There was a smattering of natural science, and not much else.

Typically, after these general studies, graduates went into an apprenticeship in a profession: divinity, medicine, law, dentistry, or veterinary science. The professional course of study was ad hoc. It was tied only loosely to the main Harvard curriculum. A student could enter directly into vocational studies without passing first through Harvard College—or any college. Students then could go into professional training without much more than a high school diploma.

This educational system would not have been a dire problem if the world had been meandering along as usual in the two hundred years that separated Harvard's founding in 1636 from the Panic of 1857. But by that latter year, although Harvard hadn't changed much, just about everything else had.

ABOVE ALL, INDUSTRIALIZATION ALTERED THE HUMAN RELATION-
ship with the planet: how long we lived, where we lived, whether we
lived in single-family dwellings on the land where we raised animals
and crops for our own needs, whether we moved en masse into cities and lived in apartments or tenements and worked for salaries in
order to have funds to purchase goods from those who specialized in
their production.

To reduce a dynamic and complex process to but one example,
consider people's changing eating habits. Starting at the beginning of
the nineteenth century, it would become more common for people to
buy their family's meat at the market than to raise and butcher their
own animals. That may sound like a simple, even trivial, change. Yet
as the great environmental and labor historian William Cronon has
shown in detail, in consumer practice it was emblematic of shifting family, social, community, national, economic, political, labor,
immigration, health, lifestyle, and demographic relations. It also reveals why a different kind of professional education was desperately
needed by Eliot's day.

Take the case of a rural New England farm family in 1820, raising
a small herd of cattle, plus tending chickens, a garden, and a hog or
two. The entire family performed chores to run the farm and household. Everyone learned a little bit about everything—from household management and horticulture to animal husbandry—usually by
doing it, with only some labor differentiated, typically by gender.
Knowledge and practices were passed on from one generation to the
next and from older children to younger.

That familiar single-family farm arrangement began to change
when the first slabs of meat from western cattle were sold in New
England markets at lower prices than locally raised beef. Suddenly,
the small farm was not sustainable. In its place grew the complex,
specialized forerunner of today's agribusinesses, requiring railroads, shipping infrastructure, meatpacking facilities, and so on.
No longer could a single family live off the land, raising the produce and animals they needed to survive and selling or bartering a
few additional cows or pigs to pay for goods they could not supply

for themselves. Many farm families moved from the country to the city to find work to provide income to buy the food that, a generation earlier, they would have produced for themselves.

While reducing the need for the cottage industry and the rural single-family farm, this new economic dynamic increased the need for specialists who could manage and regulate every stage in the new, mechanized, large-scale agricultural operations. Specialists were needed, for example, in the sanitary slaughter, packing, and distribution of processed meat. Professional associations were created to establish the standards for credentialing different kinds of regulatory experts. Vocational schools and universities began to train inspectors as well as those who independently certified the inspectors. The workers were supervised by managers who themselves had specialized training in highly differentiated processes, from transporting livestock to feedlots to maintaining the railroads that delivered the cattle.

A new range of professionals was required to design the human, mechanical, legal, and fiduciary apparatus of meat production and to manage every part of the meat production process. Professionals had to certify the safety of these operations, calculate profits, adjudicate conflicts, unionize to protect workers from exploitation, provide social services for those who could not work, and on and on. These are not skills people learn in traditional ways by putting into practice knowledge gleaned from a parent or an older sibling.

Nor are they occupations that supply workers with the personal satisfaction that might have come from owning a small shop or a farm, where pride in the work is deeply integrated into all aspects of everyday life and community. In the agribusiness model, employees labored for a salary from the employer. Any rewards or recognition were conferred by a representative of that employer, typically the supervisor. Workers were rewarded not for their personal or individual characteristics—autonomy, intelligence, knowledge, creativity, and so forth—but for achieving the goals (or production quotas) determined by a supervisor who, in turn, was required to meet goals set by his or her supervisor. Employees did not work specifically to produce goods necessary for their own and their family's survival, although their survival probably depended on their ability to work. With the arrival of industrialization, workers were separated from their work, and the work was separated from their existence and community. This is what Karl Marx called "alienated" or "estranged" labor: people's labor became an object that existed outside themselves and that was controlled by others.

The raising of animals, for example, was separated from their slaughter. People were not consuming meat from animals they had raised themselves. The meatpacking industry was divorced from the consumers of the meat. Earning an hourly wage standing in one spot all day creating uniform-sized pieces of sirloin, flank, and rump steaks from carcasses that arrived via assembly line removed individual responsibility from the entire process, responsibility to the once-living animal and to the humans who would eat it. When the bottom line was all that mattered to the company and its shareholders, the divide between labor and safety was likely to be large, if not vast. This created the need for new worker protections. The federal government hired a phalanx of safety and health officials to regulate and safeguard labor, safety, and sanitation. Previous generations didn't need regulators and bureaucrats because safety and hygiene were tied directly to their survival and that of their family and community.

What happened in the cattle industry, as Cronon observes, had parallels in virtually every other industry of the time, with similar movement from family- and community-based activities to specialized, hierarchical operations, all of which required trained workers, overseers, and bureaucrats.

This is where formal education entered the picture. The great education project of the nineteenth century, in the United States and in industrializing Europe, was to train farmers to be factory workers and shopkeepers to be managers, supervisors, regulators, bureaucrats, and policymakers for the new industries. Enacting compulsory public education was one response to the need to train factory workers. In England, where industrialization had been under way for decades, the Factory Act of 1833 was a good example of the relationship between the factory and the school. The act raised the age at which children could work in factories to nine years and reduced the number of hours a day that children could work (nine to twelve hours, depending on the child's age). It also mandated that two hours of each day be set aside for schooling. As Marx and others noted, this schooling was structured less for students' self-realization than to shape compliant factory workers. Classrooms were regulated as carefully as was the shop floor, with nailed-down desks, standardized curriculums, and division of knowledge into discrete subjects to be studied for a specific amount of time each day.

There is nothing "natural" about this way of learning, but it was a good match for that new world of mass production. As people moved away from farms and cottage industries into cities and factory work, many were concerned about the fate of children amid these enormous social shifts. Compulsory public schooling was embraced as a way of stabilizing, regularizing, and preparing youth for their future in a changing world. In the United States, between 1852 (Massachusetts) and 1918 (Mississippi), every state eventually enacted laws mandating students be educated at the state's expense. Each state set the ages at which kids had to begin school and when they could leave school. Each state regulated the number of days children had to attend school, the number of hours of school they had to attend each day, the extent of school holidays, and, in some cases, they set curricular requirements, too.

Along with these changes, led by capitalist education reformers, politicians, ministers, and business leaders, there was a push to expand higher education in the famous colleges and universities of New England that dated back to colonial times. From the time of the Constitution until 1820, a new college opened, on average, every two years; by the end of this period, the average rate was three or four a year. By the time of the Civil War, the United States boasted nearly a thousand independent, decentralized institutions of higher education that enrolled close to 150,000 students.

For most of the nineteenth century, these tended to be small, denominational colleges, averaging fewer than ninety students each.

Some colleges, established by white settlers less as educational ventures than as a means of advertising the potential of the frontier, existed before there was compulsory K–12 education in their region. They were poorly staffed and financially dysfunctional, and they often lacked textbooks and facilities of any kind. Professors were paid in chickens, eggs, pigs, or not at all. Often a "college" existed in name only on promotional materials.

The need for specialized training across the spectrum of society—from farms to factories—is perhaps best exemplified in the push to create a system of publicly funded universities that could address the needs of those living in rural areas of the country while participating in the larger processes of industrialization, agribusiness, and mass production. In 1862, near the start of the Civil War, Congressman Justin Morrill proposed what came to be known as the Morrill Acts, which allowed the money from the sale of federal lands to homesteaders to be repurposed as endowments given back to each state to fund "land-grant" universities. Each eligible state was allotted thirty thousand acres of federal land, either within the state's borders or in the homestead lands beyond. Proceeds from the sale of this land could be used to establish educational institutions. During the Civil War, Southern states were prohibited from participating in this program; yet, in 1890, under the second Morrill Act, the same benefits were extended to the former Confederate states. The point was, in the words of Justin Morrill, to make higher education "accessible to all, but especially to the sons of toil."

Land-grant colleges transformed American society by extending the reach and mission of higher education far beyond those of the Ivy League schools that embodied the Puritan college model. The rationale for many of these land-grant universities was to bring the new science of agriculture and its concomitant social and economic developments to rural America: the schools would educate and professionalize farmers. Scientific crop rotation, animal husbandry, and soil enhancement were all part of modern farming, a subject to be studied at university, not simply learned from elder generations.

Yet these land-grant universities were not vocational in a narrow sense. Consider this lofty statement of purpose from the Morrill Acts: "Without excluding other scientific and classical studies and including military tactics, to teach such branches of learning as are related to agriculture and the mechanic arts, in such manner as the legislatures of the States may respectively prescribe, in order to promote the liberal and practical education of the industrial classes in the several pursuits and professions in life."

Almost all of the universities established were public (MIT and Cornell are two exceptions). At the end of the Civil War, when the second Morrill Act extended the land-grant universities into the former Confederate states, a new provision was added that resulted in the creation of historically black colleges and universities (HBCUs).

Because the Morrill Act funding disallowed racial segregation in the new schools even as many Southern states legally segregated blacks and whites, HBCUs were established proximate to Southern (white) land-grant institutions to technically fulfill the terms of the Morrill Act. This is one way in which higher education participated in the racist and racialized "separate but equal" laws of Jim Crow accepted as a "compromise" during Reconstruction.

In 1869, when Charles Eliot addressed the shortcomings of existing institutions of higher learning in his manifesto "The New Education," he purposely excluded the land-grant universities from his critique. Because they were only "four or five years" in conception and only a few months old in terms of "actual work," it was too early to judge how innovative they might be. Like others of his time, however, he was aware that these regional public universities offered a different model for higher education, one far more connected to the needs of their communities than anything the Puritan colleges had to offer. Indeed, a majority of the founding presidents of land-grant universities had graduated from the elite colleges of New England (including Harvard) and were unprepared to reconcile the discrepancy between their education in Greek, Latin, and mathematics and the mission of the new universities rising from the soil of East Lansing, Michigan, or Ames, Iowa.

Against a growing national recognition that citizens of an industrialized America needed a relevant higher education, Charles Eliot led revolutionary transformation at the nation's oldest and most prestigious universities. If change was happening everywhere in America, Eliot argued, institutions of higher education certainly needed to reflect it in their curriculums. In their antiquated state, Harvard and the other Ivy Leagues could not be trusted to train competent leaders of the new universities, corporations, professions, government offices, and other rapidly changing institutions.

AT THE TIME OF THE PANIC OF 1857, IT WAS ASSUMED THAT A HARvard professor would be independently wealthy and would not need to earn an income, certainly not by teaching. For Eliot, his Harvard salary was symbolic, more honorarium than living wage. After the financial panic, his tutor's income was all he had. He worried that he would have to "abandon chemistry, and instead go into business in order to earn a livelihood."

Caught up in the excitement over new forms of higher learning and how they could contribute to the burgeoning new industries of the nation, Eliot decided to postpone his entry into the business world and, instead, pursue the business of higher education reform. Europe had already gone through extensive educational transformation, so, in 1863, Eliot used an inheritance from his grandfather, supplemented by a loan, and set out on an extended trip to Europe to study the new research universities flourishing in Germany and France. With his wife, Emily, and their two sons—one a toddler, the other still an infant—Eliot set himself a rigorous course of study of the superior European system of higher education, including the vocational schools, which were older and more developed than the new American land-grant universities, and the distinguished universities dedicated to training Europe's elites.

As were many of his American contemporaries, Eliot was drawn to the University of Berlin (later renamed the Humboldt University of Berlin), which had been established in 1810 by the liberal educational reformer Wilhelm von Humboldt. Like Harvard, the University of Berlin was designed for elites, not for the general population, and was dedicated to cultivating the talent of future political and intellectual leaders. The rationalist foundation of the university meant that it concentrated on the idea of *bildung* (building) the whole man (women were not admitted).

Disciplinary in structure, the curriculum at the University of Berlin was far more expansive than that of its American counterparts. Humboldt himself had passionately championed the humanities—literature, history, modern languages, aesthetics, and linguistics (his own field)—which he saw as continuous with, rather than separate from, the crucial study of natural science, engineering, and technology. He believed every field of study required foundational principles based on logic, reasoning, and the connectedness of knowledge.

The Humboldtian university was cosmopolitan, with the goal of making its students citizens of the world. It combined research and teaching, science and the arts, all considered necessary schooling for the socially responsible individual. Inspired by its founder's Enlightenment belief in rationalism as a social good, a hallmark of this new research university was what we now call "academic freedom"— freedom to pursue research without regard to the religious, political, economic, or intellectual leanings of university administrators or ruling political parties. The university promoted the development and interchange of free, independent ideas that could lead to the betterment of society. Humboldt had emphasized that universities should be subsidized by the state, not driven by capitalistic market demands and pressures.

Eliot also studied the French system, which was based on a different model of higher education. Whereas the German university emphasized selection, diversity, and choice, the French system was rooted in the "universal," meaning standardization and regularization of the curriculum, requirements, and admissions procedures. Eliot studied carefully the advantages and drawbacks of each system, comparing the more prescriptive French system with the German emphasis on choice, the ability of students to choose their elective courses and the professors who would direct their research.

Because his broad aim was to consider the impact of an advanced system of higher education on society, Eliot augmented his study of the universities with interviews of people from all walks of life, from shop floor workers and milliners in France to corporate leaders and even princes and princesses in Germany. He interviewed people who attended university and people who did not, people in professional occupations and those in poverty, students as well as professors, professional educators and college dropouts. He wanted to assess the societal effects of the university, as perceived by the widest segments of society.

He noted that in Europe, especially in Germany, all of the universities had been founded by the aristocracy, including the so-called polytechnics designed for skilled tradespeople. This resulted in a system of education that was virtually free for students undertaking advanced training and in a workforce far more skilled and knowledgeable than that in the United States.

Eliot applauded many of the reforms he saw during his tour of Europe and had significant reservations about what might or might not work in the United States. He knew Americans would not accept a federally funded, top-down, uniform, national university system. From the beginning, education in America had been a local responsibility. Mandatory or homogeneous reforms would not be possible, so he concentrated instead on making Harvard and other elite universities models of change for other institutions to follow.

One area where Eliot's thinking deviated strongly from that of European educators was the idea that young people should be funneled into a vocation early. In Europe, children aged ten to thirteen were sorted into educational tracks that directed them either to the university or to the vocation-oriented polytechnic. They were also assigned to study a specific subject or discipline. Students didn't specialize in theoretical chemistry and then swerve into education as a college sophomore, for example. Eliot, by contrast, upheld the

American idea of higher education as a formalized opportunity to rethink one's vocation and retool toward a different future.

A combination of shrewd choices and fortuitous timing enabled Charles Eliot to transform Harvard and create the American research university. While on his information-gathering trip in Europe, Eliot was offered a lucrative and impressive opportunity: a major textile mill, Merrimack Company of Lowell, Massachusetts, wanted him to be, essentially, its CEO. He would be paid the exorbitant salary of $5,000 a year and given a house to live in for free.

Because one of the main reasons he had toured Europe was to figure out how American higher education could produce more corporate leaders, especially in the manufacturing sector, the offer to run a company was tempting. He could have employed his training in chemistry in the factory, combining his intellectual and his business interests.

He had another job offer, too. The new Massachusetts Institute of Technology, one of the few private land-grant institutions, was just opening its doors to its first class. Eliot decided not to go into business. He accepted a position at MIT, becoming its first professor of chemistry, at a salary of $3,500, significantly more than he would have earned at Harvard.

Harvard was then going through a challenging period. In quick succession within a decade, three presidents—all trained as ministers—had resigned or died in office. At the same time, more and more leaders in the business community started to agree with Eliot that the college was doing a poor job preparing its students for the modern world.

While he was a professor at MIT, Eliot published the long, scathing two-part essay, "The New Education." The essay caused a stir and put Eliot at the center of a national debate on the scope and purpose of higher education and what was needed to radically reform the university for industrial society.

To the surprise of most observers, when the Harvard Corporation found itself locked in a dispute over who might best lead the college in its time of internal turmoil and external disapproval, Eliot's name was proposed. Not everyone found the idea acceptable.

Some members of the Harvard Corporation balked, whereas others saw Eliot as the practical visionary the institution needed. Eliot was not a clergyman or a classicist, the two vocations most central to Harvard's identity. Nonetheless, on October 19, 1869, at the age of thirty-five, he was elected and then inaugurated as president of Harvard University.

He began his term with a bang. Most inaugural addresses, then and now, are drenched in platitudes, but Eliot opened with a clear articulation of changes he would pursue during his tenure. He insisted that Americans were not ignorant by nature. He blamed—as did many Europeans—poor schooling as the problem: "Not nature, but an unintelligent system of instruction from the primary school to the college." In his view, the real question was not "what to teach, but how." He put his colleagues on notice that, in his role as president, he intended to enact far-reaching modifications of the university.

And from the start, he led decisively, restructuring the most basic elements of the academy into new courses, fields, disciplines, and requirements. He changed working conditions for professors and preferences and admission standards for students. He extended the offerings of the university to formal medical and professional schools, for which he raised funds. He joined with the most important capitalists of the era to finance enormous institutional growth and rehabilitated everything from the admissions procedures to the graduation requirements, from athletic offerings to race relations.

He was in constant contact with other education leaders, including Andrew D. White at Cornell and James Angell at the University of Michigan, as well as the founders of three private regional research universities, Daniel Coit Gilman (Johns Hopkins University), William Rainey Harper (University of Chicago), and David Starr Jordan (Stanford University). Together they formed networks and associations that included virtually every other college president in America and began to redefine the university as a place and a means for training professional managers who could thrive amid the economic, technological, and social dislocations of the late nineteenth and the early twentieth century.

For all his concern with a relevant education, Eliot was opposed to the idea of a strictly technical, vocational education such as that offered by Germany's polytechnic universities. He believed vocationalism did not produce the intended result: "To make a good engineer, chemist, or architect, the only sure way is to make first, or at least simultaneously, an observant, reflecting, and sensible man, whose mind is not only well stored, but well trained also to see, compare, reason, and decide. The vigorous training of the mental powers is therefore the primary object of every well-organized technical school. At the same time a well-arranged course of study . . . will include a vast deal of information and many practical exercises appropriate to the professions which the students have in view."

In 1909, forty years after he took the job, in a letter to his friend Edward Everett Hale, Eliot listed what he considered to be his greatest achievements:

I. The re-organization and ample endowment of the Medical School.
II. The re-making of the Law School under Langdell.
III. The re-building of the Divinity School on a scientific basis with a Faculty containing members of several denominations.
IV. The establishment of religious services on a voluntary basis under a board of preachers representing several denominations.
V. The requiring of a previous degree for admission to all the professional schools except the Dental School, which is moving in the same direction.
VI. The administration of the University as a unified group of departments—one undergraduate department and many graduate schools.
VII. The perfecting of the elective system as a system.
VIII. The increase of the endowments and of the number of students.
IX. The remarkable rise in the scholarly quality of the men appointed to teach in the University.

It's an expansive list. Of special note is how much Eliot concentrated on professionalization and admissions requirements for the new professional schools. This meant, for all of Harvard faculty as well as students, a new emphasis on research, specialization, and credentialing, changes that would have a necessary impact on Harvard College, too. Each of Eliot's nine top achievements necessitated extensive transformations of other aspects of the university as well. In order to change instruction to allow for a wider range of interests and talents (electives), Eliot had to reconsider the university's admissions standards and allow in students with a wider educational background than one in Greek, Latin, and mathematics. In order to expand the size of the student body and improve its quality, he looked for applicants who were not descendants of elite Harvard alumni. Perhaps even more remarkably, in the name of excellence, he championed what we would now call "diversity" as crucial to improving and modernizing the intellectual life of Harvard, making it less insular and less provincial. Unlike several of his predecessors, he did not oppose admission of either Jews or Roman Catholics. He also admitted African Americans, including a young man who would go on to become one of the most famous sociologists of the twentieth century, W. E. B. Du Bois, the first African American to earn a PhD at Harvard. Because the most brilliant students were frequently not the wealthiest, Eliot also raised an endowment and offered students financial aid.

Although Eliot could not imagine women on the same campus as men, he very much supported women's education, a progressive stance in Victorian America, when many scientists and medical professionals argued that learning could tax and even destroy women's reproductive capabilities and diminish their maternal instincts. In his 1869 inaugural address, Eliot noted: "The world knows next to nothing about the natural mental capacities of the female sex. Only after generations of civil freedom and social equality will it be possible to obtain the data necessary for an adequate discussion of woman's natural tendencies, tastes, and capabilities." He quickly reassured his audience that he had no intention of subjecting Harvard to an experiment in gender equality: "It is not the business of the University to decide this mooted point."

Yet in 1879 he was receptive when a Cambridge businessman, Arthur Gilman, came to him with a request. Gilman had started the Private Collegiate Instruction for Women, known then as the "Harvard Annex," and later renamed Radcliffe College. Gilman offered Harvard faculty bonus salaries to teach there so that his brilliant daughter and other young women could experience a first-class education. Gilman asked Eliot whether the relationship with Harvard might be formalized. Eliot agreed, and he and Gilman enticed a number of prominent local women to take leadership roles, including Elizabeth Cary Agassiz, the wife of the famous naturalist Louis Agassiz. She would become the first president of Radcliffe College. Other Harvard faculty members were persuaded (and paid well) to teach the young women of Radcliffe a more comprehensive array of subjects than they would have encountered at many of the women's colleges of the time: modern languages, philosophy, music, history, political economy, natural history, mathematics, and physics.

Perhaps Eliot's most important and lasting contribution, inspired by the Humboldtian university, was his emphasis on student choice. He believed students should be allowed to choose both courses and professors. Allowing students to choose their course of study meant that the university would need to adapt to the trends that emerged. The rush of students into certain fields and courses taught by particular professors showed which academic areas were in demand and others that were in decline. New, advanced courses in the most desired areas had to be added and new faculty hired. This necessitated new graduate programs to train the next generation of professors in those fields and that room be made in the existing faculty. Eliot designed handsome retirement and pension packages to incentivize strategic retirements, a previously unheard of practice. Again, each change was connected to others, and the whole system was reengineered at once.

To promote new fields of research and to reward faculty excellence, new criteria for advancement had to be developed. New faculty, like new students, were not accepted solely because they were descendants of Harvard alumni, and it was no longer assumed that instructors had trust funds to supplement their income. Eliot raised the typical Harvard professor's annual salary from \$3,000 to \$4,000, making it possible for them to support a family. He developed a system for advancement and tenure inspired by the German research university's emphasis on the primacy of research and intellectual freedom.

Writing in 1909, on the occasion of Eliot's retirement as president of Harvard, Eugen Kuehnemann, a visiting professor from Germany, considered his accomplishments. Whereas Eliot had provided his friend Edward Everett Hale with an unannotated list, Kuehnemann was more expansive. He noted:

> A new spirit had to be infused into this new organism. There had to be a complete change of methods as well as of aims, and, what was still more, a raising of the standards of work was imperatively needed in all the departments. The easy-going pursuit of prescribed courses was to give way to real study, determined by the student's own resolution and on his own responsibility. The drill system with its merely practical aims was to be replaced by a thoroughly scholarly training befitting the dignity and importance of the learned professions. But the most urgent task was to determine the proper relation between general education and professional training. Only those possessed of a general education, acquired by independently chosen study in the college, were to be admitted to the professional schools. That was the final aim. Truly, the very conception of American education was involved in the momentous decision of these questions.

The features of the modern American university that Eliot invented, experimented with, implemented, or institutionalized during his long presidency make an impressive list: majors, minors, divisions (humanities, social sciences, natural and biological sciences), credit hours, degree requirements, grades, the bell curve, deviation from the mean, class rankings, certification, general education, upper-division electives, ability to choose professors, optional attendance policies, professionalization (credentials, accreditation), graduate schools, collegiate law schools, nursing schools, graduate schools of education, collegiate business schools, Harvard Annex for women (later Radcliffe College), competitive scholarships, financial aid, college entrance exams, capital fund-raising campaigns, living wages for professors, tenure, sabbaticals, faculty pensions, school rankings, new courses and subjects (including natural history, algebra, laboratory physics, geometry, modern languages, American archaeology, and anthropology), secularization, and optional prayer (the first American college to end compulsory prayer).

Many of these were profoundly new, even radical features for American higher education. Most were in place by 1909 and fully institutionalized across numerous institutions by 1925. Not a single item needs explanation for anyone reading today because they remain the basics of the university we have inherited. As Eliot's accomplishment, that's remarkable. As the continuing infrastructure for higher education in the twenty-first century, it's the problem.

THE TRANSFORMATION OF THE PURITAN COLLEGE INTO THE MODern American university—*our* university—happened at a specific historical moment in response to extensive societal changes wrought by industrialization. In leading that revolution in higher education, Eliot and his colleagues were part of the *zeitgeist* of industrialization, data-driven scientific methods, quantifiable outcomes, professionalization, specialization, new modes of manufacturing, and new ideas about labor and management. The presidents at the nation's most elite institutions of higher education financed their ambitions for higher education reforms by working with the wealthiest industrialists of the day. University of Chicago president William Rainey Harper joined forces with oil magnate John D. Rockefeller, and President David Starr Jordan with railroad magnate Leland Stanford. Eliot worked closely with these and many of the other industrialists of the day.

The philanthropists involved in the transformation of higher education—Carnegie, Rockefeller, Cornell, James Buchanan Duke,

Marshall Field, Cornelius Vanderbilt—were known by another name to the general public: robber barons. They differed from one another greatly in political persuasion and personality and yet shared many assumptions about the importance of professionalism and productivity. Like Eliot and other educators, they also believed in the prevailing business and management theory in the United States in the 1880s and 1890s. They were in step with (and sometimes directly influenced by) the work of the architect of "scientific labor management," Frederick Winslow Taylor, whose principal objective was to apply quantifiable or "scientific" measurement to labor to increase economic efficiency and productivity.

Although Taylor began his studies in factories, he believed his practices for measuring inputs and outputs pertained to all labor, including that in corporate boardrooms, professional associations, and universities. He presided over the American Society of Mechanical Engineers and worked to institute and regulate top-down standards for that field. He would go on to become the first professor hired by one of America's first collegiate business schools, the Tuck School of Business at Dartmouth, and worked to translate scientific labor management into academic practice. Standardization of labor practices, of measurements, of productivity quotas became key to the management of factories and assembly lines—and came to influence a new approach to higher education that increasingly relied on quantitative metrics as the means for certifying quality and expertise. Eliot knew Taylor's work, and Taylor knew Eliot's.

Taylor's time-and-motion studies were designed to maximize the efficiency of specialized labor. The distinctive feature of an assembly line is that no longer is one person skilled at all or many aspects of making a product. Instead, production is divided into separate tasks, and each person is trained to complete one operation, on time, on the assembly line, over and over and over, with maximum expertise and efficiency. Taylor argued that each task could be accomplished at greater and greater efficiency if certain principles were followed. Those principles included the specialized training of every employee, evaluation of those employees, and addition of managers trained to supervise and measure worker efficiency. Taylor favored a hierarchical system by which supervisors in factories instructed those who worked for them to be as regular, repetitive, and machine-like as possible. Workflow was designed to be consistent; a worker was expected to work at the same pace at the end of a long day as at the day's beginning. Human working life, in short, was fitted to the rhythms and necessities of the machine, and human outputs and efficiency were judged by standardized measurements, all of which we know as "Taylorism" today.

Taylor developed his ideas while working as a manager in a pig iron factory. The son of a wealthy family, Taylor attended Phillips Exeter Academy and passed the entrance examination for Harvard with honors. He planned to go to Harvard Law School to follow in his father's profession. Instead, like a forerunner of Bill Gates or Mark Zuckerberg, he decided that industry, not law, was the future. At the pig iron factory, he invented his theories of scientific labor management. His new science measured how much pig iron a laborer could be incentivized to carry in a ten-hour workday and set quotas for how much workers should be able to carry and how fast. He called those who met the quotas "soldiers" and those who did not "malingerers." He rewarded the former and had no problem penalizing and even firing the latter.

In designing college education to prepare students for a world increasingly shaped by industrialization and, later, by Taylorism, Eliot and his colleagues embraced specialization, standardized analytics, and constant evaluation by peers and supervisors. Led by Harvard, nearly every elite university moved to a system driven by selective admissions testing and measurable outcomes, the higher education equivalents of Taylor's worker productivity calculations. Universities divided knowledge into distinct and specialized departments (disciplines, majors, minors, and combinations of required courses and electives), at least partly inspired by Taylorist theories of the division of labor and the efficiencies of each worker mastering one specific part of a job using a particular method. Professionalism in higher education became almost synonymous with specialization, in sharp contrast to earlier historical ideals of what it meant to be learned, such as the "Renaissance man," a multitalented, versatile, visionary, cross-disciplinary thinker. Specialized academic training and reputation were consonant with Taylorist and other forms of industrial age management philosophy that emphasized the efficiency of job descriptions that defined specific prerequisites, functions, duties, and responsibilities. The new field of "human resources," which gained currency in the 1890s, fed off of and into Taylorism as well as into the founding mission of new graduate schools, professional schools, and research universities, which organized knowledge around production of relevant, peer-reviewed research within a specific discipline or professional association.

Even the nation's liberal arts colleges followed suit, reorganizing their curriculums in ways that resembled Harvard's: two years of general education before students chose a major and possibly a minor, too. The New England Association of Colleges and Preparatory Schools, which Eliot helped to found, designed rankings and accreditation systems by which the nation's diverse institutions of higher education could be compared, judged, and ranked. Each and every aspect of an institution was judged by an implicit or explicit system of values, often measured quantitatively by such inputs as "selectivity" or "admission rate" and by outputs such as attainment of high grade point averages (a new concept and method for reducing knowledge to a letter or a number). Harvard and the other Ivy League research universities became the implicit standard against which the merit of every other college and university was judged. Expanding educational opportunities beyond the descendants of alumni, in other words, lent new weight to admissions exams and importance to selectivity (and rejection rates) and contributed to the elite institutions gaining top rankings that other institutions aspired to.

In keeping with this new emphasis on rankings and metrics, educators at the top institutions created the College Entrance Examination Board (CEEB) on December 22, 1899. Based at Columbia University, the CEEB was charged with designing more uniform entrance exams. The CEEB created written exams that anyone could take in the fields of botany, chemistry, English, French, German, Greek, history, Latin, mathematics, physics, and zoology. The exams also allowed for comparisons of the student bodies across the different colleges and universities that administered them. The higher the aggregated exam scores of a university's students, the higher the ranking of the university.

Students, faculty, and whole institutions increasingly were graded by predetermined and measurable sets of values at the same time that Taylorism replaced experiential, quality judgments with supposedly scientific time-and-motion studies that quantified the productivity of shop floor workers. He also devised new accountancy methods and scheduling charts for middle managers and executives. Eliot's university, like Taylor's management theories, emphasized the relationship between time and knowledge. The invention of the "credit hour," for example, necessitated standardizing the requirements and regulations for how long students had to be in school and in a classroom ("contact hours"). The prescribed numbers of hours per class session per course per year and per degree were concurrent features in the realms of management and academe.

The distance from measuring worker productivity carrying pig iron in wheelbarrows to determining college admission to elite universities by standardized test scores is closer than we would like to imagine. Influenced by Taylor's ideas that every worker should be held to production quotas and that specialized labor is more productive than general competency, Eliot and other educators of the day designed the modern university to train the nation's elite to assume their role as leaders of the industrial age. They would be trained to become the professional-managerial class in a time of rapid technological, scientific, social, and economic change.

Eliot's innovations—now mandatory, standardized, and regulated for well over a hundred years—may have been useful to the creation of the professional-managerial class required by a newly industrialized and urbanized country. The features of the modern university designed to train and to measure specialized knowledge production were desirable because they enabled people to be pigeonholed into hierarchical corporate structures. Eliot's university was designed for stability on the basis of an apprenticeship model where students were tested on the knowledge they have coming into the university and tested in each course on the way to a degree in a specific field where specialists had defined the degree requirements. What constitutes "excellence" and a "field" in the first place is still based on standards established by the elite universities.

Eliot's system did not make innovation easy on a structural level, even if one of his goals was to train fully rounded and independent-thinking graduates. Nor was it flexible, adaptive, geared to the circumstances (economic or regional) of the institution or to the varying abilities of students. In fact, it narrowed what *counts* as aptitude and intelligence, as creativity and ingenuity, to that which can be tested according to standardized metrics—intellectual production quotas—established in advance. It is no wonder that the same era that produced all of these interrelated institutional features of higher education also invented "giftedness" and "learning disabilities," new terms to account for human differences, to address the fact that some otherwise exceptional and admirable students had shortcomings that simply did not, quite literally, "measure up."

In the modern university, what Fredrick Winslow Taylor called "scientific labor management" was translated into what could well be called "scientific learning management." The worldwide preeminence of standardized testing today can be traced back to these roots, when a streamlined, standardized answer was considered "scientific" and a good index for intelligence, aptitude, or achievement. This must have been baffling to earlier educators, for whom recitation, oratory, debate, and other forms of performance ranked high. Because we have so thoroughly accepted these machine age ways of thinking about education, it is hard to peel back all the assumptions to see how historically specific they are. When we do, it is surprising to notice that many of the notions that shape formal education today really are archaic, even odd.

Many progressive educators, at that time and in the intervening decades, have protested the reduction of all the different ways we learn, think, and know the world to machine-gradable test scores and all the pedagogical and curricular corollaries to standardized testing. John Dewey, Maria Montessori, and progressive thinkers at the turn of the twentieth century objected to reducing humans to test-taking trainees checking off boxes on the way to a degree. A hundred years of sophisticated, thorough learning research and theory—Paulo Freire's critical pedagogy, Howard Gardner's multiple intelligences, bell hooks's activist learning, and Carol Dweck's growth mind-set—separate us from the prevailing thinking at the time of the creation of the research university. A century of studies has revealed what learning is, how people learn differently and in different circumstances and in different fields, how people perform in groups, and how being invested in one's own projects and following them through from initial idea to completion and implementation teach incomparably more than any standardized test can measure.

Yet we have not incorporated these findings about active learning into the institutional practices of most of our elite universities. Quite the opposite. Graduate students who plan to become college professors undergo rigorous training in their field of specialization but almost never take even a single course in pedagogy. They rarely know much at all about the research on new (or even old) ways of teaching and learning. If apprenticeship (learning the way your adviser learned) is the institutional ideal, then faculty have no reason to understand how to teach their students more effectively. Faculty operate under the assumption that their graduate students learn by imitating faculty advisers the way these advisers learned to imitate their own mentors. Pedagogy is irrelevant. So is change.

We rely now more than ever on tools and ideas championed by Taylor and incorporated into the infrastructure of the modern university by Taylor and his colleagues. Consider the SATs, the gatekeeper for college. The first multiple-choice exams that could be graded by a grid or grade sheet (later, by machine) were developed in the early twentieth century. They met a need: new laws requiring students to stay in school until age sixteen had been passed, effectively transforming secondary education from precollege training for the elite into mass education for everyone, including the millions of immigrants arriving in America at the time. There were not enough teachers to give every student individual attention and elaborate written feedback. The tests automated the complex process of learning assessment, reducing knowledge to one best answer among four or five distractors, and were easily marked by an untrained grader using an answer grid. The inventor of the single-best-answer timed test was a doctoral student at Emporia State University (previously Kansas State Teachers' College), Frederick J. Kelly. Inspired by the new methods for determining IQ (intelligence quotient, ca. 1904), he developed the Kansas Silent Reading Test in 1914. These ideas were entirely of their moment. If Model Ts could be produced cheaply and effectively by standardization and automation ("any color you want so long as it's black"), then so could learning.

Here's a sample test question designed by Kelly and included in his 1914 dissertation: "Below are given the names of four animals. Draw a line around the name of each animal that is useful on the farm: cow tiger rat wolf." The dissertation continues: "The exercise tells us to draw a line around the word 'cow.' No other answer is right. Even if a line is drawn under the word 'cow,' the answer is wrong, and nothing counts. . . . Stop at once when time is called. Do not open the papers until told, so that all may begin at the same time."

Drawing a line under rather than a circle around means I don't get into Harvard? By 1925, this timed multiple-choice test, in a form anyone today would recognize, became the Scholastic Aptitude Test. Ninety years later, a good score on the SATs continues to guarantee admission to college, even though many of the assumptions behind multiple-choice testing have been discredited. Is a perfect score a testament to intelligence or passivity? Is it a sign of aptitude or affluence and access to teachers trained to "teach to the test"? Does it yield insight into someone's creative potential and ability to change and learn and relearn, or is it a good indicator of exactly the opposite? The United States tests earlier and more often than any other nation on the planet. And our overreliance on tests is only the tip of the iceberg. We've been honing and perfecting, regulating and expanding Eliot's system of higher education for a century.

ELIOT'S UNIVERSITY HAS HAD A GOOD, LONG RUN. YET IT NO longer prepares young people for the conceptual, epistemological, economic, intellectual, and social demands of the complex and often disturbing world we live in today. Even the most basic categories in Eliot's time simply do not hold in our post-Internet world. What is the division of "work" and "leisure" in a world where everything I do—my work life, personal life, social life, political life—and all the information and requirements of who I am and what I do comes to me on a smartphone that fits in the palm of my hand?

More and more, I will have an AI-driven device set up in my home that *tells me* what I want to do based on data it silently, watchfully gathers as I go about my days. I can enter my nineteenth-century office building, walk down the corridor that splits each department and discipline at my university into physically separate spaces, go into my private office, and then, with my door closed and myself cordoned off from the world, turn on my desktop computer and the entire world—personal, social, and professional—comes tumbling in all at once. Conversely, when I finally escape on vacation as far away from the office as I can manage, I cannot make a call on my smartphone without seeing an email from my department chair that requires an immediate response. Very little in the higher education process of today prepares us for managing the integrated, merged, and chaotic work and home lives most of us are now experiencing.

Ours is not the world for which Eliot and his colleagues created majors, minors, graduate schools, and professional schools. Indeed, many of the professions for which individuals now train in the most rigorous ways no longer exist in a way that makes sense. For example, many medical students end up earning a second degree in another field because medical school doesn't prepare them for the way medicine is practiced. Occupations for which an advanced degree—

including graduate degrees and professional school degrees—was required are rapidly being outsourced, offshored, or reduced to low-pay, insecure, "ambient" work (contingent, with no labor protections, no job security, and no benefits). That's true for accounting, journalism, computer programming, and college teaching.

As you will see, colleges and universities have not simply stood still since Eliot handed down credit hours, tenure, the nursing school, and so on. Most institutions are constantly adding new programs relevant to the world today. Whether creating programs on genome ethics, data science and society, or race and law enforcement, universities work hard to address the most pressing issues of the times.

In fact, nearly every college and university today hosts parallel systems. On the one hand, they offer traditional majors, minors, departments, and disciplines that bear remarkable resemblance to those created for the industrial age university. Traditional departments hire new faculty members and are responsible for their promotion and tenure. College rankings, too, tend to be based on productivity in these core disciplines that look like the Harvard and Radcliffe curricular core of 1900 (modern languages, philosophy, music, history, political economy, natural history, mathematics, and physics). Job listings for new professors are advertised in the bulletins of the same professional associations that award grants and fellowships to graduate students and new professors, making it hard to stray too far beyond the boundaries of traditional disciplines.

Yet the real action at most universities and colleges is happening outside these traditional areas, in institutes, initiatives, and interdisciplinary groups that typically span the inherited structures, that are often inspired by the most innovative research of the faculty, and that usually offer students opportunities to engage in original research, real-world projects, internships, or experiential learning outside the various requirements and assumptions of the traditional majors. Interdisciplinary programs tend to exist in a somewhat uneasy or even antagonistic relationship with the core departments. They are also most vulnerable to cutbacks. Because the movement to make college more "economical" by cutting "frills" is so closely tied to ideological goals, often the most relevant programs with the most flexible career opportunities are the first to be eliminated.

The traditional infrastructure of the contemporary university remains remarkably similar to what Eliot and his colleagues designed. Yet it is no longer serving our students well. Charles Eliot and his colleagues redesigned American higher education in response to the changes in the nineteenth century that had altered the conditions of life and work and that required, as they saw it, a new kind of specialized, measured, quantifiable approach to educating the nation's youth.

It was a brilliant answer to massive transformation that occurred a hundred years ago.

It's what we're saddled with today—and what many of us are working very hard to change.

2 COLLEGE FOR EVERYONE

GLIB, NARCISSISTIC, AND QUICK TO PALM OFF THE GRUNT WORK TO
someone else, Jeff fit to a T the stereotype of the callow young lawyer
on the make, his suits as shiny and pricey as his Ivy League pedigree.
Then everything fell apart. With his degree exposed as issuing forth
from *Colombia,* the for-profit degree mill, not from the famous Columbia University, Jeff was suspended from his law firm, disgraced
and disbarred. He resolved to start over.

As in all morality tales, Jeff's plummet from social grace ended
up being his saving grace, maybe even his salvation. His detour from
a life of great material rewards became an opportunity to find deeper
human riches. Even with intermittent backsliding on his way to a
moral path, Jeff gradually dropped his defenses and learned humility,
patience, hard work, and respect for others. Slowly, step-by-step, he
traveled a long road toward happiness. He grasped a second chance
to live life on a different scale—better, more human, humane. His
path began at Greendale Community College.

Meet Jeff Winger, played by actor Joel McHale, the star of the
cult NBC comedy series *Community.* Created by comedian and

writer Dan Harmon and based on his experiences attending community college, the plot of *Community* is straightforward. Still at square one on his winding road to salvation—that is, an associate's degree— Jeff is determined to seduce a fellow Greendale student, Britta Perry, a radical activist and high school dropout who is returning to community college after traveling around the world. To get closer to her, Jeff invites Britta to join him in a study group. She agrees. But because she really intends to work, she invites several classmates to join: Abed Nadir, the Palestinian-Polish popular-culture trivia addict who sits somewhere on the ADHD spectrum; Troy Barnes, the handsome African American jock who uncomfortably reveals he is a geek at heart; Annie Edison, the insecure young brainiac working to overcome social anxieties and a high school addiction to Adderall; and Pierce Hawthorne, the affluent, closed-minded senior citizen "returning student" who (played by the perfectly unctuous Chevy Chase) spouts platitudes of self-discovery to anyone he can bully into listening.

This is the eccentric, diverse cast of characters commonplace on sitcoms. In the segregated world most Americans inhabit, rarely does one actually encounter such diversity in everyday life. Except perhaps at an actual community college, where one finds people of all ages, backgrounds, races, economic classes, religions, and forms of intelligence, preparation, and determination. What is shared among this singularly diverse social group is a common goal: gaining an education. This TV *roman à clef* gets the demographics right. As our elite universities become ever more bastions of the 1 percent, with exorbitant tuitions that only the affluent can afford, community college works in the opposite way, by being open to those who need that second chance.

Welcome to college for everyone! Most of us grasp the purpose of community college. What we understand less is that all the rest of higher education has much to learn from these low-status schools. Because its mission, structure, and institutional design are almost the mirror image of Eliot's research university, community college offers a counterpoint to Eliot's university, above all a release from the tyranny of selectivity. Community college thus offers us a host of ideas for the new education.

The biggest difference between Eliot's four-year institution and the two-year community college model is mission. Whereas the research university puts its institutional reputation first, community college prioritizes student growth. Rather than beginning from a fixed standard of what counts as expertise—as recorded by a GPA or SAT scores—community college takes any student at any level in order to help that student reach their goal. You could be, in the example of *Community,* a disgraced and disbarred lawyer starting over from the professional and moral bottom or a former prescription drug addict or a lonely senior citizen seeking companionship or a smart, beautiful, formerly middle-class young woman who spent a little too long backpacking around the world in search of herself. None of these potential students is likely to be admitted to Stanford or Harvard because none is going to boost either university's rankings or likely add to its future glory.

The strength of community college and its ability to innovate and directly address the needs of its constituents lies in the fact that it is not part of the same ranking system used for four-year colleges and universities. If you are a new president at a four-year university, whether Harvard or a larger state school, one of your main goals is to increase your school's ranking, because improving rankings is seen as improving quality. Improved rankings also make it seem as if a new president is doing a good job.

The single fastest way a president can improve a university's ranking is to become more selective, because a chief factor in rankings is the admittance rate. Selectivity comes with other bonuses, too. Because you are recruiting better-prepared students, you almost automatically raise your institution's GPA levels, retention rates, and graduation rates, all without making other institutional improvements. Because public K–12 education in the United States is financed locally, we have one of the most unequal public education systems of any developed nation. Because local school systems are tremendously uneven, owing to class and de facto racial segregation, raising "standards" (that is, admission selectivity) means you are also likely to be selecting from a pool of wealthier and better-prepared students.

One result is that more of your students are likely to be full-time students. Although 62 percent of students in college today also work, more do at the large public universities than at elite privates, and far more do at community colleges. Holding down a job, not surprisingly, slows your time to graduation and affects your academic performance. Without the pressures of outside employment responsibilities, students who don't work are more likely to graduate sooner.

It's a perfect, closed circle. More elite students from more elite families in more elite K–12 schools more often end up at elite colleges and universities, where they graduate faster. Of course, in such an approach to admissions you limit diversity, racial and economic. Because of how economic and racial segregation work in our society, you are also likely to have fewer black, Hispanic, and new immigrant students. Community colleges are more diverse because they are not chasing rankings—and they are not chasing rankings because of their founding mission.

The infrastructure of the research university is based on exclusion, sorting, selecting, and ranking; the infrastructure of the community college is based on inclusion, remediating, improving, and offering first chances—and second, third, or however many are required for success. As a result, the way professors teach, the way students learn, and the metrics for success are different in community college. In the research university, those carefully selected students are judged against an implicit standard of excellence and expertise, represented by a distinguished faculty. In community college, virtually everyone is admitted, and the task is not for the student to replicate the expertise of the professor but, rather, for the student to gain the basic literacies required to move ahead.

By definition, community college centers on the student because there is no preset, a priori admission standard or criterion of selectivity based on a presumed, ranked hierarchy of status. There is no implicit or explicit ranking with Harvard and other elite universities at the pinnacle, setting the standards against which each and every student, professor, department, and institution is judged. A great community college keeps asking who in its community is not yet being served—disabled vets, the newly paroled, senior citizens, refugees, undocumented workers, stay-at-home moms—and figures out alternative ways of helping them reach their goals.

When your mission is to accept everyone, everything else about your institution has to support every student's success. This means low tuition and fees, access to financial aid, academic flexibility and variety, basic literacy and numeracy training, basic language and cultural training (including for immigrants), specialized skills-training opportunities based on the specific and up-to-date occupational requirements of a local community, professional certifications to augment traditional degrees and diplomas, personalized attention (with an emphasis on advising and small class size), extracurricular components, and online course offerings to supplement local courses and offer flexibility to those juggling the scheduling demands of school, jobs, and home life. The community college is set up to focus on the student—not the professor, not the profession, not the discipline, all of which are central to the status of the research university.

There is as much variety across different community colleges as there is across the array of four-year institutions. Some are primarily designed as trade schools or for specific vocational training programs, a role increasingly important as secondary schools abolish vocational training in the face of cutbacks. Others are designed to be feeders into four-year research universities and so duplicate the general education patterns of the first two years of traditional schools.

However, by design, community colleges are not mere substitutes for the first two years of a four-year college or university. They are student-centered, and this means their goal is to improve student knowledge, starting from whatever students come in with. The general education courses cannot assume that students enter college with the basics that solid, middle-class high schools provide in history, literature, the arts, social science, natural science, and math. So, rather than reject students as "unprepared" (as a four-year institution would), community colleges embrace the students and help them fill in the gaps in their knowledge and preparedness.

No wonder, then, that at a recent two-day workshop on leadership and peer mentoring for undergraduates from all over the City University of New York (CUNY) system, several of the students who were currently enrolled at four-year colleges after having completed an associate's degree at CUNY's two-year colleges came to me genuinely alarmed to plead that I talk to our system-wide CUNY chancellor: "You have to tell him. You have to let him know there's a terrible problem at our four-year colleges. Everything is backward there. It's almost as if they don't care about us, as if we don't count. Students are failing and getting lost!"

These were all exceptional students, A students, at three different (and selective) four-year colleges in the CUNY system. They were shocked when I informed them that, no, there wasn't something terribly wrong at these four-year institutions. These universities were actually doing what they were designed to do: "weed out" students who weren't prepared, who weren't "ready for college," as the phrase goes. Four-year institutions do not make it their job to nourish each and every student, from any background, to success. At their first gathering as a freshman class at a four-year institution, the dean of students often tells students, "Look to your left. Look to your right. Only one of you will be walking through graduation." At community college, the two who didn't make it would be welcomed with open arms and challenged to find a place from which they could build toward success.

At a faculty meeting at a four-year institution lamenting the poor preparation of incoming freshmen, the likely topics might be how to maintain standards and prevent grade inflation. At a community college faculty meeting confronting the same circumstance, the discussion well might center on how to address the need for remediation of students suffering under the current regime of rampant high-stakes testing and the corrosive effect of so much teaching to the test.

Like Jeff Winger smirking his way through his first day at Greendale in *Community*, we are unused to thinking of the community college as having something to offer the rest of higher education. We have internalized value systems that put community college at the bottom. "Santa Monica Community College is basically Grade Thirteen" one of my nieces was told, derisively, by her friends—even though it was the ideal college for her to hone her dream career to be a fine jewelry designer and to found her own business. Appreciating what we can borrow from community colleges means suspending over a hundred years of valuing the credential over the student, of valuing the mastery of expertise over actual learning, and of requiring that students learn from experts rather than empowering them to become more expert (at whatever level) themselves.

FROM ITS NINETEENTH-CENTURY BEGINNINGS, COMMUNITY COL-lege was intended as an alternative form of postsecondary education, not as a "lesser" institution in the four-year model. It was planned with a different standard of inclusiveness entirely. It was not de-signed to educate a professional-managerial class, the new kinds of leaders who could take America into an ascendant role on the global stage. It was not set up as an "also-ran" to four-year universities but, rather, was conceived with a distinct function and purpose.

Before 1850, only a handful of two-year institutions offered some form of postsecondary training, mostly teacher training. The great boom came in the decade from 1909 to 1919, when the number of community colleges nationwide grew from about twenty to nearly two hundred. Called "junior colleges," they increased in number at the same time that secondary school expanded beyond elites bound for college. The passage of state laws requiring students to stay in school until their mid-teenage years meant there was a general teacher shortage. There was also a shortage, specifically, of vocational education teachers. As high school became more inclusive, new voca-tional subjects were added to the curriculum, but, because the four-year colleges did not teach these vocational subjects, there wasn't a robust mechanism for training vocational teachers for secondary schools. Both factors led to the doubling of the number of junior colleges after World War I. New junior colleges were sometimes private, sometimes public, and they included church schools and for-profit schools offering specialized vocational teacher training.

As with four-year colleges, the new community colleges were designed specifically to meet the economic challenges of industrialization but with a focus on non-elite students. The global economic changes occasioned by industrialization required a more skilled, better-educated, more cosmopolitan or "worldly" population, or what might loosely be thought of as a literate middle class. This was, of course, one of the main reasons Eliot strove to remake and expand American higher education. But more than three-quarters of those who graduated from high school in 1900 did not go on to college or university, commonly because they did not have the desire or the financial resources or the flexibility to go away from home to a residential college. Community colleges offered training in specialized skills, a low-cost form of advanced education that could be pursued without disrupting one's home or work life.

Joliet Junior College is considered to be the first official modern-day junior or community college. It began as a combination high school–community college at Central High School in Joliet, Illinois. Students could attend the high school even after graduation to pursue specialized and advanced work in teacher training, vocational education, or citizenship (a general civics curriculum). Soon, the higher education component was moved to facilities away from the high school campus. Since the founding of Joliet, more than a hundred million people have attended community college in the United States.

From the start, community colleges had several distinctive features. Often, they were small overall and emphasized small class size. Unlike most four-year institutions, they opened to women early on and often emphasized training elementary school teachers. In states such as Missouri, which did not require that grammar school teachers have a bachelor's degree, it was common for over 60 percent of community college students to be women preparing to teach K–8 public education. Early on, community colleges became places where immigrants and minorities went to college, for economic reasons and because many residential colleges operated under overt or covert racist (e.g., segregationist, anti-Asian, and anti-Semitic) admissions policies.

Today, there are 1,166 community colleges in the United States, and about half of US undergraduates attend community college. For many of society's poorest, newest, and often most ambitious, determined, and potentially productive members, community college is their hoped-for route to the middle class and out of poverty. Approximately 44 percent of students with family incomes of less than $25,000 per year go to community colleges directly after high school graduation (compared to 15 percent of high-income students). Some 38 percent of first-generation college students go to community college first, whereas only 20 percent of those whose parents graduated from college do. Nearly half of all Hispanic students, 31 percent of African American students, and 28 percent of white students begin at community college. Community college is also a disrupter of the so-called school-to-prison pipeline, in which secondary school "zero tolerance" policies increase police involvement in schools and in students' lives. By admitting students who have come out of the criminal justice system and by sponsoring programs in prisons, community colleges are a small force against America's shameful distinction as the world's leading jailor.

Community college *works*. Average community college students earn significantly more income over their lifetime than do individuals from the same demographic groups who do not earn either a professional certificate or an associate's degree. One large-scale study of community college students from six states shows that students completing an associate's degree earn an average $5,400 a year more than students from the same background who do not complete the degree, a remarkable statistic given the high percentage of students who enter community college from families earning less than $25,000 a year. Nearly a quarter of those with associate's degrees earn more than the median earnings of those with bachelor's degrees. Community colleges rank higher than elite four-year universities if the standard isn't selectivity but what is known as the "social mobility index," a measure that calculates the difference between the income level of one's family upon entering college and the income one achieves at graduation. Community college truly offers people a way into the middle class.

Community colleges don't measure their success in supposedly objective measures of "excellence." They admit everyone with a high school diploma or who has passed the General Educational Development (GED) test, regardless of college entrance exam scores or prior academic record. Sixty percent of first-year students cannot take first-year college classes without some kind of remediation, typically in writing, reading, and, especially, mathematics. If our educational mission is to ensure that each student learns and thereby moves into a position of greater knowledge, then we must throw out many of the metrics higher education generally uses, including the bell curve, which dictates a predetermined grade distribution for success and failure. Structurally, many large public and private universities control the flow into certain majors through the academic ritual known as the "flunk-out course," typically a very large introductory lecture class in a subject area that can be graded by a standardized exam. Introductory math, statistics, and organic chemistry typically fall into that category where only a small percentage of students earn As. If the pre-med or math majors then require a certain grade point average for admission to the major, the lack of an A in that introductory course can be fatal to a student's career ambitions. That gatekeeping structure is antithetical to the mission and the curricular design of community college.

The bell curve and the flunk-out course work only when a deficit model of pedagogy is employed, when the professor has the expertise and evaluates students backward from that standard, excellent to failing. In the community college mission of knowledge for everyone, "I don't know" is a baseline, a starting place toward success, not a signifier of failure.

As selectivity at top private and public institutions rises, as GPA and test scores correlate ever more closely with affluence, and as income inequality grows, it is not surprising that we see soaring numbers of kids diagnosed with "learning disabilities." In the deficit model, poor scores are a problem of the learner, not of the instructor or the institution. Educator Carol Dweck calls this the "fixed mind-set," the idea that intelligence and talent are basic, inherent qualities. The opposite is the "growth mind-set," the idea that one can learn, build on one's foundation of learning to learn more, and increase one's capacity to learn by reflecting on one's own learning accomplishments and methods, and that anyone and everyone has the capacity for growth. Community college begins from a pedagogy of acceptance. Any growth constitutes success. The student is at the center.

WHEN PROFESSOR JOSHUA BELKNAP TEACHES ENGLISH AS A SEC-ond Language (ESL) at Borough of Manhattan Community College (BMCC), he might find himself in front of twenty-five students who each speak a different native language. The coordinator of BMCC's ESL Lab, he uses a pioneering method of language instruction called a "translingual learning model," a method that sees multilingualism as a benefit, not a deficit. One of the paradoxes of American culture is that elites prize being able to speak more than one language, multilingualism. Yet, for immigrants, accents and other traces of an original language are marks of shame. Translingual learning methods attempt to remove that stigma.

Before teaching his first English lesson in a given semester, Belknap assigns his students a project: they must research two especially notable features of their native language, write up their research in a short, formal paper, and present their linguistic research to their classmates in English. Before anyone focuses on improving their English grammar and syntax, the students have been allowed to be linguistic experts, authorities on the unique features of their language, and exemplary researchers who can communicate their ideas as a contribution to the group and relate perspectives on features of English that might prove tricky. English isn't a "superior" language; the students are not "inferior" for not knowing it. They all come to the class with a rich store of other language abilities, and, from one another's research, they gain sophisticated knowledge of the kinds of semantic, semiotic, and grammatical features that constitute a "language." They are learning this in English, of course, before they have even begun formally studying English.

This is the paradigm of all active, student-centered knowledge transfer. The instructor finds out from students what they have to contribute and then creates opportunities for them to contribute what they know, challenging them to expand their capacities and often expecting far more than is expected in a normal, passive learning environment, where students simply need to learn what's required and pass a final exam. Belknap's students present their research in front of their peers and on a topic of great individual pride, yet in a new language—a scary prospect for any language learner, and even more so for immigrants. In active learning, you encourage students to use their existing knowledge as the foundation for gaining more knowledge. Ideally, you then let them contribute in some way to the public good, whether that is the community of the classroom or beyond it. Their accomplishment, in other words, is not something that only the teacher sees (and grades) but is part of a common project of everyone learning together. "Start Here, Go Anywhere" is the motto of the Borough of Manhattan Community College, and Professor Belknap is starting his ESL students off on the right foot for that journey to who knows where. They'll be ready.

You cannot use a deficit model of learning if your goal is student success. Not knowing isn't a deficit, a problem, or a source of shame but rather is precisely the inspiration and motivation for being in school in the first place. Not every professor at every community college gets this right, but they should if they are living up to the principles of inclusion, student-centered learning, and success in the world beyond that are central to the mission of their institutions.

This approach to teaching is possible because, unlike most professors at four-year colleges and research universities, community college teachers actually train and prepare for teaching. They don't just teach the way they were taught by their graduate school professors—the apprenticeship model of learning where you imitate your mentor. They actually study effective methods for teaching students at any level. Like K–12 teachers, community college professors take pedagogy seriously.

It is one of the peculiar inheritances of Eliot's reforms that the art of teaching is not factored into the system of hierarchical, institutional ranking. Nor is it factored in a significant way into the reward and recognition systems for faculty at four-year institutions. Good teaching counts. In decades of faculty meetings about hiring or tenure, including at two of the most elite private universities in the country, I have heard countless comments on someone being "a good teacher." That said, it is rarely factored in to promotion decisions in the same way that publication is, and there's no benchmark for it in the national rankings. Even the way we measure teacher effectiveness in four-year universities is an impoverished, flawed method: student evaluation forms. We know student evaluations track with racial and gender biases, that they don't have much to do with how much a student has learned, and that they have negligible value in helping teachers improve at their craft. It's shocking in this age of sophisticated data collection that four-year institutions haven't found better ways of assessing teacher effectiveness.

Once again, we can learn from community colleges because improving pedagogy is key to their mission. In putting the student at the center, professors at community colleges strive to find the best ways to break through whatever lack of preparation, lack of aptitude, or fear students may think they bring to the enterprise of learning and to help individual, specific students learn something new.

"It's not just the periphery but the center and everything else that is different when your mission is changing the bottom, not the top," insists President Gail Mellow of LaGuardia Community College, in Long Island City, Queens.

Located in the renovated Ford Instrument Company building, which once served as a manufacturing plant for World War II military materials, and other adjacent low-rise urban buildings, LaGuardia has eighteen thousand students in fifty different majors, including liberal arts, health, math, theater, science, business, and technology. Approximately 58 percent of the students are full-time, 42 percent part-time. The students come from over 160 different countries and speak an astonishing 127 native languages. When you step inside LaGuardia Community College, you have to reverse-engineer your assumptions about higher education. As President Mellow says, "Four-year colleges and universities talk about selectivity, the grade point averages, or the test scores of the students they accept. We take the top 100 percent." She is passionate about the school's mission to elevate, serve, and address the intellectual, social, cultural, and material needs of those our society considers the bottom tier. It could not be further from the ideal of selecting from an increasingly narrow top. When you take the top 100 percent, Harvard's values cannot be your yardstick.

President Mellow has a high, almost girlish voice, an open face, and expansive gestures. She has presided over this community college for fifteen years. She strides the modern, industrial, glass and steel urban campus as if it were her living room, picking up a piece of paper and throwing it in the trash, making a note of a gash in one of the wooden doors, mentally plumping the pillows as she goes. She has a smile and a greeting for everyone, and they smile back. President Mellow wants LaGuardia to shine—and it does. Widely regarded as an exemplary community college, LaGuardia's luster comes partly from President Mellow's leadership, energy, and pride. She is respected and emulated by community college administrators everywhere.

When we tour LaGuardia's theater, she frowns at the condition of the carpet. "That will change this year!" she insists. "Our students and faculty produce some of the best original theater in this city. We are a training ground for incredible talent. We can't have this place threadbare."

She does not want the buildings disrespected and will not tolerate disdain for the students or faculty. She uses the words "talent" and "brilliance" often and is tough-minded in throwing contempt right back at those who disparage community college. "You get some types who think a community college is training refrigerator repairmen. There's nothing wrong whatsoever about repairing appliances as an occupation—and our students who earn professional certification, in any field, do better in their professions and in the world. That's a source of pride for everyone here. But vocational certification is not the only reason you would come to LaGuardia—or even the main reason. Our three core competencies for which we want to prepare each and every student are inquiry and problem solving, global learning, and integrative learning. Our signature competency is the second one: global learning. Our students come from all over the world. We are better at global learning than just about any other college or university anywhere."

LaGuardia's motto is "Dare To Do More." That begins with President Mellow. In her high heels and black jacket trimmed in leather, she could be a CEO. Her look is strategic. She wants the students at LaGuardia to aim high in their lives beyond school. "We have students who walk from Flushing to take one class and then walk back to get to their part-time, minimum-wage job," she tells me. "That's ten miles each way. They are determined to get an education no matter what. You tell me we aren't training our future leaders!"

President Mellow conveys warmth and also a determination to see each and every one of LaGuardia's students succeed. One of her pet projects is the President's Society, informally known as "The Bossy Moms." It's a leadership society for full-time students who have maintained a 2.5 grade point average for at least eighteen credits. Students who join receive a $1,000 stipend, which, for many, offsets the need for another part-time job. They commit two hours a week to the program and attend an array of extracurricular cultural events, speeches by industry leaders, motivational talks, and other kinds of professional development opportunities. They focus on career planning, public speaking and networking events, cultural appreciation, community service, and leadership. There is an unabashed etiquette component, an introduction to middle-class cultural literacy. Members of the President's Society gain free admission to cultural events plus a Metro card to get to them. There is also a stipend for professional clothing and a "dress for success" personal shopper at one of the department stores, who guides them in choosing appropriate interview apparel.

"Community college is about identifying people who don't have other opportunities for success in the world," Mellow says. "Our society doesn't offer these students random goodies—scholarships, opportunities, respect. We try. We give them a chance. It's the opposite of selectivity. Our rankings don't depend on how many applicants we turn down. It's about what we do to ensure success for people where every odd is stacked against them. When you focus on the bottom, everything else has to change."

This goes against the grain of "standards-based" education and exposes the truth of "objective" testing: what is supposed to be about achievement, test preparation, and hard work is often about material and cultural conditions, about—for want of a better term—existential hopelessness. Lani Guinier calls this the "tyranny of meritocracy," in which those who do or don't do well on standardized tests have the illusion that the tests are about intrinsic merit, not about test preparation that correlates with income level. Student-centered education, which community college champions, doesn't allow students to be written off as academic failures, the future fixed at zero.

College for everyone is not an easy end to attain, however. Community colleges face all the challenges of a truly diverse student body, with diverse levels of preparation and radically diverse career goals. They are the most financially underfunded institutions in higher education and have experienced the worst cutbacks of all in recent years, even as they have become more and more valuable to students. The Delta Cost Project, a nonpartisan agency dedicated to analyzing funding in higher education, notes that historic enrollment increases in community college combined with steep declines in per student revenues from state appropriations mean that, currently, the subsidy for community colleges is less per student than it was a decade ago. Given these cutbacks, tuitions are rising and faculty are vastly overworked and underpaid. A majority of courses at community colleges are taught by adjunct or contingent faculty who make less than $2,000 to $3,000 per course, with no benefits and no job security. Calculated on an hourly basis, that salary is equivalent to between $10 and $15 an hour.

Those who achieve their associate's degree and then move on to four-year institutions also run into structural problems. Until recently, there weren't even data on the number of students transferring from community to four-year colleges, and the data remain scant. What we know suggests that it is slightly easier for students to enter a four-year research university from high school than from community college. According to the National Association for College Admissions Counseling, the national overall acceptance rate from secondary school is around 69 percent, and from community college around 64 percent. The pathway from community college to elite research universities remains almost nonexistent.

College for everyone faces formidable obstacles, in other words. And yet, for many students, community college offers an unparalleled opportunity. Dr. Jade Davis, associate director of Digital Learning Projects at LaGuardia Community College, puts it eloquently: "The students are not high risk, but high stakes. Every choice and every moment they spend imagining a future for themselves that is different than the narrative society has given them is a high-stakes moment. Coming to LaGuardia instead of working or doing something else is a high-stakes decision when you live in a household that has an income of only $25,000."

JOHN MOGULESCU, DEAN OF THE SCHOOL OF PROFESSIONAL Studies at City University of New York, ended up at Brown University for athletics, he insists, not for academics. A tennis and basketball star, he would have been surprised, at age eighteen, to learn he would be heralded as one of America's most important visionaries in the field of public higher education, his work cited in speeches by none less than the president of the United States. Over a long career, he has worked with virtually every government agency in the city of New York and developed programs for working adults, for adult and continuing education, for workforce development, for language immersion, for adult literacy, and for GED preparation. He's developed special training initiatives for city and state workers and for welfare recipients. He led the team that developed the City University of New York's seventh community college, the Stella and Charles Guttman Community College, a radical new institution specializing in outdoor, experiential, hands-on learning supplemented by classroom work.

Mogulescu's most recent project has garnered national attention for its early and exceptionally promising results. He supervises Accelerated Study in Associates Programs, or ASAP, a program that has done what no other has: it has doubled and, in some schools and programs, even *tripled* graduation rates. "We have your back. And your books. And your Metro card." is one of the slogans of the program, a succinct way of letting students know that their success is the program's goal.

Dean Mogulescu ushers me into his bright, unfussy office in midtown Manhattan, a few blocks from Herald Square. He doesn't have much truck with academic pretension. He insists he got into public education by accident, the same way he got into Brown. He ended up teaching at a public elementary school in Fort Green, New York. He began there without ever having done a day of teacher training. "It was the hardest thing I've ever done. Period. I was twenty-two. The kids were ten and twelve. They were great kids, but it was exhausting and I knew I couldn't keep up with them."

He'd always wanted to be a social worker, so he went back to school and earned his master's in social work and went into community organizing, based out of New York City College of Technology. Working with his mentor, Fannie Eisenstein, and a small cadre of talented educators, he helped build programs in adult literacy, second language instruction, and GED completion for immigrants, workers, welfare recipients, people with developmental disabilities, and prisoners.

"Really, there was one uniting objective in all of this: How do you change the city? How do you get low-wage workers out of low-wage work?" Under CUNY chancellor Matthew Goldstein, one of Mogulescu's assignments was working with the public schools and forging connections between them and CUNY. He began to build a team, mostly using grant funds, of highly skilled people who didn't necessarily have conventional doctoral or other advanced degrees or even traditional academic experiences.

"We had values, mission—and a lot of energy. And so Chancellor Goldstein came to my group and presented us with a problem: we have community colleges, but we're not graduating anyone. Ten percent, twelve percent. That's not good enough. We have to do better." They went to Mayor Michael Bloomberg for money to fund an intensive program to find a better way, promising a 50 percent graduation rate. The mayor came up with $6.5 million for the first year of the program and $19 million over three years.

"The chancellor said, 'Can we really do this? Can we deliver?' I said, 'I have no idea, but we'll try!'" Mogulescu helped put a planning group together, and they began asking what they could do differently, what would be important, what could move the needle.

"We had a team from all over—literacy, English language ed, math ed. The main thing was we weren't traditional thinkers. We knew how to make change—and we knew what universities could do. We were willing to consider new kinds of solutions, new options that hadn't been tried before. Our question, every minute of every day, was: What do we have to do differently to see this happen?"

From day one, they set up an assessment protocol. For each experiment they tried, they used an experimental group and a control group that continued in the traditional methods.

"We'd test and look at the results. If it worked, if the persistence rates increased, we'd focus there and build on it. Some of the changes didn't seem that revolutionary. They didn't cost a lot, didn't require some fancy corporate sponsor or some shiny new technology. There were no headlines in the *New York Times*. Then, with two groups side by side, we would look at the results, not the promises, but real results. What we found *was* revolutionary. We got results. We kept going like that, trying new ideas, comparing the new with the old, building on what worked."

Mogulescu is right: their new ideas don't seem revolutionary in themselves unless you consider that, unlike most education reforms, these treated students as full human beings with complex lives, not just test takers or statistics. Mogulescu and his team concluded that they could easily offer certain simple material benefits that could drastically change outcomes for students.

"Metro cards was a big one," Mogulescu says. A one-way trip on the New York City subway costs $2.75. Almost everyone going to community college has to take the trains, spending at least $5.50 a day. "If you have to think each time you have a class, do I spend the money on going to school or on food, it adds another disincentive at the most basic level, right when you should be doing the opposite. Some sacrifices people just won't make in order to get an education. Feeding your kid is one."

The experimental group of students who received Metro cards and other modest material assistance began outperforming the group who had to make that grueling, soul-crunching choice—school or food?—day in and day out. They also started to believe that CUNY believed in them.

ASAP's other methods seem just as basic—and as profoundly against the grain of so much historical and contemporary thinking about higher education, from IQ and multiple-choice testing in Eliot's time to the voguish commercial educational technology sector that focuses on tools and outputs, not on the whole student. ASAP targets commonsense factors, factors one can change and address quickly and easily and, given that CUNY is woefully underfunded, inexpensively. The program looks at the busy lives of its students and intervenes where it can to remove obstacles that block the successful pathways through school.

Although many ASAP students hold down jobs, one requirement for everyone in the program is that they must be full-time students. ASAP comes with intense and individualized advising on everything from course selection to study habits. Students join the program in cohorts and offer one another peer mentoring, team spirit, camaraderie, as well as a sense of moving together, with their group, class, and cohort. The program also attends to the everyday realities of living at or near the poverty line. If you have no margin of error, then one mistake—a missed student loan check, for instance—can spell the end of a community college career. If there are gaps in financial aid—Pell grants or other funding that doesn't come through—ASAP counselors are ready to find ways to bridge the loans until your check comes.

Mogulescu and his team have also streamlined the pathways to a degree. ASAP operates only in a limited number of degree programs to ensure good advising but also so it can guarantee, again, within the stressed budgets of an urban public community college, that the course offerings students need to complete an associate's degree are available. At a later date, more programs will be added, but for now, in a limited number of majors, advisers coordinate the sequencing and scheduling of each and every prerequisite and advanced course to make it as easy as possible for students to complete a degree on time. Multiple sections are available at different times to fit complex work, school, and life schedules. Attention is paid to the reality of jobs, families, commuting. Advisers look for bottlenecks and try to eliminate them.

Every university—even Harvard, even Stanford—can learn from ASAP. What we are seeing, especially at our major public universities but also at the elite private schools, is that students on the largest scholarships are also the ones most likely to graduate with high tuition debt, to need paid work that extends the time working toward a degree, and to drop out without a degree because the everyday costs, the debt, and the juggling of multiple roles are overwhelming. ASAP is for community college students, but the model can be imported by any university that adopts student success as the chief metric of its own excellence.

In ASAP, the structural change that spells success is that deans all work together on everything—curriculum, financial aid, scheduling, pedagogy, and advising—instead of separating into bureaucratic silos (a dean of students maintains a separate turf from the dean of faculty, for example). The goal is to ensure that student needs are addressed from every perspective. Integrating the administrative functions happens only occasionally in four-year institutions and constitutes a departure from current technological remedies that purport to "save" college by assuming that it is about "content delivery." The focus in ASAP is on the student, not the tools, consonant with the mission of community college. This should be the mission of all higher education institutions, of the new education designed to prepare students for a world in flux.

"Constant advising is important here, too, because it turns out that, by staying in continuous contact with the students, they help us," John Mogulescu notes. "The students know the problems before we do. ASAP wouldn't work without them working with us. They let us know where we need to pay attention. You can't fix problems if you don't know they are there. The students know, but in the past they'd be discouraged, assume the system couldn't be fixed or was rigged against them, or that they didn't have the power to change. Now, they know we want to hear from them."

No one could believe that well over 50 percent of students in ASAP would graduate on schedule, up from 23 percent. Some CUNY ASAP programs now have a 60 percent graduation rate. And, because assessment was built in from the beginning, administrators didn't have to bring in a special team to measure what had happened and why. The program has data on every change, what worked, what didn't work, where there were positive results, and where a change hadn't really made a difference. A new city government didn't dampen enthusiasm for ASAP. Mayor Bill DeBlasio put up the funds to expand the program. ASAP started with 1,192 students in the first cohort. In 2016, the number of participants was 25,000.

Dean Mogulescu is convinced the ASAP principles are so clear and simple they could be replicated anywhere, including at four-year institutions and liberal arts colleges. At community college, the translation is easy because the infrastructure for student-centered learning is firmly in place. At four-year institutions, in addition to all the other rankings and ratings and accreditation criteria, a new one might be added for how each student is being assessed, not just by standardized tests but also in progress toward a degree. A school might build in checkpoints for students who might be losing their way as well as small material forms of support. To do this requires some institutional redesign because financial aid is separate from student services and academic advising, but this would be far less costly to the institution than having a student drop out of school without graduating.

Given ASAP's success rate, it now practically pays for itself. A very large percentage of CUNY students live below the poverty line and are on financial aid. By proceeding expeditiously to graduation, ASAP students free up financial aid and resources for other students. Of course, most important of all, graduates become contributing members of society. "ASAP has turned failure into success and become an incredible engine of social mobility," Mogulescu says. Indeed, because he also oversees workforce education and work placement for the city, Mogulescu can help students with career placement and the city with finding the best new employees.

That's what community college should be. It is a model that all colleges and universities can learn from. But Mogulescu doesn't stop there. He believes that higher education has to be actively, persistently involved in every part of civic life, and he agitates for a living wage in the kinds of jobs for which community college prepares its students. He shakes his head mournfully when I mention the studies that repeatedly show that just having an associate's degree, though it likely improves life outcomes, doesn't guarantee someone will have a middle-class life.

"It's true—but is that the fault of higher education or society? If we are doing our job, preparing students, giving them the so-called skills they need to thrive—math and reading and writing plus skills in majors that are useful and contribute to the city's welfare—then society has to do its part and make sure those jobs are worth having, that the people who do vital, important work in our society are compensated for that work."

Like President Gail Mellow, he is determined to help community college graduates be as ready as possible for the workforce. But he also hopes that his ASAP students have the confidence to be social reformers, not just passive workers. As educated voters and taxpayers, they can contribute by working together to ensure that educated citizens aren't living below the poverty line. College graduates not finding well-paid jobs is too often presented as the "crisis of higher education," Mogulescu insists, when it should be talked about as the "crisis of American life, the end of the middle class."

Outside the dean's glass office door, coworkers gather up papers, preparing to leave for the day. He waves to some of the workers and notes that they aren't actually going home. They'll all be heading to a workshop at one of the CUNY campuses for an hour, maybe two, before they are off for the night. He nods at a big "Education That Works as Hard as You Do" banner in his office. "Hard work only gets you so far. Graduating on time can make you ready for a job. But there's another part of this. If you are going to get low-wage workers out of low-wage work," he says, "you can't do it alone just from an education side. You also need a society that values and is willing to pay for the labor that allows it to function. If we don't accept the status quo as an absolute in education, we can't accept it in society either. We are committed to doing better. We can do our part—we can give them a good education, we can ensure they graduate. But if the jobs they are going into are paying seven dollars an hour, then that's not the fault of higher education. That's the fault of a greedy society."

So many studies blame higher education for not preparing students for remunerative work. You can read the stories, see the bar charts. Graduates with a bachelor's degree don't earn as much as they should; those with an associate's degree earn even less. The implication of such data is that education is failing this generation, that education needs to be doing a better job, really concentrating on skills, on workforce readiness.

As Mogulescu says, "It's not higher education's fault that our graduates don't make as much money as they should. If the going wage for healthcare aides is kept artificially low, say, eight dollars an hour, it doesn't matter if we are turning out great healthcare workers. That's not an education problem. It's a social problem."

The language of a "crisis of higher education" makes it seem as if the problem is only that higher education is in crisis. As John Mogulescu points out, higher education can and must fix many things. But broader social problems must also be addressed. "That's not saying higher education is perfect," he insists. "We hope ASAP will be a model that lots of places will modify for their own needs, their own students, but really try. It works. It seems simple, maybe too simple, but it's not magic. We just asked 'who are these students? What about their life in and out of school makes them drop out, give up?' And then we focused all our energies and resources right there."

THE ECONOMIC DOWNTURN AND THE HIGH COST OF COLLEGE (especially residential college) mean more students are seeking a cheaper way to earn a bachelor's degree. Over half of all college students today are enrolled in community colleges. Increasingly, even the children of professional, college-educated parents consider community college as an option. This shows a pressing need to integrate community college graduates into the flow of life at four-year colleges and research universities because those who achieve an associate's degree and then move on to an institution that grants bachelor's degrees face challenges. Data suggest that, where four-year colleges do not allow transfer credit or where they put up other impediments to community college transfer students (such as preventing them from applying for college scholarships or honor societies or receiving academic awards), there are disparities in graduation rates between those who begin at and those who transfer into four-year colleges. However, where transfer of course credits is easy or seamless, the graduation rate for community college transfer students is indistinguishable from that of the rest of the student body.

Community college, as Jeff Winger learned, views students as unique human beings confronting challenges of many kinds, both academic and personal. At LaGuardia Community College, making sure students know how to dress for an interview and how to conduct themselves is part of the informal curriculum. At Borough of Manhattan Community College, a baseline of knowledge of how one's native language works is a key ingredient for learning English as a second language. What we can learn from all of these community colleges is that higher education should not be about the selection rate. It should be about the success rate, about giving all students an opportunity and the best possible chance to do well, in school and after.

Understanding the different mission of community college helps us see the assumptions embedded in the rest of higher education, assumptions so deep they can be difficult to detect. In computer science, if you notice something unusual in a software program, you ask whether it is a feature or a bug. In the modern research university, failure is a feature, not a bug. The entire apparatus of the research university is based on weeding out: selectivity at admission, rankings based on selectivity, and the funnel from general education into a major and increasingly specialized courses that narrows much more for admission to graduate or professional school. By contrast, community colleges are designed not only to accept everyone but also to do what they can to help each student reach a goal, whatever the goal. Success is a feature.

A first step in revolutionizing higher education is being aware of these legacy assumptions. A second step is recognizing other models that respond to different assumptions. It is challenging to rethink the ways structures and methods might actually hinder mission. It is rare for any institution to examine its assumptions this deeply. Yet it is essential if we are going to revolutionize our traditional colleges and universities.

Thinking about community college is important in its own right, and it helps us think deeply about the assumptions of all our colleges and universities and consider alternative ways they could be responding to the realities of students' lives today. I am not arguing that elite, Research One institutions such as Harvard and Yale and

Stanford and Columbia (not "Colombia") and Princeton and Duke should suddenly transform themselves into community colleges, forfeiting selectivity. That isn't going to happen and it shouldn't. These schools have different histories, purposes, audiences, intentions, and cost structures. Rather, I'm suggesting that even these top institutions have much to learn from institutions that are designed such that all students are supported on their way to mastery, no matter where their journey begins.

Metro cards. Cohorts. Inclusion. Bridge loans. Advising the whole person, not just the "student as customer" or the "student as credential seeker." All of these are part of the larger mission of community college: teaching students to learn how to learn, to build upon their experiences and knowledge, to engage in original research, and to contribute to their community. Eschewing the deficit model and embracing active learning and emphasizing teaching, learning, and student progress as key components of a successful college—whether a community college or a four-year institution—these are all key elements of the new education.

3   AGAINST TECHNOPHOBIA

My husband, Ken, remembers studying trigonometry in middle school around the time that the first solid-state, pocket-sized electronic calculators came on the market. They were pricey, about $250. All the smart kids were thrilled by the amazing things you could do with them.

Calculators were banned from his math class.

The students were required to pretend these exciting new devices didn't exist—at least, not in the classroom. Their well-meaning teachers were sure that if they allowed the students to use calculators, the students would become dependent upon them and their math skills would suffer ever after. Instead, Ken was taught to do trigonometry using a slide rule.

In retrospect, that seems ridiculous. Why would calculators hurt your ability to do trigonometry, but slide rules would not? The answer can be summed up as "technophobia," a fear of the new and a fear of change as embodied in new technology, especially technology that the young seem to master with ease but that makes their elders feel clumsy, out-of-date, and yearning for the good ole days. Ken's teachers weren't focused on their students' ability to do mental calculations (a good, foundational math habit) but were worried about them relying on a new device instead of the old one. It is common, in the history of technology, for adults to be sure that the latest device—the one that wasn't around when they were growing up—will somehow do irreparable damage to the younger generation. For teachers, a common technophobic response is to ban from the classroom devices that are becoming ubiquitous everywhere else.

We are in this situation once again. It's not electronic calculators that are being banned; many schools find those quite acceptable. And of course it would be difficult to find a slide rule in any classroom these days. But many educators and pundits have spent the last two decades banning (or calling for bans of) laptops, tablets, and mobile phones from classrooms. They draw from and are abetted by researchers whose studies—some more convincing and thoughtful in experimental design than others—"prove" that college students who have an electronic tablet in the lecture hall don't pay as much attention to the lecture. (Is that really surprising?) Or they show that taking notes on a laptop makes for lower grades on final exams.

The results of these studies have been popularized in best-selling books that portend doom for the device-obsessed younger generation. These books warn that "Google makes us stupid" and predict that social media will make our children "alone together" ("if you don't learn how to be alone, you'll always be lonely"). Whether in the lab or in advice books, technophobia always starts from a baseline of nostalgia. What is new is measured against some glimmering memory of a golden past before the Internet, when everyone was smart and self-sufficient and no one felt lonesome.

I'm skeptical of these technophobic arguments. My personal history plays a part in my skepticism because I spent a decade of my life researching the impact of and reaction to the last information age in human history—the industrial age that ushered in mass printing and that, in the United States, coincided with the drafting and passage of the US Constitution. With the advent of steam-powered presses and machine-made paper and ink, books became cheap to print and for the first time in history middle- and working-class people could own (or borrow from the new lending libraries) popular books. Before that, you might own a family Bible, a Psalter, and a primer, but suddenly reading was a "thing," and the young couldn't get enough books, especially popular novels featuring dashing heroes or victimized heroines whose everyday work and lives resembled their own. Thomas Jefferson and John Adams were only the most prominent people who insisted that wasting your time on such sensational tales made you stupid and, yes, lonely and isolated from the "real world." Pundits in 1790 wrote articles like "Novel Reading, a Cause of Female Depravity." Novels were thought to "mesmerize," "capture," and "tyrannize" a reader's attention and volition. Many of the technophobic arguments one hears against modern digital technologies and their cultural offshoots—tablets or video games, Google or Wikipedia—sound to my ears like the Founding Fathers railing against the rapt young novel readers of their era.

In our day, some professors have not only banned devices in lecture classes but have written about how and why everyone else should, too, with all the earnestness and good intentions of Ken's middle school trig teacher. For the sake of argument, let's say taking notes longhand is "better" for students than taking notes on a laptop. Even if that is true, what good is forbidding students from using laptops in class if everywhere else in their lives—in their days outside of school and in their future work—they are using some computing device to take notes? Doesn't it thus make good, common sense to come up with ways of teaching the best, most efficient, and smartest ways of using their devices, rather than issuing a blanket rule to "ban" them from class?

Our students carry smartphones more powerful than the IBM 360 mainframe computers that NASA used to put men on the moon. It's no surprise that a standard-issue lecturer loses the competition for students' attention. Sometimes, of course, we should tell students to put their phones away, but we also need to be rethinking the lecture, which, if I'm remembering my undergraduate days correctly, often couldn't compete successfully with the student newspaper for my attention. The real lesson for the new education is that we need more active, creative ways of teaching that put some of that computing power to good pedagogical use. It's odd and even irresponsible that formal education is the one place where we're not using the devices on which we do our learning all the rest of the time.

If you want students to succeed not only on a final exam but in everything else in life and work, it makes little sense to ban the devices essential to life and work outside of school. It seems sensible to, instead, teach the skillful, critical use of these tools. If the purpose of formal education is to prepare students for what comes after graduation, we should not be forbidding learning of the kind that they will experience beyond school.

It seems so logical, and yet to make this switch requires a re-examination of our deepest assumptions about the role and function of formal education. As we have seen, especially in the modern college and research university, every structure and infrastructure of academe puts the *institution* at the center—not the students, not the professors. All of those inputs and outputs, selection processes and graduation requirements, entrance exams and certifications that were designed between about 1860 and 1925 are now veritable fortifications against professors dedicated to progressive, student-centered, active learning. This is less the case in community colleges, but everywhere educators are skittish about innovation that makes them feel insecure about their skills. We all (including parents) came up through and were trained by a system of formal higher education in which students were rewarded for mastering and emulating the expertise of their professor. What happens when a young person is more adept at a shiny new learning device than are her parents—and her teachers?

Well-meaning educators have created a lot of anxiety, in students and even more in their parents, around the Internet. After all, *they* learned the good old way, before computing devices—and *they* are in control, the authorities at the front of the classroom calling the shots, knowing what's best.

My students were typically born after 1993, the year the Internet exploded, and they find this stance as silly as Ken and his fellow trig students found the edicts against calculators. Ken and his classmates would have been delighted to learn that, when the first slide rules were invented in England in the seventeenth century, most educators responded with alarm. The math profs who invented and used them typically did so covertly. They were afraid powerful dons or magistrates or religious leaders would find the slide rules sinister, even profane. Many Christians of the time believed the use of mechanical devices that allowed humans to exceed their God-given abilities was heretical. As Galileo and others could testify, life didn't go well for scientists who were thought to be of Satan's party or who dared defy the authority of the Church. Even Sir Isaac Newton feared public reaction. He and his students used their slide rules in secret, behind closed doors.

The impulse toward technophobia dies hard. And we're all complicit, not just educators. Every older generation defends cherished practices. This is a problem for those of us invested in educational reform because, for thousands of years, the role of the educator has been to institutionalize and authorize traditional ways of knowing as a bolster against the incursions of the faddish, the distracting, the shiny, and the new. For all our talk of innovation, on some level, most parents want educators to maintain standards, which often means being the gatekeepers, testers, and sorters of the worthwhile from the dreck, protecting tradition and authority, saving us from our flightier impulses. The citizens of Athens forced Socrates to drink hemlock as punishment for poisoning the minds of youth. That lesson haunts most profs.

Yet innovation happens, and adventurous students and professors always seem to come up with a way to use it. Ken's middle school friends did as Newton had done: they practiced math the accepted way in school and, in private, away from school, they played all kinds of trig tricks on their calculators.

Here's the paradox: Ken's teachers were positive they were helping to arm students for their future by not letting them use the device of the future.

Here's a second paradox: Ken's slide rule–versus–calculator tale isn't his only allegory of education and technological change. In high school, he was given a choice in his driver's ed class between learning to drive a car with a manual transmission and learning with an automatic transmission. Following logic similar to what he followed in trig, he went with an automatic. To this day, he grumbles about that decision, especially when we find ourselves in a foreign country having to pay double to rent an "American-style" car to accommodate his need for an automatic shift. Slide rules no longer exist. Stick-shift cars still prevail just about everywhere but in the United States. That's the trouble with technological change. It's never easy to tell what will or won't last. This is a reminder of why we invest formal education with the authority to be a bulwark against technological fads. How do you decide what is the bathwater and what is the baby?

If the goal of higher education is to prepare young people for the world beyond, it's clear that technology must have a role. At the same time, we must be more thoughtful about what that role should be. Transforming higher education for the twenty-first century is not about throwing a lot of tech into classrooms. What we need instead is to rethink higher education so that our students are digitally literate—so that they understand, gain insight into, and maybe even exert more control over the technologies that have changed and sometimes dominated our lives and will do so even more in the future.

TODAY'S MATH CLASS FOCUSES ON RELATIVELY PRIME (OR "COPRIME") numbers. Professor Derek Bruff of Vanderbilt University explains these are numbers that share no common prime factors. 34 and 45 are relatively prime because $34 = 2 \times 17$ and $45 = 3 \times 3 \times 5$. They have no prime factor in common.

Follow? If you do, you are like the top 10 percent of the students in Bruff's cryptography class. Bruff makes sure his teaching inspires those students—and the other 90 percent in his classes too.

Trim, clean-shaven, and affable, with unfussy steel-rim glasses and an enthusiastic, engaged speaking manner, Derek Bruff is a born teacher. In addition to being a professor of mathematics, he directs the Center for Teaching at Vanderbilt University. Improving the student learning experience is what gets him out of bed in the morning. He's on a mission. He loved college, and especially math, but knows that "nine out of ten students have math horror stories."

Math is a subject for which each thing you learn builds on what you already know. "One bad math teacher," he says, can ruin someone's interest in math for life, so his aim is to do the opposite. He wants to ensure that students leave his class with the same good experience he had as a student. His teaching methods derive from his mathematical training as well as his reading in the work of the renowned educator Benjamin S. Bloom, who reversed the old idea that students had innate abilities or inabilities and replaced it with the idea of "mastery learning." In mastery learning, you take each student from where she is and build her up to a point of mastery of the next most complex concept, then build on that. Failure is not a constant state but a problem of the instructional method that fails to grasp what the student knows or doesn't know in order to help her find the path to greater and greater mastery. A student doesn't only learn math. She learns how to learn, how to take what she knows and extrapolate answers to other questions. It's a skill that serves her in every subsequent challenge she faces.

In a traditional math lecture on relatively prime numbers, the prof would stand at the white board scrawling equations. It's Bruff's estimate that 10 percent of his students understand such equations already and they're bored to death. Ten percent struggle to learn. Eighty percent are so lost they give up the struggle and tune out. Since Math 101 is typically a flunk-out course for students hoping for a STEM major and a career in science, there's often a feeling of despair in the class. The ones who want to succeed badly enough, perhaps so they can go on to medical school, hire a tutor to get them through the final exam. The rest stare into their smartphones, wishing they were anywhere but there.

That's not what happens in Prof Bruff's math class. He often teaches with clickers, a relatively simple technology that collects student responses to his questions and projects their answers for everyone to see and analyze together. Most lecturers scoff at clickers and might even scoff at them as being the stuff of game shows, not higher learning. Yet they are gaining currency and respectability, thanks in part to Harvard physics professor Eric Mazur's advocacy of them. Clickers are often used in "flipped" classrooms, where students read the material beforehand and then, instead of sitting passively in a lecture, respond to questions or problem sets posed by the professor. The professor can then see how many came up with the right or wrong answers, respond, give feedback, and then pose a similar problem so students can try again. This turns a large lecture class into a two-way dialogue, with real-time feedback and students working in pairs or teams to find solutions to increasingly complex problems.

Professor Bruff sets them a task: "Generate pairs of three-digit relatively prime numbers." He has them submit their answers on the clicker polling system and he submits an answer too—a deliberately wrong one. All of the answers are then projected on a screen overhead.

Everyone examines the rows of answers, looking for their own. Professor Bruff next informs the students that at least one pair of numbers on the screen is incorrect and has them work in small groups to identify it. The room is suddenly abuzz with activity as each student huddles together with a few classmates. As it turns out, today there's a second wrong answer, submitted by one of the students. Even better! Everyone is talking, calculating, testing, totally absorbed in the exercise. Cell phones sit ignored on desks.

Keep in mind that Professor Bruff has never lectured this class on how to determine relatively prime numbers. The students are exchanging information, teaching one another, giving one another hints and advice. Within a few minutes, he asks for a volunteer and calls on a student to explain how she confirmed 493 and 611 shared no prime factors.

"How did your group figure it out?" Bruff asks her.

She says that $493 = 17 \times 29$ and $611 = 13 \times 47$ so that makes them relatively prime. She explains that her group divided each number by larger and larger primes. The method they used gives him an opportunity to extrapolate to a larger principle that he wants the students to understand: "Multiplying numbers is easier than factoring numbers."

Bruff is pleased with how this class session is going. He next asks a few more students to explain their methods for arriving at correct answers. Educators call this "metacognition" or "reflection": pausing to think about how you learned, understanding different ways of solving the same problem, and extending your method to other outcomes and applications beyond the immediate problem you are solving. Some theorists believe the most important learning of all happens through reflection because this is where the student begins to grasp her own principles and best practices for future learning. These are key ingredients to learning beyond the test, to learning that can be applied to the rest of your life.

It turns out that, in their group work on relatively prime numbers, Bruff's students hit upon a method that, structurally, is important to a much larger mathematical problem with vast practical implications. "It's the main idea behind public key cryptography," he says. They discovered how to use prime numbers to generate codes, one of the most important security systems of the open Internet, used for digital signatures and for legal and other sensitive documents, among other things.

Bruff will build on this foundation of knowledge, trusting collaboration, and growing confidence all semester. He is quick to point out that the clickers are only a tool. They aren't magical devices that do learning for you—or evil ones that prevent you from learning. The key is to use what advantages technology offers to make the most effective learning possible. Peer instruction is his principal pedagogical method. Everyone is engaged, everyone participates, and the devices aid the interactive learning process. If they didn't have clickers, they could come up with a workaround using paper and pencil. The point is a method of interaction that requires students to actively engage with the material and try to figure it out for themselves. The opposite method—using a fancy digital tool, but in a way that does not require active student participation—is not effective. Without a well-designed new pedagogical method, technology alone does not help students learn. It is no different from lecturing and scrawling equations across the blackboard. Slide rules or calculators? The lesson here isn't what tool you use but how you use it.

Derek Bruff writes about his teaching methods on his blog *Agile Learning*. The term comes from principles of agile software development. These principles date back to the late 1950s, when developers writing computer code elaborated a method by which they could "iterate" together. They would self-organize into teams composed of people with different skill sets who could add to one another's code, allowing for continuous feedback and improvements. The ideal was not to labor alone in attempts to write perfect code. That never happens anyway, because no one person can see all of his own mistakes. Coding requires other "eyeballs," in programmers' parlance. The ideal was to publish code quickly and then to rely on one another to see any bugs and correct them.

Bruff uses agile software development as the basis for how he teaches math. "Learning is social," Bruff notes. "You can spot one another's mistakes and help one another to learn much more easily together than you can on your own. It takes away some of the anxieties around failure and math."

Bruff applies agile learning methods even in the more daunting courses he teaches, like linear algebra. "No one's there because they want to learn about matrix algebra, vector spaces, and eigenvalues," he laughs. "They're only there because it's required. My objective is for them to understand why linear algebra is useful, why it is relevant, why they are being required to learn what they are learning."

For this course, he doesn't start with clickers but with photocopies of the Monopoly board. He points out that photocopies are a technology, too.

"Monopoly is a terrible board game, really. There's no strategy to speak of. Basically, the only decision you have to make in Monopoly is whether or not to buy a property. Everything else is just rolling dice. That means you need to know if a property is going to make you money. You have to know how frequently a given property will be landed on by other players—and how much they will pay you in income if they land on your real estate. You have to model how often people land on property relative to how much you make from them." As he explains, Jail has a huge impact on probability because people spend a lot of time in jail. The squares right after Jail get hit most frequently.

As Bruff tells me, "You can model all of this with Markov chains but, rather than begin with a lecture on what those are, I have the students work in pairs and strategize. I tell them to ignore Go To Jail and Community Chest, to simplify the model, and come up with odds for how often you land on any square." He notes that they tend to easily figure out that, when there are no contingencies, all the spaces are landed on equally over time. Even the most anxious and math-averse students get it right. "That's a confidence builder," he smiles. "Then I have them pair up, throw in Jail, Chance, and Community Chest as factors and add a few other rules. We talk about how that changes our model. I give them problems and prompts along the way and pretty soon they are figuring out probabilities for every square, for every roll of the dice."

One hundred students, annoyed they have to take a required math course, are now excited to learn something that has obvious practical implications, not only for winning their next Monopoly game but also in other real-life situations they know they will encounter. They've seen the tip of the iceberg and can't wait to see the rest. Statistics is a puzzle, a problem, a mystery, and, instead of being baffled, they now are seeing statistics as something they can use.

"After they begin modeling the ways different rules change various probabilities, I then introduce the terminology of a matrix," Bruff says. "They've just seen one. They've helped build one themselves. They didn't even know that was happening. They are making models that help them understand interesting problems. They're even making predictions. Next I have them Google 'Markov chains' and find out all the more complex models that are based on this one very simple formulation. You can model populations with what they are learning from Monopoly. In fact, you can understand Google itself since the page rank algorithm uses the same method."

Vanderbilt is far removed from the world of community college, and yet Derek Bruff's goal is consonant with the inclusiveness of community college learning. He wants everyone to learn and comprehend regardless of their prior training or ability, and his ambition is to show students how classroom learning can be applied significantly in the world beyond. He doesn't care whether he breaks the curve with his classes; he's not worried about "grade inflation." His goal is to provide an atmosphere in which students learn and feel confident speaking up about what and how they've learned.

Vanderbilt is a highly selective research university, and he admits that some of his mathematically gifted students don't need his flipped class to succeed. Some even resent it at first. "Quite frankly," he says, "some of these students are very good at 'doing school.' For some of my students, the math comes really quickly. I could teach directly to those students, but I find that 90 percent of students do not know what they are doing. So, I figure, why not teach so everyone learns more, the ones who are good at math and the ones who struggled with math in high school and think they got in to Vanderbilt as some fluke."

As he tells it, some students "just want to come hear me lecture so they can take notes, pass the class, and never think about linear algebra again. College is traditionally supposed to be about teaching—it's all about the prof, the prof's status, the prof's ideas—not about what you, as a student, are learning." Learning requires more engagement from the student; it also requires more imagination from the faculty than simply standing at the front of a lecture hall for a few hours and reciting what you already know. "There's what some educators call a 'mutual nonaggression pact' between faculty and students: you don't ask too much of me, I won't ask too much of you. But even the students who begin resenting having to work in class, to talk, change about halfway through. I can feel they are eager to be there—they realize they are actually learning, they can see how mathematics is useful, they're finding examples in everyday life."

Ample research supports his pedagogical method. In a 2014 analysis of 228 different studies of STEM teaching and learning comparing the efficacy of lectures ("continuous exposition by the teacher") to active learning ("the process of learning through activities and/or discussion in class, as opposed to passively listening to an expert"), active learning won hands down, yielding greater success rates, completion rates, and higher exam grades than the traditional lecturing methods. It also took less time for students to master the material and methods.

Great professors who use technology intelligently in the classroom do so to spark new connections and knowledge. Middle school teachers might use a calculator as an active learning tool to allow their students to find sine, cosine, and tangent trigonometric functions. This becomes a starting point, from which they go on to learn more complex trigonometry and to apply it to areas they are passionate about: astronomy, programming, acoustics, optics, biology, chemistry, computer graphics, and other subjects far beyond the syllabus of eighth-grade math. In other words, technology is a tool—and so is trigonometry.

Derek Bruff smiles with pride. "About 99 percent of students leave the class convinced this is a better way to learn. The fifty minutes we've spent together every Monday, Wednesday, and Friday has been worth their time."

As impressive as Derek Bruff's pedagogy is, it's not likely to convince more traditionally minded teachers that new technologies can contribute to learning. Technophobia is not only a fear of what technologies might do to our brains, or our social lives, or our ability to learn. It's also a fear of losing a useful skill. This is a perfectly rational fear, because that is indeed often a consequence when we embrace new technologies.

As a case in point, in 1837 when a geometry professor at Yale introduced the radical new technology of the blackboard, insisting his students use it to draw conical sections and write out equations, his students felt this demeaned their vaunted abilities at rote memorization and mental calculation. They rioted. Yale stuck by the prof. Thirty students were suspended and threatened with expulsion if they did not apologize. Contrite, they eventually returned, and were reinstated to good standing. The chalkboards stayed.

The Yale students weren't entirely wrong in their anxiety about those chalkboards. What they portended was a new relationship between intellect and industrialization that was about to turn higher education on its head. Memorization and declamation could carry one a long way in a ministerial world where the elite was small and homogenous, but it certainly could not do so in a world increasingly shaped by steam engines. For that was what was implicit in the chalk marks. Not only was science becoming too complex for simple memory but also the value of memorization and oration was declining as books, newspapers, journals, and magazines packed with information became ubiquitous. The Yale students feared a loss of status. Recitation, rote memorization, and Latin grammar were no longer sources of power in a world where the wit and wisdom of the popular author or the professional journalist held greater sway than the minister at the pulpit.

What features of the twenty-first-century world outstrip our pre-Internet capacities? Professionalization and specialization were higher education's responses to industrialization in Eliot's day. For our era, the ability to search and research—sorting, evaluating, verifying, analyzing, and synthesizing abundant information—is an incredibly valuable skill. With the advent of Twitter and fake news, as well as the digitization of vast archives made accessible for the first time, these active learning skills should have a far larger role in higher education today.

What is often seen as a pernicious development—our dependence on our devices—has an upside. Whereas research confirms that we are, in fact, tied to our devices now, it also reveals that our devices serve as "transactive" memory aids, enabling us to encode, store, search for, and retrieve information in a way that helps us find answers more efficiently than we were able to do without these devices. We now rely on our devices for information we used to commit to memory, but we also, because of our devices, have incomparably more information at our fingertips than ever before. Some traditionalists insist, as did those Yale students in 1837, that memorization should still be important. It's clear that memorization is no longer as significant to our daily lives as it once was, and that's a good thing because it is also clear that we are no longer memorizing all the facts that, a few decades ago, it was thought necessary to commit to memory.

Research also reveals that memorizing less does not damage our cognitive abilities, as we once thought it did. Needless to say, myriad things still need to be memorized and become habitual to be effective in one's life (language learning, basic math principles, how to drive a car, dance steps, game rules, etc.). However, many things we once memorized we now just Google—and we're not necessarily the worse off for doing so. We are now in the second decade of testing for effects of the Internet on cognition, and the results are looking much more positive than they did in the earlier, more transitional stage. To summarize dozens of recent studies: the Internet does a poor job helping us do the things we did before the Internet existed in the same way that we did them before the Internet existed. Which is almost a tautology. The converse is also true: the Internet does an excellent job helping us do the things we do with the Internet and other forms of new, interactive technology.

As with just about anything else—learning to walk or play tennis, write C++ computer code, or perform brain surgery—practice matters. Not practicing tennis means your tennis game declines. Practicing tennis, though, doesn't improve your ability to write C++ computer code. Ken's eighth-grade teacher was perfectly correct that calculators did not help him improve his ability to use his slide rule. However—and here is what educators so often miss—Ken and his pals would have been able to apply trigonometry in so many more exciting ways had they been able to rely on their calculators for certain functions that they could then build upon. In metaphoric terms, the calculators would have freed up their brain space to conceive of more challenging, complex trigonometric applications based on their calculations.

In short, we should allow devices in classrooms more frequently than we now do because sustained, careful, critical practice with devices helps us use them better—and that's a good thing for us and for society. Finding the most creative, engaged ways to employ technology in the classroom helps bring Charles Eliot's university into the twenty-first century—but *only* if the technology introduced is part of a classroom and pedagogical redesign that takes maximum advantage of the transactive capacity suddenly at the students' disposal. The professor can't just opt out by introducing technology but must think deeply about what the technology can do, what the students can learn with it and about it, and how devices can help students think together, remix one another's ideas, iterate, respond, and contribute to an evolving whole.

In my classes, I allow my students not only to take notes on their laptops but also to take collaborative notes on a web tool such as Google Docs or the open-source platform Hypothes.is, where they all contribute notes, annotate them, drop in links for further reading, and basically set up a back channel for questions they want answers to during class. Whether I'm teaching Survey of American Literature, This Is Your Brain on the Internet, or The History and Future of Higher Education to beginning students or advanced doctoral students, everyone learns more when everyone is learning and contributing together. One cannot underestimate the social component of learning. I find my students learn more and dig deeper when they all contribute. As in Professor Bruff's classes, they also learn better methods for finding and mastering content, including web literacies that will serve them in their future.

To the horror of technophobes, I like to say that if we profs can be replaced by a computer screen, we should be. I mean that as a challenge, not as an admission of impending defeat. Every class should be an opportunity to do that which no screen can do—including offering students the opportunity to understand, create with, and also critique all that is going on in the background of our screens.

You teach students to be literate in a digital age by doing, by interacting, by evaluating technology—not by banning it in formal education, the one place where they should be learning the wisest ways to use it.

STANFORD UNIVERSITY PROFESSOR EMERITA ANDREA LUNSFORD is everyone's ideal English professor. Graceful, with snowy upswept hair and reading glasses perched on her nose, she has a face both reserved and kind, with the wise half-smile one associates with Victorian portraiture. Don't let her look fool you. She is one of the most innovative researchers in the country. She studies the impact of the Internet on student literacy and all the ways this generation's particular transactive and digital literacy skills can be maximized to help them lead more successful lives, in school and beyond.

Lunsford has studied student literacy all across the nation, leading numerous research projects with different methodologies. The most famous and extensive is the five-year Stanford Study of Writing. It was designed to address this question, often raised by worried alumni and parents: Are digital devices destroying the literacy of students at Stanford? If the digital age is harming students at one of the most selective universities in America, the rest of us are sunk.

The Stanford Study of Writing, begun in September 2001, is one of the most extensive studies of this generation's actual knowledge and how it influences what they think and write. Two hundred forty-three first-year students were invited to participate by submitting their writing, whether expository classroom writing or personal writing. One hundred eighty-nine students committed to the project. They also agreed to participate in an annual survey, and a fifth of the pool was interviewed in depth annually. In 2006, once all of the data were collected digitally, assessment of the massive archive of over fifteen thousand pieces of writing plus the interview and survey data began.

That students were willing to grant access to such a quantity of academic and personal writing is extraordinary. They submitted their research papers as well as emails, blogs, social media writing, journals, creative writing, and even scripts for videos. Lunsford was curious about not just how well these high-performing students wrote in their classes but also how they felt about assigned writing. She also wanted to investigate how often, and in what styles, students wrote outside of class.

Lunsford found that, contrary to all the hand-wringing, students today, including those who reported spending significant amounts of time online, are good writers. However, she found their writing had a distinguishing feature that makes it different from the writing of previous generations she has studied, a difference that she and her colleagues attribute to their time online: this generation is unusually adept at *kairos,* a rhetorical term meaning the ability to assess your audience and shape your style, tone, language, and technique for that audience.

"On social media, audiences are everywhere," Professor Lunsford wrote in a paper analyzing the data. "Online, it is hard to tell who is the writer and who is the audience because response is instantaneous. This generation of students understands that well, and we saw it in the way they adjusted the tone, vocabulary, forms of address, even the humor depending on to whom they were writing. That's an exceptionally sophisticated kind of literacy, to be able to control for effective communication to a specific audience."

Interestingly, Lunsford found few traces of the traits that other pundits assume characterize student writing today—shallowness, stupidity, distraction, or loneliness. She and her team simply did not find, in any of the qualitative or quantitative methods they used, any evidence for an erosion of literacy due to the time students were spending online. The only clear negative she came across is that students enter Stanford with a higher level of confidence in their writing ability than they possess when they graduate, possibly, Lunsford conjectures, a consequence of their professors reminding them repeatedly of how social media use is destroying their intellect. She surmises it may also be a consequence of all the individual feedback their writing receives. At Stanford, students are given an enormous amount of individual attention. Some 35 percent of classes have fewer than ten students. The students write a lot and receive expert, individual, and often critical feedback. They become stronger writers in the process. They hear and absorb the critique but don't seem to believe that their writing ability has improved because of it.

Another of the study's findings is that students do not do particularly well in writing papers just for the sake of writing papers. Rather, students value writing that "makes something happen in the world." From a traditional writing teacher, this is a serious criticism of this generation. In the typical five-paragraph essay, for example, the writer employs a prescribed method, almost a formula, to shape each section of the essay, and you don't deviate from that structure even if your audience changes. Nor do you need to because, in the traditional five-paragraph essay, the audience is unchanging: it's the professor. Students learn to write essays that only they and their professor will be reading, in a form and format that are rarely used beyond the classroom.

For anyone dedicated to higher education designed for what comes next, students' desire to write to make something happen in the world is a cause for excitement. That's how Professor Lunsford views this finding. She encourages her students to discover the best ways to use their writing for a purpose. Perhaps, instead of a conventional term paper, they might conduct a research study about colon cancer and turn it into a white paper and a poster for a community public health event. Or maybe they write an op-ed for the local newspaper on how Stanford might change its cafeteria purchasing options to increase relationships with neighboring farming communities. She seeks to bolster her students' already strong sense of *kairos* by encouraging them to write on important topics and then define and address an audience beyond her, beyond her classroom.

Virtually every serious study of Millennial reading and writing habits confirms what Professor Lunsford has learned in her quarter century of studying digital age student literacy. It turns out, for example, that Millennials read more than any generation since World War II. But, again, you would miss the depths of their literacy if you used traditional assessment methods. What they read most voluminously during their teen years is young adult literature, a publishing category that barely existed before the Internet. Many of those youngsters waiting at midnight at the local bookstore for the latest Harry Potter volume had video games in their hands and didn't see that as a contradiction. On the other hand, those avid young digital readers have also grown up to read distinguished, contemporary prize-winning books, including graphic novels, works by young immigrant and minority writers, books by writers from other parts of the world, and even poetry, especially by new authors; their annual book reading, as adolescents and as adults, outpaces that of preceding generations. Like that first generation of novel readers in the information age, which began around the time Thomas Jefferson was president, young people clamor to read literature relevant to their lives, reflective of those lives, and relative to the social and technological challenges they face.

What Andrea Lunsford sees in her classes is that students' constant interactive lives online, rather than making them dumber or lonely, make them more connected and engaged with one another, with the larger culture, and even with printed, old-fashioned books. In her field of rhetoric, this manifests in a kind of literary urgency. This generation wants to know what is important and wants to communicate what they know. Writing well is important to them, and they judge themselves more and more strictly the longer they are in college. Writing a term paper for the sake of writing a term paper, one that will be read only by the instructor, seems pointless, even ludicrous. Why write just for the sake of a grade on how you write? That is antithetical to the purpose of writing: communicating, connecting, persuading, interacting. *Kairos*.

Working from similar assumptions about the writing and reading commitments of students today, Professor Juana Maria Rodriguez has found ways to restructure her classes so that her students engage in original research and writing with an active social purpose. In the Department of Women's and Gender Studies at the University of California at Berkeley, Professor Rodriguez teaches LGBT 146, "Cultural Representations of Sexuality." In this course, students not only read a number of complex, dense theoretical texts but also conduct original archival and ethnographic research. However, where formerly they wrote up their findings in research papers, now they use results to identify and correct weak, erroneous, or missing Wikipedia articles on major lesbian, gay, bisexual, and transgender (LGBT) scholars, theorists, and performance artists.

As recently as 2007, some departments, colleges, and universities were still "banning" the use of Wikipedia (not that this was enforceable). Technophobes assumed Wikipedia was bad, just as they felt suspicious of clickers—it had to be because it was produced in a way antithetical to top-down, scholarly, expert-driven, peer-reviewed scholarship. Wikipedia is crowdsourced, and you do not have to be a certified expert with a PhD to contribute to it. Many, therefore, opposed its use.

Professor Rodriguez reasoned otherwise. If it is bad but open to editing, why not have students use their research to contribute to the world's most widely used encyclopedia? She challenged her students to make improvements in entries. She enlisted the help of the editors at Wiki Education Foundation, a nonprofit that bridges Wikipedia and academia and that is dedicated to helping professors craft classroom research and writing assignments to improve Wikipedia's scholarly accuracy and coverage. WikiEdu also works with professional librarians to expand the public's access to library resources and academic professional associations to find ways to ensure that fields are being covered as thoroughly as possible.

In LGBT 146, Professor Rodriguez teaches students professional research skills, including how to authenticate accurate and reliable information sources, how to address controversial subject matter with professionalism and accuracy, and how to cite sources properly, skills our society as a whole needs desperately. She is often surprised by the results even though she has high expectations of her students. For instance, her students discovered that the influential cultural critic José Esteban Muñoz, whose tragic death at the age of forty-six rocked the LGBT academic community in 2013, had been addressed by only two scant paragraphs on Wikipedia. "José Muñoz finally got a page that might begin to approach his significance," Rodriguez says. "My students also created pages for Essex Hemphill, Justin Chin, Martin Wong, Gil Cuadros, and some local Bay Area queer luminaries: Adela Cuba, Chili Felix, Cecilia Chung, and a beautiful page for tatiana de la tierra. They also added to a host of other pages. They are a start towards making Wikipedia a more queer, colored, inclusive, and accurate space."

Most people, looking from outside, might think that a gender studies course, one on queer performance art, would have no relevance to the students' future jobs. Yet, Professor Rodriguez has taken a subject area about which her students are passionate, with a commitment that grows out of a deep sense of personal or political identity, and has designed a course that, like Bruff's, is based on mastery learning that will influence how they learn everywhere—in other classes and in their future work lives. The research, reading, writing, and online-editing skills they gain give them an advantage at competitive entry-level job positions. Because Wikipedia provides analytics that track every change to every entry, her students explore the methods and power of data analysis. In the course of creating their entries, they compile annotated bibliographies of all of the work they do, and they use an open-source tool called Zotero to collect their citations and references and to make them available online to fellow researchers beyond their classroom. Many entry-level positions now require web and digital skills that many students at elite institutions simply do not possess. Rodriguez's students aren't just mastering a subject matter about which they care deeply but are also defining and managing a complex project and working through, individually and collectively, the best way to realize it, from inception to completion. They are learning how to write for a real-world audience and how to contribute meaningfully within a set of institutional rules and practices.

Uniting the projects of Derek Bruff, Andrea Lunsford, and Juana Maria Rodriguez is a deep understanding of how the traditional classroom can be redesigned to help prepare students for the challenges their generation faces. What also unites them is a conviction that a professor should use the technology best suited to the needs of students. It is the ideal way to empower the next generation to use the avalanche of information at their fingertips in a purposive, responsive way to make possible their own future success and, ideally, their contribution to a better society.

EVAN MISSHULA IS A PROFESSIONAL PROGRAMMER WHO IS ALSO earning his doctorate in computer science. An open source and open access advocate, Misshula is passionate about coding, and especially about the need for more women and minorities to enter this field that is changing all of our lives. His goal is to train the next generation of programmers and technology designers to care not just about innovation but also equity. He has finished his coursework at The Graduate Center (CUNY) and, while he writes his dissertation, is teaching two courses. One, "Databases and Datamining," is offered at the John Jay College of Criminal Justice (CUNY).

John Jay is 40 percent Latino and 21 percent black. Nearly half of the students are first-generation college students. Misshula uses open-source content in his classes and to develop new software, but he hadn't applied the Internet's open-source, agile methods to his teaching before. He decided to give it a try. Instead of a traditional final exam, he challenged his undergraduates at John Jay to come up with an app that made a "public contribution." He left the nature and scope of that app up to them.

Two of his students, Nyvia DeJesus and Marta Orlowska, asked if they could develop an app for recently released prisoners. They developed *Jailbreak-my-life*, a mobile resource guide that provides interactive information to help former prisoners schedule their lives. After years of confinement, where everything is scheduled and choices are made for them, released prisoners can find the challenges of managing time and scheduling meetings formidable. Some wind up back in prison for missing meetings with parole officers or other required appointments. DeJesus and Orlowska decided to incorporate a Google Maps application programming interface so users could find the nearest, essential resources such as food, jobs, free tutoring, counseling, and health care. They used a modern stack of Node JavaScript, HTML5, and React programming languages to build their app.

Taking the *kairos* principle to the next level, Misshula registered his students for the Women in Technology Hackathon for Good. A hackathon is a largely unscheduled free-for-all. Hackathons are invention marathons where participants, gathering in spontaneous teams, sometimes work feverishly all night, everyone learning from everyone learning, as they proceed together toward a goal. Some people come to pitch projects. Others walk around, find something they are interested in, and sign on to work on that project with others for the day. There aren't directors or referees of any kind. It's all a bit haphazard and works more because of the goodwill and energy of the participants than from any careful planning by the organizers. That fluidity is what you sign up for. There's usually a purse and a prize for the winning teams, but the process, the new skills they learn on the fly, and the networking are the real reason so many programmers flock to onsite and online hackathons.

Thousands or even tens of thousands of hackathons happen around the world every year in education, in the nonprofit world, and in industry. New York City even maintains a website devoted to all of the hackathons going on at any given moment—civic hackathons, environmental hackathons, technology hackathons, music hackathons, educational hackathons, community activism hackathons, diversity hackathons—all in one weekend in one city.

When you go to a hackathon with a project, you typically set a goal for the concrete product you want to "ship" at the end of the day; on the hackathon website you post specs about your project, your team, and your ideal collaborators. People drift by and tune in to your conversations and decide on the spot whether they want to work with you. You post the open-source code as you are iterating throughout the day and, after the meet-up, a virtual hackathon continues online, with others pitching in to improve and finish a project you all care about. If you are used to conventional business models and project development, this process sounds problematic, to say the least. Amazingly, it works.

The open-source hackathon reverse-engineers just about everything in Charles Eliot's university. There's no hierarchy; no credentials are required. Hackathon participants don't ask and don't care whether you have a PhD or work for Microsoft. They want to see whether you are good at working with others, soliciting contributions and participation from everyone, to arrive at a goal. At a hackathon, the goal is to do as much as you can in a limited amount of time. Because the project is also open source and online, you can return to it later, after the hackathon is over, to improve it through iterating, modding, remixing, and morphing until it reaches the right stage of excellence.

The purse for the Women in Technology Hackathon is small, but finding potential partners, employees, and other talent for future collaborative projects is the main reason so many people show up. Professor Misshula's students, DeJesus and Orlowska, were seeking partners with whom they could work to finish their *Jailbreak-my-life* app. They ended up pairing with two professional developers, Sara Morsi and Igor Politov, one of whom was a recent alumnus of another CUNY school.

And they won. They won the best overall award for a female-led team and the prize for the best use of the Harmon API (application programming interface).

Winning wasn't the end of the matter. After the hackathon, all have continued to work together at the intersection of computer science and law enforcement. The project has turned out to have an indelible impact on all of their lives. The undergraduates reached out to Jeffrey Coots, director of the From Punishment to Public Health initiative at John Jay College of Criminal Justice, to try to raise money to produce the app and make it free for recently released prisoners. DeJesus, who moved to Texas with her family a year after the hackathon, determined she would continue her career as a programmer working with the criminal justice system. Orlowska accepted an internship at the Defense Intelligence Agency and was offered a permanent position in DC. Evan Misshula now teaches computer science to undergraduates at John Jay and has also begun teaching the computer programming language Python to detainees at Rikers Island, as well as data management and descriptive statistics to students in the New York Police Department's Executive Master of Public Administration program. It is hard to imagine a more edifying conclusion to a trip to a hackathon by a professor and two of his star students.

The steam engine and other industrial age inventions harnessed the strength, speed, and power of the machine to do jobs that no one human could perform alone. The Internet and all of the computational technologies developed since its invention harness the interactivity, connection, participation, and access of massive numbers of humans and all the data that we produce, to accomplish work at a scale and speed almost unimaginable. It is hard to think of any aspect of our lives that has not been changed by this technology.

The new education must not only recognize this reality but reimagine higher education that takes advantage of the digital skills our students bring to college while also training them to be full, critical, creative, and even skeptical participants in this technology-driven age. Technophobia is no longer acceptable—in the classroom, in the structures of higher education, in the curriculum, in the pedagogy. Technophobia hamstrings our youth instead of preparing them. It limits them instead of arming them to deal with the complexities of a world, a workplace, and a future that most of us cannot begin to grasp or predict.

4 AGAINST TECHNOPHILIA

It is January 2013. The NEW YORK TIMES has proclaimed 2012 to be "The Year of the MOOC"—the massive open online course. Best-selling author and Times columnist Thomas L. Friedman hails "a budding revolution in global online higher education." He insists MOOCs will transform all of higher education and slash the skyrocketing cost of tuition. Why stop there? "Nothing has more potential to lift people out of poverty," Friedman insists, than the MOOC.

Three elite universities—Stanford, MIT, and Harvard—are leading the MOOC charge, spinning out for-profit (Coursera and Udacity) and nonprofit (edX) companies that will host and stream video lectures delivered by eminent professors from a consortium of a dozen or so top universities.

My university—Duke—is one. We've partnered with Coursera, a company started by two former Stanford computer science professors, Daphne Koller and Andrew Ng, with an undisclosed amount of venture capital. MOOCs deliver "courses" in the form of a sequence of digitized video lectures posted to an interactive Learning Management System hosted by Amazon Web Services. These courses are free to auditors or, if you wish, you can pay a $100 fee to take a verified "Signature Track" that offers a certificate to those who watch all of the videos and pass the multiple-choice, machine-graded tests. The MOOCs are open admission, available to anyone older than eighteen years the world over, not just college students. I have been invited to teach a MOOC on the history and future of American higher education.

I feel a bit like Ken's middle school trig teacher. I am skeptical of this newfangled technology whose advocates promise, in the business jargon of our day, to "disrupt" the status quo in higher education. The MOOC pedagogical model of experts pontificating in half-hour videos feels retrograde to me, a digitization of the tired, passive, broadcast model of education, the one-way transmission of information straight from the expert's mouth to the student's ear. Ample research shows that this model has very little impact beyond the test. I want much more for my students: I want them to ask hard questions, instead of merely memorizing answers, and I want them to leave college with confidence in their ability to tackle the most complex problems they encounter. The multiple-choice tests and the idea of a certificate of completion are offensive. This is not my idea of college. I'm suspicious of the MOOC business model, too. Coursera pays me a modest fee to make the six half-hour videos, an add-on to my regular Duke job. I don't see how this arrangement by a for-profit company could lower Duke's operating expenses or reduce student tuitions. Will students and faculty profit intellectually as the investors accrue monetary gains? And the idea that MOOCs will lift the masses out of poverty is ridiculous—technophilia at its worst.

If technophobia means a fear of slide rules, blackboards, calculators, clickers, or laptops in the college classroom, technophilia can lead to giddy and unrealistic notions about what technology can do, cure, and offer. Technophilia can make you lose your critical marbles, so to speak, cede away your rights, your data, your privacy, and just about everything else to Google, Apple, Microsoft, or any other company that powers your ebooks, your GPS, your children's toys, your appliances, your transportation, even the pacemaker that keeps you alive. Ownership activists Aaron Perzanowski and Jason Schultz discovered just how smitten people are with technology in an experiment they concocted using a dummy website that promised free software downloads to customers who signed a terms of service agreement. Ninety-eight percent of users assented to terms whose first sentence ceded away all rights to their "first-born child."

Our complacency in the face of the technologies that run our lives should make us even more determined to ensure that our students have the computational literacies they need to prepare for their future. Technology—now more than ever—should be the starting point for deep, thorough, critical analysis. Videos of famous professors from elite universities packaged by other famous professors who formerly taught at elite universities will not "transform" higher education except perhaps in an unfortunate way, reinforcing and spreading the nineteenth-century passive, hierarchical models of teaching and learning.

Seymour Papert, a pioneer in the field of artificial intelligence, was an influential learning theorist and a passionate advocate of student-centered learning. He dubbed his particular computer-inspired variation on student-centered, active learning "constructionism." He championed the idea that the best way to learn—especially in the post-Internet world of interactive communication—is literally by constructing something: making, doing, exploring, experimenting, trying, failing, analyzing the failures, and trying again. For K–12 learning, he wanted to put younger children and older children with a range of skills and backgrounds in the same classroom so that they could learn together. He wanted kids with physical or cognitive impairments to be part of the "constructing," too; if you grow up with a disability, your whole life is a creative workaround. As cofounder of the MIT Media Lab in 1985, Papert mixed experts and nonexperts, specialists and novices, computer scientists and artists. The Media Lab was a place where students and faculty, together, could explore, reflect, build, design, and improvise new tools inspired by new ideas and new tools. He believed that a teacher's role, especially in the computer age, was to provide "the conditions for invention."

Watching video lectures is the opposite of constructivist learning. I dig in my heels with Coursera. I'll make the course videos, I say, if they let me try an experiment. I want to see whether I can work with a group of actual, face-to-face onsite students to, together, turn the conventional MOOC form into something student-centered, not just for the onsite students but also for the thousands taking the MOOC online. Instead of conventional term papers, I will challenge the onsite students to design creative and challenging ways to wrangle the eighteen thousand online registrants of the MOOC into an interactive learning community. Papert warned that "nothing could be more absurd than an experiment in which computers are placed in a classroom where nothing else is changed." If MOOCs simply repeat industrial age hierarchies, curriculums, and pedagogy, they will only replicate the current absurdity of those traditions on a massive scale.

To their credit, Daphne Koller and Andrew Ng do not oppose my ambition to include thousands of online students in an interactive seminar. As engineers, they are interested in what we might learn from the project. They put me in touch with others who are experimenting with MOOCs. At the University of Pennsylvania, Professor Al Filreis is running "ModPo," a MOOC in modern poetry that doesn't use videos. Filreis gathers a dozen students together each week. One class member "assigns" a poem of her choosing to all Coursera participants. Once a week, they videocast their live discussions on the Coursera platform and invite anyone in the world to call 215-746-POEM to contribute to the conversation. Difficult, arcane contemporary poets who previously had a small audience are suddenly selling chapbooks and gaining notice worldwide. International participants nominate poems by their favorite poets, too, contributing to a rich syllabus of world poetry.

That format won't work for my history-based course, but Prof Filreis's deviation from the MOOC model is a useful precedent. Before the onsite seminar students arrive for the semester, I assemble a small team to create the videos. Some graduate student assistants and a few technical staff, a first-time producer, and I all set out to make a MOOC. Instead of hiring professionals, Papert-like, we learn together, writing, filming, editing, recording, and uploading the six half-hour videos to the Coursera platform. I'm the one on camera for these DIY videos, so, at the end of each one, we have an "extras" feature where we turn around the camera to show viewers everyone who helped make the week's lesson. We explain the various tools we used, from video cameras and software editing programs to cue cards and websites like Lynda.com, which offers instruction in all of these things. In addition, we invite viewers to construct their own videos in response to ours and upload the link to our course website.

Our first four videos provide some Anglo-European context for what is mostly a history of US higher education, with each half-hour video concentrating on a key moment in that history: the founding of the land-grant universities, the redesign of the Puritan college into the modern research university, the GI Bill and the Great Society's expansion of higher education, and the defunding of higher education over the past forty years. The final two videos focus on the future, proposing new ideas for transforming higher education. They offer techniques for active, student-centered learning designed to prepare students for the tumultuous, interactive time in which we all now live, and they invite members of our worldwide MOOC community to contribute their own alternative pedagogies.

In addition to the proprietary Coursera platform for interaction, we build an open-source online web space on which the onsite seminar students will host their forums, blogs, wikis, and whatever other kinds of online interaction they come up with. We make that content available publicly and for free to anyone who wishes to access or contribute to it. I hope that both the content of the videos and our student-centered methods will transform the static MOOC format and influence methods used in lecture halls and seminar classrooms taught by our eighteen thousand students all over the world. We're evangels for this new education. We decide to give our course a jocular name to signal our grand ambitions beyond the standard MOOC: "The History and Future of (Mostly) Higher Education: Or, How We Can Unlearn Our Old Patterns and Relearn for a More Successful, Fruitful, Satisfying, Productive, Humane, Happy, Beautiful, and Socially Engaged Future." We give it a Twitter hashtag: #FutureEd.

After the MOOC videos are finished, I turn my attention to the actual face-to-face seminar and the students who are charged with leading this grand experiment. Like Papert, I believe the nineteenth-century model of "age-graded" and discipline-restricted education limits and homogenizes the learning experience, so I open my seminar class to undergraduate, graduate, and professional school students in any discipline and extend invitations to students at all the universities in the area. My course description is intentionally vague and provocative. I am looking for twelve to fifteen truly daring and technologically adept students who will take this brand-new experimental MOOC form "to the next level." I warn that this will be the most demanding, creative, and time-consuming course they've ever been part of.

Students sign up from Duke, the University of North Carolina, and North Carolina State University. From the registration permission list, I select fourteen gifted and vastly different students for this challenge. Among them are a nineteen-year-old psychology major, a twenty-year-old aspiring educational reformer, a thirty-something Iraq War vet working toward a master's degree while rehabbing combat injuries, doctoral students in fields ranging from Caribbean history to computer science, a former philosophy professor returning to earn a degree at the Sanford School of Public Policy, and two students (a photographer and a graphic artist) working toward master of fine arts (MFA) degrees.

When the *Chronicle of Higher Education* finds out what we're up to with #FutureEd, the editors invite me to write a column documenting each week's activities, both in the onsite seminar and in the eighteen-thousand-person MOOC. I suggest instead that, because we're promoting student-centered learning, the seminar students should write the columns, not me. Although this is unprecedented, the *Chronicle* editors agree to experiment, too. Contrary to Daphne Koller's frequent pronouncement that higher education hasn't changed in two thousand years, everywhere we go, we are finding people who want to be "disrupted," including in ways more conceptually and pedagogically innovative than with MOOCs.

"Let the revolution begin!" Thomas Friedman intoned. We're ready.

PROUD AND A LITTLE NERVOUS, FOURTEEN STUDENTS ENTER OUR classroom for the first session of #FutureEd. They don't know much about what the semester holds except that they have been selected to lead a revolution in the university as we know it.

I don't say a word as they take their seats; they haven't seen a syllabus. Yet, they are primed, eager to disrupt the disrupters, laptops at the ready.

I hand out pencils. And index cards.

"Pop quiz," I proclaim, tapping my pencil imperiously against a blank index card.

"Who invented the printing press?" I ask, in my most conventional, professorial lecture voice. This is the old one-way transmission model of education, where the professor poses the questions and the students supply the right answers.

I produce an analog timer from my computer bag. "Put your pencils down when you finish. You have ninety seconds," I say in the same officious tone.

They exchange puzzled glances, but once the kitchen timer starts ticking loudly, they turn to their index cards and write. These would-be disrupters of higher education, these eager revolutionaries, snap into Good Student form.

This is how we are training youth today. It's the pattern we most need to break. If the school bell was the symbol of nineteenth-century public, compulsory education—training all those farmers to be machine-like factory workers—the timer is the symbol of twentieth-century, high-stakes summative testing. With the advent of Taylorism, it was no longer enough to think. You had to be able to think on time, to pick the "right" answer among specified choices fast, to supply as many right answers as you could before the timer went off.

The timer epitomizes the outmoded production model of learning that confuses *standardization* with *high standards* and reduces success to the answering of questions simple enough to be graded by a Scantron system—when, in fact, our era demands dexterous, innovative, and interactive thinking. This is a ludicrous and irresponsible way to prepare students for a world in which online attackers can shut down a website and totally disrupt our lives by bringing down central servers. Before the October 22, 2016, cyberattack on the New Hampshire–based Internet performance management company Dyn, most of us weren't even aware that the much-touted Internet of Things had transformed our toasters and other household goods and even our kids' toys into unwitting collaborators of malicious hackers. What else is our technology up to that we don't know about? The complexity of the world we live in is far beyond the imaginings of most of us old enough to remember a time before the Internet, and our educational system is doing little to change that for the younger generation. We subject the average American schoolchild to approximately 110 timed, high-stakes, standardized tests on their way to high school graduation; most of these tests were developed in a format that has not changed much since 1914. The misalignment between how we are training our youth and the world they must contend with could not be more glaring.

All the students have put down their pencils. They didn't need ninety seconds to write "Gutenberg."

They have no idea where I'm going with this. They are more than a bit disappointed. None of this feels exciting, experimental, or revolutionary.

#FutureEd is #sad.

ONLY A VERY FEW YEARS LATER, WE'VE FORGOTTEN THE MOOC madness that took over higher education in 2012. Technophilia does that: you become so dazzled by all the hype about the future that you forget the past and lose your way in the present. Even when technology dashes your hopes, you are willing to buy the next shiny toy, and the next, and the next. You forget the consequences of the last failed promise. Surely *this* technology will solve all our problems. Isn't the problem with higher education that professors are stodgy and resistant to change? Isn't it better to hire CEOs and programmers and for-profit companies to disrupt higher education using the best new tools? Don't we all really need to step aside and let Silicon Valley make a real difference in our colleges and universities?

We now know that MOOCs did not do what they promised—slash tuition costs, offer first-rate education to anyone in the world, end global poverty. In fact, they have in some cases had pernicious effects. At one major institution, the University of Virginia, MOOC mania so engulfed the Board of Visitors that they precipitated an unexpected resignation of a respected and effective new president, Teresa Sullivan, allegedly because she didn't jump onto the MOOC bandwagon during the summer of 2012. It took Eliot and his colleagues sixty years to redesign the research university. Perhaps they reasoned that, in the Internet age, with MOOCs, surely UVA could do it in sixty *days*! Although faculty and student protests led to the reinstatement of President Sullivan, the notion that higher education was on the "brink of a transformation" because of MOOCs was an opinion held far beyond Virginia.

MOOCs aren't the shiny new thing anymore, but large and powerful companies will dangle other technologies, promising innovations. Technophilia and technophobia harm in both directions. Jumpy administrators and faculty can make hasty, poor decisions to adopt the latest technological gadget so as not to seem old-fashioned or passive. Or they might resist all new ideas—even good ones—because the previous technological miracle they invested in flopped.

That's why I began my first meeting with the #FutureEd seminar with this archaic routine of index cards, pencils, and timer. It wasn't sadism but a classic pedagogical technique called "defamiliarization," a method that puts students in a situation where suddenly they question what they thought they knew and examine what they take for granted. Before they took over a leadership role with thousands of international MOOC registrants, I wanted them to think critically about several key characteristics of the higher education we've inherited: technology, the timed test, pat answers like "Gutenberg," the teacher's authority, the broadcast model of pedagogy—all components of higher education that the so-called revolutionary MOOC reproduces on a massive scale. Although these were curious, risk-taking students—they would not have enrolled in this seminar otherwise—they were also excellent students, accustomed to A and A+ grades. They were well trained to the assumptions and practices of formal education.

Sir Francis Bacon insisted that knowledge is power. The French social theorist Michel Foucault admonished us to think about who controls knowledge and who gets to make it, enforce it, and rebel against it. Following them and other thinkers, I wanted my #FutureEd students to be asking: Whose knowledge? Power for whom? What does it mean when venture capitalists want to transform higher education by reproducing at scale the one-way model of teaching? Though such a "solution" might have been appropriate in the age of the emerging broadcast technologies of the telegraph, radio, and film, a defining quality of the Internet is that your audience can speak back to you, regardless of your status and power. Why aren't we educating for an era in which the skills of connecting and constructing are more important than ever? Is the MOOC really a revolution in learning or, like another era's horseless carriage, a mechanized version of what already exists? Can canned lectures delivered by elite professors help students think and learn for themselves? Are we even wise to be teaching online, making content—our information, our secrets, our consumer habits, our bank accounts—available not only to Google and Coursera but also, possibly, to government surveillance and malicious hackers? Are we ceding to Coursera and other for-profit technology companies the educational equivalent of our "first-born child"?

"I have a proposition for you," I tell the fourteen students in #FutureEd. "If you believe what you wrote on that index card, you can hand it in now and you have a guaranteed A for the course."

"But what happens if our answer is wrong?" Claire asks.

"Well, you'll flunk, of course," I say.

There is some uncertain laughter.

"Is there an alternative?" Max asks.

"Sure! You can turn over the card, take another ninety seconds to answer the question using any devices you brought with you. Do some research. Go beyond Wikipedia. Use any method you want—just make sure to verify your findings. If you don't believe in your current answer, see if you can come up with a better one! Who *really* invented the printing press? Ninety seconds."

Before the timer starts ticking, the students are talking to one another, strategizing who will do what. I hear one student say she can create a Google doc where they can put any information that seems relevant. Another suggests that they use the open-source Zotero reference management tool to track their citations.

I've done a version of this student-centered research exercise probably twenty times now in different classes and workshops, and the same thing happens every time. If students know it is permissible, they turn to one another even before they turn on their laptops. Millennials have recently been dubbed the "We Generation" (a revision of the earlier "Me Generation"). I think the collective term is more accurate. In my long teaching experience, they are by far the most accomplished generation at productive collaboration. Whenever I hear commentators say that smartphones and laptops have made students isolated and narcissistic, I know they haven't sat in on a class designed to encourage students to work together creatively.

"So, did Gutenberg invent the printing press?" I ask after the minute-and-a-half burst of energetic, engaged research and dialogue.

Everyone laughs. Over the next ten minutes, they fill me in on what they've learned. They found that Bi Sheng developed the basics of movable type in AD 1040, during the Song Dynasty, using porcelain tablets that could be rearranged to produce and then reproduce over a hundred thousand Chinese characters. This technology was exported to Korea, where, later in 1377, metallic typefaces were invented and used to publish the *Jikji,* the world's oldest extant books printed with movable type. Chinese and Korean prints and printed books, along with several versions of the printing technology itself, traveled between East and West on the Silk Road with spices, fabrics, ideas, art, math, and science. In 1450, Johannes Gutenberg created his printing press for the limited number of alphabetic characters of European languages. The Gutenberg Bible was published in 1455, and the rest is history—Western history.

"Did you know any of this before?" I ask.

No.

"Have you ever been challenged in a classroom to use all the information you have available to you on your phones and laptops to supplement or even question the authority of the knowledge you're presented with?"

No, again.

I note that they would not even have had access to most of what they discovered in ninety seconds before Wikipedia offered us all a platform on which anyone in the world can contribute just about any kind of knowledge, as long as it could be verified by external sources. Even our most extensive research libraries are dominated by Western accounts of history that often (even in scholarly sources) fail to acknowledge non-Western innovation. Wikipedia and other open sources are vast, global stores of crowdsourced knowledge that provide alternate versions of the history we've come to accept.

Unfortunately, this hasn't changed the syllabus of formal education very much. Technology is ideology. Technology is epistemology. How we know shapes what we know, but we have not yet fully grasped the different ways that our new access to global and local stores of knowledge should be revolutionizing higher education. We can be doing so much better.

"What if I were one of those professors who bans laptops and other devices—?" I ask.

"Gutenberg would have invented the printing press," Claire quips, before I can even formulate the whole question.

"And if you are asked about the inventor of movable type on the Graduate Record Exam?"

"Gutenberg," they say almost in unison. The tone is angry now. You don't have to tell students today that a lot of what they learn in college, despite the high cost of tuition, is antiquated.

"If we do it right, everything in our MOOC on the history and future of higher education will address these concerns," I insist.

"Do you know who invented the index card?" Barry, a computer science doctoral student, asks. It's a question an open-source programmer would raise, because it's about the tools we're using. The index card, he informs us, has quite a lineage, and one that is relevant to our experimental class. It was invented around 1760 by none other than Carl Linnaeus, the father of modern taxonomy. The Swedish physician aspired to categorize and arrange in hierarchies all the world's plants and animals—including humans—assigning everything a phylum, a genus, and so forth for his *Systema Naturae*. He cut heavy paper into standard-sized cards and stored a discrete bit of information on each, which enabled him to reorder his data while keeping each datum distinct.

In *Systema Naturae*, Linnaeus also divided humanity into four races based on continent of origin and skin pigmentation. He specified "temperaments" for each race, and, because of his hierarchical assumptions, those who were not white northern European Christians were assigned demeaning and lesser characteristics. He called Asians "luridus" (yellow), intending all the etymological meanings of *lurid*: sallow, ghastly, wan, horrifying. He had a fifth category of humanity beyond these four racial categories: "monstrosus." Into this category went people with all imaginable disabilities, as we would now call them, including genetic differences, cognitive differences, even cultural differences.

Barry tells us how Linnaeus's index cards and his hierarchical classification system were taken up in the 1870s by Melvil Dewey, a librarian at Columbia University, creator of the card catalog and the Dewey decimal system. In the 1890s, edge-notched cards were invented that could be sorted and hung from a long, needle-like rod. In the 1960s and 1970s, these notched index cards became the basis of early computational databases. Some of the culturally biased classification hierarchies, trailing all the way back to Linnaeus, persist deep in the binaries—1s and 0s—of modern computing. Technology can often seem objective, as if it operates without or beyond prejudice. That's not true. If humans are biased, so are human-created algorithms. It takes systematic analysis to understand the biases technology retains, automates, and replicates.

"How many index cards did it take to make Wikipedia?" Barry asks provocatively.

After a silence indicating that the other students aren't exactly sure, Barry reminds us that Wikipedia was created without a taxonomy. He's been an editor on Wikipedia and knows that one of its distinguishing features is its lack of preestablished hierarchies and taxonomies. There are over five million separate entries in English Wikipedia alone. You can create an entry on the history of the VCR, Marvel comic characters, queer performance artists, or just about anything, and it will "stick" as long as you can cite an existing secondary source. There are plenty of value judgments and lots of contested spaces on Wikipedia, but there aren't rules that make some entries count as "knowledge" and other entries "superstition." That's how an entry on movable type can include Bi Sheng's contributions—it didn't have to fight against a taxonomy that categorized Asians as "luridus" and therefore incapable of having contributed to Western "inventions."

"Wikipedia is a free online encyclopedia that aims to allow anyone to edit any article and create them" is the first line in the "Wikipedia" entry on Wikipedia. Any topic is eligible as long as it has had mainstream media or academic journal coverage.

Barry recites some basic (and rigorous) rules that Wikipedia enforces before it will allow information to be published as "verified." Some criticize Wikipedia for having too many regulations for reliable content; as of 2014, the complicated governing policies ran to more than 150,000 words. Barry initiates a discussion of the differences between peer-reviewed and crowdsourced scholarship and between reliability and regulation.

Leslie, one of the two undergraduate students in the class, raises her hand. She's been conducting research on her iPhone as we speak. "Only 8 percent of Wikipedia editors are women—over 80 percent of American librarians are women."

"So 'open' doesn't necessarily mean egalitarian," I summarize, on the first day of our massive *open* online course. Epistemological lightbulbs are going off everywhere.

The index card gambit worked. I don't need to lecture them. That's the point of active, student-centered learning. You set the conditions for invention, set challenges, and let students go from there. MOOCs structure knowledge in one way and broadcast from one source to many participants, reiterating a very old model of knowledge and power. It is our task to figure out how to set the conditions for invention for the thousands of registrants of #FutureEd.

When I challenged the onsite students to find the best ways to turn this MOOC into an active learning experience for the Coursera students, they decided to coordinate online office hours so that, day or night, a MOOC participant anywhere on the globe could have a real-time interaction with an actual onsite #FutureEd student. Sleep deprivation became a key issue with the course because just as a student's three or four office hours were ending in the wee hours of our morning, some other country was waking up. New participants would see the dialogue that had unfolded in another time zone and would jump in. My students often came to our actual class meetings exhilarated and exhausted from a global twenty-four-hour workday.

Together, the onsite students devised many different ways to counter blind technophilia and one-way pedagogy, turning Coursera's for-profit MOOC into a DIY peer-to-peer learning experience. They joked that we were leading a Meaningful, Ornery, and Outrageous Course. Using social media and an open educational blog, we put out a worldwide call for "co-teachers," and seventy professors and academic administrators volunteered to host their own local seminars each week on some aspect of the MOOC's subject matter. Each was like a fast-food franchise, except no uniformity was required; on the contrary, we urged these distributed, worldwide seminar leaders to augment the US history with their own supplementary or alternative national, regional, and local histories, using the Coursera platform, Facebook, Twitter, and the open-source blogging websites they developed to remix the content and supply a counterhistory.

In Dunedin, New Zealand, a group of educators watched the videos each week at a McDonald's because that's where the bandwidth was reliable and free. They ran Twitter chats after each video, adding content about the impact of New Zealand's colonial history on its forms of higher education as well as information about Maori language inclusion and resistance. Other groups convened in Bangkok, Cairo, London, Rome, Oslo, Cape Town, and Lima. Often they posted their own forum topics in response to the Coursera videos, usually several a week, and sometimes dozens of MOOC participants would pile on, adding facts and opinions on subjects such as alternative grading systems, language reform movements, and the role of missionary schools in indigenous communities. Two different discussion groups began meeting independently in the online virtual world Second Life. In Ecuador, a participant named Vahid Masrour made beautiful mind maps each week that charted the video lesson and its global evolution.

In addition to the array of other social media they used, the #FutureEd students orchestrated two digital hackathons on an open website, each lasting approximately twenty-four hours. The first was an extension of an assignment I use to begin almost all of my classes: students use an online tool to collectively write a "class constitution," essentially the terms of service for our semester together. I've done this with up to fifty students at a time, but inviting eighteen thousand to participate was something new. In the end, nearly four hundred people contributed ideas and language to the #FutureEd constitution, resulting in dozens of surprising "index card" moments.

One of the most provocative discussions came after an American participant wrote: "Knowledge is a public resource that should be open and accessible to all people, allowing for freedom of expression, dissent, and critique." That sounds logical, but a student at the National University of Singapore pointed out that "critique" is a Western style of rhetorical argument and isn't valued in the same way in Asian cultures. She reported on a joint program between NUS and Yale University in which the Singapore students balked at the term "critical thinking." The Asian students found what Americans thought of as critical thinking to be rude and naive. They believed it presumptuous for students in an introductory course to critique eminent philosophers or world historical figures. There ensued an eye-opening side forum on the relationship between higher education and the European Enlightenment, or Age of Reason. A Japanese participant added that his country had proudly rejected the idiosyncratic Western divisions of "mind," "body," "emotion," and "intuition." There is no Japanese equivalent of the word or concept of *rational*. In Japanese, you say *rashonaru*. One epistemological consequence is a body of Japanese knowledge that Westerners were unable to see as anything but "superstition" until relatively recently. Acupuncture and meditation are two of many examples. In the #FutureEd Constitution, "critical thinking" was emended with a communitarian alternative: "collective, evolutionary thinking."

The second #FutureEd hackathon was a "World Wide Timeline of Educational Innovation." After scouring the Library of Congress catalog, the onsite students determined that there was no such resource currently available. Even Wikipedia was sparse in this area. Using the collaborative online tool, one participant kicked off with: "Sometime between 3500 BC and 3000 BC, some unknown Sumerian geniuses invented a new system for storing and processing information outside the brain. . . . This data processing system that the Sumerians invented is of course writing." Someone else added an entry for 2370 BCE: "The scholar Ptahhotep completes the writing of the 'Instruction of Ptahhotep' as a guide to living and reflections for the instruction of others."

Like the complex answer to "Who invented the printing press?" it turned out that "What was the first university?" had a history different from what we believed. We learned about universities throughout the ancient world, in places like Taxila, Jixia, Beirut, Odisha, Constantinople, Bihar, Fes, the Balkans, and Cairo, that had all been going strong before 1088 and the establishment of the University of Bologna, typically called "the first university." At one point, someone corrected an entry submitted to the time line to read: "1088, Foundation of the University of Bologna, the first *European* university."

In the course of this second hackathon, one of the contributors, a student from Indira Gandhi National Open University, noted that there were over three million students at her university, the world's largest. Having an opportunity to discuss education and pedagogy with only a half dozen students at one time—even if it was remotely— was priceless. Two other participants—one at Bangladesh University and another at Anadolu University in Turkey—noted that approximately two million students attended their universities. None of them had ever experienced such a degree of intellectual intimacy as they did during the online office hours or the hackathons.

I went into #FutureEd a MOOC skeptic, and I remain one today. Yet I also saw how an intensely interactive, student-centered online community could empower students, both those in the room and those joining us from thousands of miles away. What the #FutureEd class experienced was in some ways similar to and different from study abroad. You can go to another country your junior year, live in a dorm with other Americans, have a great experience, but never really come to understand how people from another culture interpret the world. In #FutureEd, we never left North Carolina but we traveled an enormous intellectual distance by engaging with others internationally in ways that were deep and challenging.

I cannot prove it, but I have a hunch that, because the interaction was virtual, it made it easier for participants to both speak up and disagree, and perhaps even allowed more dialogue—even conflict—than if students had inhabited the same physical space. The real-time conversations were so intense that our syllabus kept changing, with different kinds of questions and ideas constantly intruding into the neat lesson plan presumed by the six initial videos. This dialogic way of knowing is foundational to the new education, a key to preparation for better lives and careers beyond school, and a way to make the university into something that is not, as the saying goes, "merely academic."

In the series of articles the onsite students wrote for the *Chronicle of Higher Education,* they ended up striking a balance between technophobia and technophilia. They were more clear-eyed, analytical, and perceptive than many journalists or professors of the day who had either abetted or attacked the MOOC craze. They took seriously their responsibility as public intellectuals who had firsthand experience with a commercial enterprise developed from outside academe and that had shaken the foundations of higher education. They didn't shy away from controversial topics. One article addressed the problems in Coursera's changing and unclear terms of service agreements and the especially problematic conditions for use of student data. Another addressed the labor issue implicit in automating college teaching. Wouldn't MOOCs make it even more likely that doctoral students pursuing a career teaching in higher education would be consigned to adjunct, part-time positions for their careers? If the point of MOOCs is to cut costs by cutting faculty positions, that doesn't bode well for the future of higher education. Yet another article addressed past educational technologies that had not lived up to their hype and predicted that, once MOOCs lost their luster, Silicon Valley venture capitalists would invest in the next new technology touted as cheaper, faster, better than actual professors.

The fourteen students had succeeded in ways none of us expected in turning an overhyped, costly, and poorly conceived idea— that watching videos was the same as learning—into what was, in fact, an active, student-centered experience that would serve them well the rest of their lives. All around the world, there were formal partings as the MOOC came to an end, sad farewells among the students who had joined us for six weeks from Australia to Alaska, Cape Town to Cardiff, Dunedin to Daejeon, and who had had intense interactions in the all-night office hours that my students had orchestrated. Against odds, they had turned a MOOC into a community.

"Here's what I see when I look outside my window," one of the MOOC students in Thailand posted to our class blog one night. He sent a cell phone image of his computer with the #FutureEd website on the screen. In the photo, you see the fingers of his left hand on the keyboard and, beyond that, his room, and, beyond that, a window. The lights of Bangkok glitter in the darkness outside.

"Here's what I see," one of the students in our onsite seminar responded, posting a photograph too: screenshot, keyboard, fingers, room, window, the world of Durham, North Carolina, beyond. Dozens of similar photos began to appear, virtual postcards from elsewhere, insisting: "I was here."

ONLINE LEARNING WILL NEVER FULLY REPLACE BRICK-AND-MORTAR institutions, but it is also certain to get better over time. Right now, over 95 percent of colleges and universities that enroll more than five thousand students also offer for-credit courses online. Unlike MOOCs offered for profit, the vast majority of these courses are taught by their home institution and fully accredited, fulfilling the same requirements as face-to-face courses. Some involve partnerships with corporations that have a beneficial effect. When Starbucks surveyed its workers to determine possible new benefits employees desired, over 80 percent listed help with finishing a college degree as a number one benefit of choice, especially if it could be accomplished with the flexibility of online instruction. Nearly two thousand Starbucks employees registered in an online program designed by Arizona State University, and Starbucks committed to pay tuition for tens of thousands more by 2025.

Yet, there is a significant downside, even, to online learning that originates within the institution: cost. In 2015, colleges and universities spent over $6.6 billion on technology, about 40 percent of it on institutional systems and 60 percent on systems with instructional and research capacity. More to the point, aggregated technology costs (from security measures to licensing agreements to hardware updates) increase every year, despite the technophiliac delusion that technology is cheap or even free. Demand and expectations have grown so great that funds tend to be assigned to technology needs often before any other category, even before investment in faculty. The hiring of underpaid, part-time adjunct instructors instead of full-time professors is a crisis now of epic proportion in higher education. As funding sources continue to shrink, universities and colleges find they must keep up their technology infrastructure even while cutting faculty and course offerings. That's a terrible trade-off.

And it's a trade-off that is crucial to consider as we design the new education. Charles Eliot understood it wasn't possible to redesign just one aspect of Harvard. Everything had to be remade at the same time. Now, we need to include technology in higher education because, simply, there is more and more technology in the world we send graduates into. Because of the importance of computational technologies, we also must design programs that train students to develop and use them wisely. We need to think critically and systematically about what works, both pedagogically and financially, and what does not.

MOOCs are an example of not only the false promises of technophilia but also how initial hype can obscure both the promises and the limitations of technology. The MOOC hysteria ended in September 2013 when the bubble burst as quickly as it had inflated. California governor Jerry Brown had hired the for-profit company Udacity for an undisclosed fee to design three online courses that would "solve" the seemingly intractable problem of too many students failing introductory and remedial math, algebra, and statistics courses in the California State University system. Unfortunately, Sebastian Thrun, the computer science wizard who invented the self-driving car and who started the MOOC craze by opening his Stanford artificial intelligence course to 160,000 members of the public, did not do better than the professors at San Jose State who had been trying to raise the pass rate for years. In fact, the National Science Foundation assessed the three shiny new Udacity courses and found that the overall student pass rate was 33 percent—*half* the success rate for comparable courses taught in the conventional way by San Jose State University faculty.

The media reaction was swift and brutal. Professors all over academe were gleeful. The great, flashy, high-tech corporate MOOC miracle—the proclaimed disrupter of higher education as we know it—had fizzled. When you overpromise, you have to outperform. Thrun was notably candid in admitting defeat: "We have a lousy product," he said in a postmortem with *Fast Company*. "These were students from difficult neighborhoods, without good access to computers, and with all kinds of challenges in their lives." He allowed that, for this group, the online platform was "not a good fit." Technology had not made learning easy and automatic, had not revolutionized how we teach students facing the greatest challenges. The San Jose State experiment exposed the fantasy that technology will "make" learning easy. It won't. That's just not how learning works.

But the profs were wrong, too. MOOCs aren't over. They have not gone away. And there is still a role and a place for good online learning. MOOCs are no longer "hot"—both Thrun and Daphne Koller of Coursera have moved on to other for-profit ventures outside of higher education. MOOCs rarely make the front (or even the middle) pages of the *New York Times* anymore. Yet, today, more students are enrolled in MOOCs than were taking them at the height of the hype. In January 2016, Coursera alone was offering more than fifteen hundred courses across twenty-eight countries to over fifteen million users, with twenty-five million students having at least started a Coursera course—that's four million more students total than are enrolled in all colleges and universities in the United States today.

Completion rates remain dismal, however. On Coursera's Signature Tracks, which offer certificates to paying students, less than 4 percent of those who watch the first video actually earn a certificate. However, 4 percent of millions is a lot of students, and, of those who complete certificates, a substantial number report that they did, indeed, realize some career or professional enhancement for their effort. MOOCs clearly offer benefits to those who have no other options and who have the tenacity to complete a full course on their own. As one commentator notes, "Online education isn't succeeding because it's better than Oberlin, it's succeeding because it's better than nothing, and nothing is what's currently on offer for millions of people."

MOOCs have also turned out to offer tangible benefits for brick-and-mortar education institutions. Recently, admissions recruiters have been looking at the students who succeed at MOOCs, especially those from low-income backgrounds. If you have the persistence to complete a self-paced MOOC, you are likely to do well in a traditional college or university, no matter how impoverished your background. Another benefit has been to smaller liberal arts colleges and universities that simply do not have the funds to staff advanced courses in all fields, such as the lesser-taught languages. MOOCs allow them to expand and extend their course offerings. Finally, millions of lifelong learners around the world have also been enriched by taking free courses online, not for college credit but for pleasure or self-improvement.

Dave Cormier, the Canadian online learning innovator who invented the term "MOOC" in 2007, well before Coursera and edX and Udacity got into the virtual ed tech business, sees the fortunes of the MOOC as an example of the natural process of higher education reform. After the MOOC hype has passed, the next stage is to find more creative ways to use online learning to offer revolutionary opportunities to more and more students. He argues that MOOCs "woke us up" and, even with their faults, made college professors see more clearly the limits of our inherited, traditional forms of one-way, transmission-style teaching. "Now that we have the technology to teach a hundred thousand students online," he says, "the next challenge will be scaling creativity, and finding a way that even in a class of a hundred thousand, adaptive learning can give each student a personal experience."

By building a student-centered experience together, all of us in #FutureEd learned more about the actual world we live in, a world of technological and human connection. We gained a better understanding and a greater sense of realism, if not actual control. That's crucial to my students' future, whatever careers they end up in. They mastered a complex set of insights and communication skills that empower them in the workplace and in life, as they raise their own children and contend with whichever technology comes next.

Who invented the printing press? I began the #FutureEd MOOC with this exercise so that my students would be cautious and thorough whenever they faced new technologies, whether encountered in the classroom or in their future careers. Skepticism was a first step. But we didn't end there. I challenged them to take charge, to make change, to turn their ideas about the best forms of learning into actual practices online. This meant they had to understand the back end of the technology, including data analytics, enough to remix and mod it. It meant they had to take the lead in using the raw material of the MOOC form to design a new kind of learning that went beyond what they were given, to mold and shape something innovative, interactive, personal, and meaningful. They were not bedazzled by that which is new and shiny. Nor were they technophobic ostriches, heads in the sand. They engaged the technology, evaluated it, and found ways to use it creatively, to fulfill the objectives they designed for it, and not simply be awed by its hype. That's not a bad start for the new education.

IN THE SUMMER OF 2016, I DROVE TO FREDERICKSBURG, VIRGINIA, to take part in a five-day workshop on critical technology. It was boot camp for academics interested in learning how to use the best educational technologies in the most responsible and exciting ways. More than a hundred faculty, administrators, IT professionals, librarians, technology designers, computer programmers, entrepreneurs, learning center directors, and graduate students (and one undergrad) gathered at the University of Mary Washington, a public liberal arts college in the University of Virginia state system. We were there to learn from researchers, technology designers, activists, learning theorists, artists, computer scientists, and a few bona fide hackers. We filed into the Convergence Center, a stunning, state-of-the-art building with cherry-red chairs that spin like tops and an airy, light-filled breakfast room that somehow morphs, like a gigantic Transformer toy, into a high-tech multimedia auditorium with stadium seating and every imaginable tech gizmo.

The participants were ready for transformation, too. Because we were in the midst of the first presidential campaign waged on Twitter and Facebook, shaped by "fake news," the participants believed their job, as educators, was to prepare students to be wiser than the often gullible traditional media. There were workshops on topics such as search engine optimization and how seemingly "objective" Google searches could be and had been rigged. At the time of the workshop, the first ten entries that came up when one searched for "Jew" were all produced by anti-Semitic and neo-Nazi sites pretending to be objective and informative. As the election unfolded, these educators had become increasingly alarmed that students, educators, the general public, and, shockingly, the traditional media didn't know the basics of authenticating information. Almost daily, reputable newspapers and television news shows were repeating lies that had been deliberately and carefully planted by trolls. Many of the educators in Fredericksburg were in a state of distress, feeling as if they had failed in their obligation to educate the public at large as well as professional journalists, whose responsibility it is to inform and alert a gullible public. "I'm not sure the Internet was worth it," one participant said sardonically in one of our small group meetings. This was the director of instructional technology at a major university. Someone else mentioned Orwell's novel *1984*. We were all shocked by the dystopic technology allegory unfolding in our democracy in real time.

The conferees were not technophobes. Nor were they prone to technophilia. Rather, they wanted to learn as much as possible about the technologies available, both the upside and the down, so that they could begin the necessary reimagining of higher education. Participants came from all over—Yale, Middlebury College, Smith College, as well as the University of Southern California and Stanford. Major public and private universities were represented as were regional state institutions, small liberal arts colleges, and community colleges. Change was in the air. University of Colorado at Denver sent six faculty and technology administrators as a cohort. They even had a dean along. They meant business, determined to make institutional change when they returned to Denver.

The keynote speaker was Dr. Tressie McMillan Cottom, a professor of sociology at Virginia Commonwealth University, the fastest-growing and most diverse university in the Virginia system. With a quick smile and mirth in her eyes, Dr. Cottom exudes an incisive wit and authority. She has thirty-five thousand Twitter followers and a new group of graduate students, and she was there to tell us how tweeting and teaching go together. She is one of the most persuasive activists on what is sometimes called #BlackTwitter, a loose network of public intellectuals who use Twitter to give issues important to African Americans more visibility and intellectual and political heft than they receive in traditional media. For example, when Georgetown University professor Marcia Chatelain was frustrated that the children of Ferguson, Missouri, were missing school because of the protests there in 2014, she used social media to develop "The Ferguson Syllabus," a free, crowdsourced reading list on race, civil rights, policy, and African American history. #BlackTwitter took up the challenge, and people from all over began contributing, rapidly creating an extensive and diverse reading list, using provocative hashtags, including #IfTheyGunnedMeDown. The contributions came from every field. One chemist offered essays detailing the long-term effects of tear gas.

Known online as @tressiemcphd, Cottom is fearless in the face of white supremacist trolls and hackers who frequently assail her with racist and misogynistic insults. She maintains her professionalism and systematically critiques or exposes them, one by one. Few of us have such courage in such a vicious public forum. She sees her role on Twitter as educational and, conversely, believes education needs to be far more "woke" (in the parlance of #BlackTwitter) to the troubling political agendas of many on social media. It is for this reason that she keynoted the Digital Pedagogy workshop and why she cofounded the nation's first program in Digital Sociology, an online master's program that is part of Virginia Commonwealth University's

Department of Sociology. She and her colleagues are starting small, with just nine students in what is being described as a "rigorous degree program [that] will prepare graduates to shape emerging local, national and global conversations about big data, privacy, algorithms, inequality and social movements." The program invites students not just to study the digital world but to help shape it.

Professor Cottom is as much a star in academe as she is on social media. She is an impressively prolific scholar. Like her Twitter commentary, her new book, *Lower Ed: The Troubling Rise of For-Profit Colleges in the New Economy*, pulls no punches. It is a devastating analysis of the ways for-profit universities exploit students, especially impoverished African American women who turn to them for one last chance to make a better life.

"There is much to critique," Cottom tells me over coffee, "but I learned two things from for-profits that we have put into our Digital Sociology master's degree. One, to keep choices limited so that students know where they are at all times and are going to a clearly delineated and attainable goal with a cohort of others on the same path at the same time. The other is to make sure students always understand why they are learning what they are learning and how it connects to a future career that they can attain."

Cottom believes her pragmatic bent dates back to her undergraduate years at North Carolina Central University, a historically black college and university (HBCU). She calls her education there the "information Underground Railroad," a world of knowledge that sometimes circulates out of sight of mainstream America, including on Twitter, blogs by black activists, and various websites. Understanding those different realms and how they interact (or fail to) is what she does now as a professional sociologist. "Inequality is what sociologists study," she says. "Disparity is sociology's bread and butter. What is unfair online mirrors what is unfair in the real world, and vice versa."

Although she was invited to VCU to create a program in digital sociology, she is convinced that, in a few years, it won't even be necessary to use that adjective. "What in the world doesn't have some online component now? Globalization of resources, outsourcing jobs, algorithms to identify who is or isn't a criminal. To sign up for the Affordable Care Act, you had to go online. Try to apply for a job at McDonald's without filing an online application. I've started an online sociology program and all of the first students are full-time professionals—in journalism, in health care, in law, in education, in computer science. They all do something with 'data' in their jobs and they are seeing disparities, but they are more and more suspicious about what those inequalities mean. That's sociology."

Widely recruited even in the currently tough academic job market, she decided to accept an offer from Virginia Commonwealth University, which made it clear that it wasn't just interested in her teaching about the sociology of African Americans or women. The university wanted Cottom to create a transformative new program for the Department of Sociology, to create a new field. The American Sociological Association didn't have a Digital Sociology section. Now, because of her program, it does.

Cottom's research on for-profit universities concentrates on the shifting of tax dollars from public institutions to for-profits and the fact that the highest burden of debt is carried by the nation's poorest students at its worst institutions. "The for-profits are designed to feed the loan industry, not for student advancement and learning." She is interested in the kind of person who takes classes online, especially at for-profit institutions, as well as those grasping at the so-called end of college credentialing offered by pay-for-play services such as Udacity, which promise jobs, but not necessarily jobs with any kind of benefits, full-time work, or security. Apple funds Udacity to train programmers in Swift, its programing language. Students pay $299 a month to take the courses and are guaranteed jobs as Apple programmers. Is it a great system, helping lift people from poverty— or yet another formerly middle-class occupation now demoted to casual labor with what Karl Marx called "surplus-value," where an employer is in a position to extract more labor from a worker for less than market value because the employer controls the market (and the training for that market)?

"These are key sociological questions, and it is astonishing that we haven't had a single program that was designed to frame and ask and do research to answer those questions before," Cottom says. "Don't you think it's overdue?" Her work is dedicated to understanding how the for-profit technology sector exploits ignorance about computational tools, the soaring cost of higher education, naiveté about privacy and personal data, and the perennial fear that higher education isn't keeping up and that the next generation will be left behind. "If you believe technology is the answer to everything that plagues higher education, you probably don't understand technology or higher education," she insists.

Cottom understands both. Intimately. She—not some Silicon Valley ed tech booster—is the perfect person to be starting the nation's first degree program in digital sociology. "We wouldn't have made the program if we couldn't be sure that our students would find jobs, good jobs, better ones than they came with," she says. The students who come to the master's program bring skills, experience, and training in fields that have been hurt or altered dramatically by technology, typically through outsourcing, offshoring, or automation, fields including journalism, publishing, radio, law, and accounting. "We know that there is a greater need for people who understand technology, who understand data, who can use it and make it—and who know enough to be critical," Cottom explains. The students learn how to use theory and analysis as deeply and thoughtfully as they wield and interpret statistics, data analytics, and social network analysis. The old "qualitative versus quantitative binary used to rule my profession, with one kind of sociologist dismissing and demeaning the other—none of that matters in the real world and, in our program, we want students to be proficient in both."

All of the students in the Digital Sociology master's program will start together and take the same courses together, in a cohort model very similar to that of ASAP, the highly successful community college program pioneered at the City University of New York. The VCU program's creators want 100 percent of the students to complete the program, and that means using the sociology and sociality of cohort learning to motivate and inspire students to help one another stay in school. We know from multiple studies—whether with Harvard students or teenagers from the most impoverished parts of inner-city Chicago—that learning with a cohort, in study groups with peers progressing along the same path at the same time, is one of the best ways to guarantee completion of a degree.

As Cottom explains, "When they are reading the classical sociologists—Emile Durkheim, Max Weber, Georg Simmel, W. E. B. Du Bois—we want them to be talking to one another, excited, collaborating, even though they may never meet one another face to face. Everything is geared to be as constructivist as possible, where the sociology theory they read connects to their own life and work experiences and vice versa. We want these students to understand what it means to be a sociologist, and that requires a cohort. This is not about unmaking our field. It is ensuring what is most relevant and important about our field is used to understand one of the most important issues in modern life."

Students will also read race, gender, and intersectional theory, including that from nontraditional sources such as black newspapers, magazines, and websites. Cottom is convinced these sources, often out of sight of mainstream media, offer practical insights into how members of marginal communities gain access to digital resources. From HBCUs, #BlackTwitter, community colleges, tribal colleges for Native Americans, vocational schools, guilds, nonprofit educational organizations, and other institutions where inclusion is the mission, students will learn more deeply about access and the digital divide than they can when "inequality" is studied only theoretically. Research coming out of the most well-funded universities often misses connections across and within institutions in black communities, for example, both online and in the world.

"How do we create space for critical thinking and engagement in the modern university? How do we create space for critical engagement online?" Cottom asks, then answers: "Finding the best ways is *my* responsibility in my role as a conductor on the information Underground Railroad."

Dr. Cottom is passionate about what her distance learning program will offer. She is adamant that this isn't a MOOC, a for-profit endeavor that will disappear once the profit does. It's an online program that is deeply embedded in a stable institution that has been in existence since 1838. VCU won't be acquired tomorrow by some conglomerate whose mission isn't education but minority recapitalization of profitable companies.

Cottom believes our students' lives are too precious to be squandered on an institution that exists for someone else's profit. For a for-profit technology purveyor, the bottom line *is* the bottom line. For higher education, the bottom line must be preparing students for the challenges they will encounter in the rest of their lives.

Tressie McMillan Cottom, @tressiemcphd, has a higher mission. She invokes a famous quotation from Frederick Douglass: "It is easier to build strong children than to repair broken men." For Dr. Cottom, in turn, that goal of higher education could not be more urgent and crucial. Being a principled, informed public intellectual on Twitter is one kind of teaching. She puts herself out there, knowing that attacks will come but also aware that what she is doing is necessary for a better future. Teaching wisely, well, and defensively—against the misinformation and exploitation—is, for her, a moral imperative. "Not only can you create spaces for critical engagement in higher education," she insists. "You are morally obligated to do so."

The new education must include programs like Digital Sociology, not just for a few students and at one campus but everywhere, on every campus. Digital or web literacy is no longer something we can consign to computer scientists. The power and influence of online interaction are rapidly becoming the most important factors in every aspect of our political, personal, and economic lives. Professor Cottom is positive that the students in the new Digital Sociology program will find jobs. They will possess skills the world needs—including how to discern and combat the ever-proliferating abuses of technology that permeate contemporary life.

The workplace demands far more graduates from programs such as Digital Sociology. We need educators to find a way between the twin pitfalls of technophobia and technophilia so that they can wisely navigate our technology-obsessed era—and prepare our students to do the same.

As it turns out, the jobs of the future require deep understanding of the technologies changing our workplace and our society. That understanding requires experimental and experiential training and the kind of grounded academic thinking that lets big ideas soar. The programs, the faculty, and the universities that understand that challenge will lead us all.

5 PALPABLE IMPACT

THEY FACE FORWARD IN THEIR SCHOOL CHAIRS. PRESUMABLY, THEY are looking at a chalkboard, just out of sight. Dressed like business-men, in white shirts and subdued ties and dark suits, the students sit stone-faced, blank. Some of the young men hold textbooks, but they're not reading them. Others sit with their faces resting between their hands, with fingers folded into gentle fists. One young man near the back has his head lowered into the crook of his arm. If ever they were passionate about learning, that time has passed. Almost identical, each face issues a silent plea for sympathy if not succor, showing hues of pain, fear, anxiety, boredom, and confusion. The scene happens to be in Japan, but it could be an all-male university or even a high school anywhere.

A professor in a sweater vest stands amid these pained young men. The painting cuts him off at the collar, below the neck. For all we know, he looks exactly like the young people he lectures.

This is a STEM class: science, technology, engineering, and math-ematics. In many contemporary discussions about reforming higher education for the digital age, pundits or politicians say everything should be about STEM, we're falling behind in STEM training, in difficult financial times we should be getting rid of anything that isn't essential and focusing on skills training in STEM fields. Is that what's going on in this painting?

With a textbook open in his left hand, this professor rests his right on the head of one of the two large, compound optical microscopes in the room. As big as the students, the microscopes each occupy a student desk, too. The round mechanical part of the microscope, technically known as a "head," has been replaced with an actual, literal human head. Its sadly expressive face is identical to those of the students in the room.

We have entered the tortured, surrealistic world of the late Japanese painter Tetsuya Ishida. His specimen is youth, the modern Japanese student. This painting is named *Seedlings*. Into what will these students grow? What are we doing to nurture them? The painting of the grotesquely anthropomorphic microscope suggests that the teacher can look down the eyepiece straight into the student's head, as if thought is a specimen to be examined on a microscope slide.

The painting is a powerful metaphor for a reductionist version of STEM education: rote, unrelated-to-the-rest-of-life, transmission-style learning, the head of the student detached, decapitated, severed, instrumentalized. We are not robots, Ishida protests. You cannot mechanize and dehumanize education by stripping away curiosity. In his view of the world, college makes students "workforce ready" in the most cynical way: school trains students to march, automaton-like, passive and devoid of creativity, from the classroom to the workplace, with nothing vital or inspired anywhere in sight.

It is a dystopian vision, certainly. Ishida made some two hundred paintings, all in the same style and with the same subject matter, in the nine years between his graduation from Musashino Art University and his death on May 23, 2005, at the age of thirty-one. Although he denied that he is the boy-man whose image recurs in his paintings, the physical resemblance is unmistakable. In a painting entitled *Recalled* (1998), young workers with the same immobile faces as the students in *Seedlings* box up other mechanical, dismembered workers as if readying defective tools for shipment. In "Exercise Equipment" (1997), a "salary man" manager jogs on a treadmill that's also an assembly line, powered by legless—literally immobilized—manual laborers who look exactly like him. Other works depict students trapped in some combination of 1950s B-movie spaceships and iron lungs, being trained to become businessmen whose arms have already been replaced by conveyor belts. Outer space and inner space are equally mechanized, tortured, and constrained.

Bosch-like, Ishida paints the nightmare of his generation, dominated by youth unemployment and underemployment, corrupt governments enforcing policies of "austerity," a school system characterized by endless homework, continual high-stakes standardized testing, and soul-crushing vocational training for jobs that do not exist. His nation's future? The "graying" of Japan is considered to be the worst in the world, a product of its citizens' longevity and rapidly declining birthrate as well as xenophobia that prevents the immigration of productive young workers. Youth are delaying having families. The high cost of education is a contributing factor to this national despair. Instead of addressing these crises humanely, Japan seems determined to eliminate anything that might counter them. In Japan, as in the West, the progressive defunding of the arts, humanities, and social sciences has made high school and university as dehumanized as Ishida already understood them to be.

This grim story of education in the twenty-first century is Ishida's personal tragedy. After graduating from high school at nineteen, this sensitive and vastly talented young man yearned to go to art school to improve his skill at creating *manga* and other comics. He wanted a career as an artist, but his father, a member of parliament, and his mother, a traditional Japanese housewife, were very concerned that this would be a disastrous choice for their son, condemning him to a life of poverty. They thought he should be a chemist, science teacher, or professor. They promised to pay for his college if he would pursue a STEM major, where he had a chance of finding a job.

Ishida moved out of his family house. He was admitted to one of the finest art schools in Japan, and paid for it himself by working part-time and living in squalor in rented rooms. He kept painting, too, and was beginning to gain recognition in Japan. He was determined to go to New York to be part of the city's vibrant contemporary art scene. He began to study English, and to save, work, paint, and work some more. He managed to save a million yen, about $8,500, on his minimum-wage earnings and hoped to rent a gallery to show his work. Then, his mentor informed him that there weren't rental galleries for artists in New York like there were in Tokyo. His savings would only see him through a few months in the city. He became increasingly depressed. His mother began to worry about him. One day, with a one-hundred-dollar US bill in his pocket and nothing else, Ishida left his apartment to go buy breakfast at the convenience store on the other side of the railroad tracks from his rented room. He was hit and killed instantly by a speeding train.

With his untimely death, one of the most powerful voices of Japan's Lost Decade was silenced. The Lost Decade has now stretched to two, with no signs of abating. Tetsuya Ishida's protest paintings have become world famous but have done nothing to change the tide of Japanese policies of educational austerity, which are aimed especially at the arts, humanities, and interpretive social sciences.

What is striking about Ishida's work is how much it both represents the situation in Japan and gives us a grim prediction of one direction in which American higher education is headed. We are hearing the cry, over and over, that higher education is frivolous, impractical, that its real purpose should be to give students "skills" and make them "workforce ready," by which is typically meant trained in STEM fields where, it is said as if it were true, there are jobs, there are futures. We've heard in the last few years that student financial aid should be tied to future "outcomes" and that colleges and universities should be ranked and rated by their job placements. In 2015, the US Department of Education even issued a tool called the "College Scorecard," a ranking system that allows you to determine how "good" your college is by five criteria: cost, graduation rate, employment rate, average amount borrowed, and loan default rate. That is one way of measuring the worth of an education. Certainly, everyone wants students to be able to find jobs. The scorecard also lists the mean salary of jobs, implying that the higher the salary, the better the job. Is that what we've come to? A school that turns out engineers or investment bankers gets a higher score than one that trains teachers and nurses and social workers and graphic designers because certain professions' salaries are higher than others'?

Ishida was not simply projecting some vision of misery. He felt real despair for Japan's future. Yet he did not live to see his darkest fears confirmed. In September 2015, the Japanese Ministry of Education issued a formal "request" (which is to say, a directive) to its eighty-six national universities that they take "active steps to abolish" undergraduate and graduate social science, humanities, and arts programs, including those in the areas of law and economics. Citing the radically declining birthrate, the Japanese Ministry insisted that funding for higher education must be cut and that it should go only to "essential" areas, specifically, to STEM. In December 2015, a decade after Ishida's death, twenty-six national universities announced—despite protests by faculty, students, and the public— that they planned to trim or possibly even close their humanities, arts, and social science departments. Funding for these areas from the Ministry of Education was already dwindling.

This is no longer an artist's dystopian vision but an unfolding government policy. The late Tetsuya Ishida's personal nightmare is being realized as national educational policy in Japan. And if some pundits and politicians get their way, something similar could happen here.

STEM IS NOT THE PROBLEM. NOR IS STEM THE SOLUTION.

It is indisputable that we need more people trained in STEM fields and that, relative to many other countries, the United States is poor at training the next generation of STEM experts. At the same time, it is hard to imagine a worse way of teaching STEM than by depriving it of any human applications and reducing it to "skills." The scientific method is grounded in curiosity, testing, iterating, synthesizing, analyzing, problem solving, inventing. Additionally, the latest research shows that study of STEM subjects by itself does not necessarily lead to better career outcomes in the near or the long term and that expertise in the humanities and social sciences very well might. The US Census Bureau report for 2014 reveals, for example, that a full 74 percent of those who graduate with a bachelor's degree in a STEM field do not stay in STEM-related occupations. Follow-up surveys indicate that many find that the "glass ceiling" is exceptionally low in STEM, and so they move into finance or business-related careers, such as real estate, which seem to offer more opportunities for advancement and somewhat more security. Most graduates working in STEM fields commonly return for an advanced degree in a complementary non-STEM field such as business, design, public policy, or even the arts. Changes to STEM fields come so fast and unpredictably that there is a supplementary industry dedicated to career counseling for those in STEM that emphasizes that you must keep learning, you must stay networked and connected with those in other fields, and you should be taking every opportunity beyond your training to enhance and develop your portfolio—skills that the relevant, cross-disciplinary new education emphasizes.

A 2007 National Academies' report, *Rising Above the Gathering Storm,* portended dire consequences if we did not improve the output of graduates trained in STEM, because of the increased technology needs in our country. Yet, at the same time, the report came to the grim conclusion that teaching STEM in a vacuum contributes to a low number of students entering these fields and low retention rates in STEM majors. A decade later, STEM educators (at the secondary and postsecondary levels) have begun to emphasize the importance of increasing the "attractiveness" of STEM education by, for instance, adding real-world experiences that show how one's STEM training is applicable and meaningful beyond the classroom. This is an important direction for STEM students. Internships, project-based learning, and cross-disciplinary skills building, especially in so-called soft skills (human and management skills rarely addressed in STEM degrees) all deepen learning and make connections between specialized courses and majors and larger issues in the world beyond college.

There are other problems with an overly simplistic and single-minded STEM obsession. Though we need more STEM graduates, we need ones trained differently and better than our current STEM students are trained. They should have a deeper understanding of larger contexts as well as flexibility so that, if their jobs disappear, they can build on their skills and find new jobs. As we are seeing, many STEM positions and whole occupations are susceptible to automation and offshoring. The Bureau of Labor Statistics recently predicted an 8 percent decline in existing STEM occupations by 2020.

Automation could well become the defining issue of the next decades. In the past, the risk to human occupations posed by automation has been countered by the "buggy whip" argument. The analogy goes that, with the invention of automobiles, buggy whip makers were, indeed, put out of work, but many new opportunities were created for auto factory workers, highway construction workers, gas attendants, and gas station owners as well as for car insurance salespeople, industrial designers, managers, and CEOs. However, no one knows whether the analogy will continue to hold. With artificial general intelligence powering robots to do everything from drive our cars to fill out our tax forms, it is not clear what new jobs will be created to offset the massive layoffs portended ahead.

In the foreseeable future, it is safe to say that the only jobs not susceptible to automation are those that require crosscutting skills of human discernment and creativity that no robot can approximate. It's impossible to imagine that AI-powered robots could displace workers in professions that require human judgment, talent, empathy, persuasive power, leadership, or even basic human touch (hairstylists, surgeons, writers, teachers, nurses, entrepreneurs, politicians, or therapists). Subjective, affective human qualities cannot be replaced by machines precisely because they offer what machines lack: an understanding of human needs, desires, requirements, and aspirations. In the nightmare world painted by Tetsuya Ishida, almost every human occupation can be replaced by robots. Except one: that of the artist. The originality and brilliance of the artist himself remain irreplaceable.

Although a degree in certain (but not all) STEM fields yields a first job more quickly than a degree in the fine arts, there is no evidence that STEM training leads to faster or higher career advancement, job security, or job satisfaction. Quite the contrary, evidence suggests that over time the tortoise humanist may actually win the career race against the STEM hare. University of California at Davis computer science professor Norman Matloff notes, "Statistics show that most software developers are out of the field by age forty." Both Mark Zuckerberg, CEO of Facebook, and Craig Barrett, a former chief executive officer of Intel Corporation, have observed that programming is a young person's occupation and the "half-life of an engineer" is only a few years. The research unambiguously reveals that STEM expertise without any grounding in interpretive and critical thinking skills may get you a first job, but it won't get you promoted. Go to any site offering special training in skills needed for advancement to become a manager and you see the same five or six skills listed: interpersonal or leadership (including cross-cultural) skills, communication, collaboration, critical thinking, and finance. If these skills are vital for promotion for those in the workforce, we should not be eliminating from our curriculums the courses that teach them.

If we want to take the phrase "workforce ready" seriously, then we have to understand what is required of today's workforce. Google endeavored to do just that in 2013 when it launched Project Oxygen, the most thorough, data-intensive study that any company has undertaken to date to understand the qualities that lead to promotion and a successful career. Google has collected data on its workforce since the company started and in 2013 began analyzing the factors that influenced who was hired, fired, rewarded, or promoted from the inception of the company as a small start-up to its present state as an employer of some sixty thousand full-time workers. Because Google's philosophy is that every manager should have technical training, it was assumed that technical know-how would be a top quality of successful managers.

Yet after a year of data mining and analyzing performance reviews, employee surveys, nominations for top company awards, and more than ten thousand observations of top managers at work, Google's list of qualities that lead to corporate advancement included, in descending order of importance, be a good coach, empower others (and don't micromanage), be interested in the well-being of your team, be bold and results-oriented, be a good communicator, be a good listener, help your employees with their own career development, and have a clear vision and strategy. On the list of factors bearing on actual promotion into leadership roles at Google, possessing a level of STEM skills to be able to guide others came in dead last. A piece in *Harvard Business Review* entitled "How Google Sold Its Engineers on Management" describes the way this data-driven company had to revise its vision of itself after sifting through the data.

If we are going to create a new education for the twenty-first century that can train students not for one job but for a sustained and productive life, we need to remember that, to paraphrase Steve Jobs, science and technology are not enough.

WHEN SHA XIN WEI SPEAKS, HIS EXPRESSIVE HANDS ALSO TELL the story, moving through the air and then landing on his computer keyboard, his fingers tapping out URLs with notable delicacy, videos appearing on-screen to illustrate complex concepts as he explains them. He has degrees in mathematics from Harvard and Stanford and is every bit the STEM prodigy. An entire wall of his office is taken up by an old-fashioned chalkboard scrawled with equations and geometric shapes. A mathematician who specializes in topology, a subfield of geometry that charts continuous surfaces, his gestures resemble the Mobius strips drawn on the chalkboards around the room: sinuous, fluid, three-dimensional. In a Mobius strip, that which is outside one moment bends and becomes the inside the next, and vice versa—a good metaphor for his vision of how departments and fields should constantly reposition themselves according to the specific project or challenge they must address. It is one of the symbols for the school he directs, the new School for Arts, Media, and Engineering.

Sha Xin Wei's research integrates disciplines across the old academic divides between the arts and the sciences, theory and practice, critical thinking and creative production, quantitative knowledge and human applications. He publishes articles on topics incomprehensible to most of us, with titles such as "Topology and Morphogenesis." In that article, Professor Sha writes: "One can use mathematics not as an instrument or measure, or a replacement for God, but as a poetic articulation." It's not clear whether this is math or philosophy, engineering or theology. In his new school, I'm not sure if those categories even make sense anymore.

You'd be mistaken to think this is futurism, science fiction, or something with no place in the real world. On the contrary, Sha Xin Wei's ambition is to train the next generation of students to make what he calls "palpable impact." To do that requires studying science, social science, the humanities, and the arts. You need to be able to understand cultural and religious traditions if you want your science to have an impact. You need to be original and creative if you want your solutions embraced by those who might at first be skeptical. Narrow specialization doesn't guarantee a future, nor does it prepare you to know how to change if your particular job suddenly disappears. He challenges students to address massive, complex, real-world questions such as: "What will life be like in Phoenix when there is no water?"

Dean Sha's program is not housed at the Hasso Plattner Institute of Design at Stanford, the famous design school, one of the most innovative and well-funded centers in all of higher education. Nor does it reside at the Media Lab at MIT, another elite and amply funded site for designing the future. Sha's school is part of Arizona State University, the public university with the largest enrollment in the entire United States, more than eighty thousand students total. This is not an incidental fact. His goal is not to train just a few elite visionaries who can create technologies that change the world for the rest of us but to ensure that students at a huge public university understand the changes occurring in their communities and are capable of leading significant, serious, meaningful technological change that is responsive to their community and far beyond.

"What will life be like in Phoenix when there is no water?" is not a question to be answered by any one discipline. Yet Sha doesn't like the words *interdisciplinary* or *multidisciplinary*. To him, those concepts are also outmoded and do little to change the structural limitations of inherited, traditional disciplines. The term he prefers is *synthesis*—by which he means a new way of tackling complex problems from seemingly opposite points of view, all of which are necessary if the solution is to hold against changing human or climatic conditions. He wants his students to grasp the math, sociology, and philosophy of any problem and see how each discipline offers a tool that's useful in solving the same problem in a different way or in arriving at alternative solutions to the same problem. The insights of artists are especially important to him. Unlike theorists (in any field), artists realize their most extravagant visions through the materials they get their hands on—sometimes literally. Like engineers, artists of all kinds must be visionary within constraints. Paint is a constraint—so is canvas, clay or metal, a piano or a tuba, a stage or a town square. Unlike engineers, they may not start with a blueprint, but they still end up with a product, an object, an event, a performance, enacted in real time and real space. Sha doesn't just want to recruit or foster dreamers. He wants students to learn how those who dream—artists—realize their vision in the real world. That's what he means by *synthesis*. By synthesizing the different perspectives and talents offered by different people in different fields, we can responsibly tackle major questions.

Sha tells me, "Think of everything you must address to answer 'What will life be like in Phoenix when there is no water?' Think of everyone you need to know how to work with, to be able to talk to, if you want to fully grasp the magnitude of such a question." His hands make a dipping curve, like a shorebird taking flight. "We aren't proposing solutions, we are trying to invent new techniques. We can teach students what we know, of course, but that doesn't take them very far now, does it? Isn't it much better to teach them how to ask about things they don't know, maybe never imagined, never thought of before, maybe problems no one can solve, answers no one knows? We do not need hypothetical questions to push the limits. We live in a time when the world's problems are of such magnitude that no one knows the answers. Yet in universities, we are still teaching as if we know. That's a deception. It's dangerous, really. If you expect palpable impact, you are challenging students to admit what they don't understand, what they don't know, what no one knows, and to begin to test ideas that could become solutions."

The approximately four hundred students in the Synthesis program learn all of the soft human skills prized by managers in the Project Oxygen study. Because no one person can possibly know everything, students have to learn how to learn from and teach one another, translating their specialized knowledge for those who operate with different principles, experience, and expertise. Collaboration across different realms is notoriously difficult—as Charles Eliot portended in "The New Education": "The practical spirit and the literary or scholastic spirit are both good, but they are incompatible. If commingled, they are both spoiled." True enough, perhaps, in 1869. We no longer have the luxury to make such distinctions. The world and its problems are too complex and resistant to traditional modes of thought.

"Sometimes the metaphor is the solution," he says. On his desktop computer screen, he calls up a Basic Science course project that required students to answer the question "How do bodies work?" In this course, students were challenged to find ways of helping stroke patients understand and contribute to their own rehabilitative progress, a particularly difficult task because these patients had lost the cognitive ability to process the feedback from their bodies that they once took for granted.

He reaches forward and picks up a cup from his desk. "Lifting this cup is easy for me. For someone recovering from a stroke, it could seem impossible. You wouldn't even know how to get there, because your basic information from your gestures, from your nervous system, is what's damaged. So we teach students to evaluate what abilities a stroke patient still has and to work from those. Work from a strength, not from an impairment. Say this patient's hearing is still fine. We challenge our students to ask how that patient could *hear* himself rehabilitating his own hand and arm. He can't count on other forms of cognition to help him heal his body but maybe he could hear his way to progress. How could we give him that tool to use?"

On the screen in front of us, we watch a solution developed by the students in introductory Basic Science. Stroke patients engage in physical therapy to regain full body movement by swinging their arms in arcs to the soothing sound of electronic music, as pure and clear as the perfect fifths made by a bow drawn across violin strings. The music, it turns out, is interactive; the notes are actually generated by their range of motion. When a patient moves his arm smoothly and correctly (which is to say therapeutically), the music is smooth, too, continuous and clear. When an arm falters or careens in a wrong direction, the music becomes choppy and discordant. In the video, the patient recoils from the unpleasant sound immediately. It's almost impossible to differentiate the music being made from the progress of the stroke victim making the music. Like the Mobius strips, cause and effect loop around one another: the beauty of the music created by the patient's rehabilitation is the feedback that inspires him to keep working to rehabilitate his arm, even against pain and the frustration of a slow process. I watch as one patient tries again and again. I see how he is listening, trying to return to the lovely, clean sound, which also means resuming the original arc and rehabilitating arm and shoulder muscles. This is what Sha means by palpable impact. The man is *actually* improving, using a method that no one had ever tried before because, after all, what medical school specialty teaches you that you can tune your ears to rehab your arm? If we were to break down the disciplinary sources of this solution that students in a Basic Science class arrived at, they would include biology, rehabilitative therapy, composing and conducting, music theory, computing, electrical engineering, biomedical engineering, nursing, kinesiology, and psychology. Synthesis, to use Dean Sha's term, is what pulls all these strands of expertise together into a solution. Undergraduates rarely see how what they are learning in one course fits with what they are learning in another, nor do they typically see their learning turned into an actual solution to a problem, in this case one that literally changes lives by improving recovery time.

"A musician studying orchestral conducting inspired this method," Sha says, and smiles. "I've witnessed experiments in rehabilitation in a well-funded, high-tech biomedical engineering lab at a private university where the disabled are encased in Terminator-style robot suits that cost several million dollars, with electrodes sending feedback that their limbs and brains can no longer supply. The success rate here is promising to be higher, at a tiny fraction of the cost. Who would have thought a musician might help engineers save lives and futures?"

We move on to the next topic. "We're working on climate change now in one student research group," Sha says. "Since we've had such a hard time getting traction in this politicized time, since there is so much debate about agency—whether humans have caused this rise in carbon dioxide emissions or whether it's something else— we're flipping the perspective. We're taking humans out of the equation. We're conducting an experiment and making a narrative: we are modeling mathematically and synthesizing climate change from the point of view of the climate itself, from the point of view of the weather. We are asking, if humans aren't the issue, what can we learn simply by charting what the weather is accomplishing in its assault on the earth? And if weather is what we are concerned with—not who is responsible, not what it will do to humans—what happens if we model what happens *to the weather* if a hundred thousand random people over the earth stop using cars for twenty years? It's like a game. How do we scale the impact on the weather? What difference will it make? What math, statistics, data analysis, visualization, and storytelling techniques do we need to go from what we know—the data we have now—to the unknown?"

Sha is convinced that only this new way of doing STEM through synthesis can begin to have palpable impact. If all the research stops because certain people or political groups don't want to believe humans are "at fault," you then have to do research that removes human culpability. What humans do is simply a variable to be measured, not a moral position to be regulated. Sometimes you exclude damaged cognitive processes to enact a cure; other times you have to work against social or cultural beliefs.

He calls this approach "modern alchemy." "When the problems exceed our current scientific solutions, the only way we can have palpable impact is through imagination. Sometimes good science requires magic." Many of the crucial problems we face today are of the same complexity and require the same amplitude of learning as how to rehabilitate when you've lost your normal cognitive ways of processing and how to gauge what life will be like in Phoenix when there's no more water. It is inspiring to know that these students, from their introductory courses onward, are being prepared to take on these challenges.

SHA'S METHODS MIGHT SOUND LIKE SOME NEW AGE GOBBLEDY-gook, an approach to big questions that appears innovative but that cannot deliver on its promises. Yet the results are, in fact, palpable. Bodies are healing, and students are learning new ways to think about connections between the brain and body, healing and emotions, science and the arts. There are other tangibles as well for these students who learn to think speculatively and boldly about urgent, lived realities. More than most, these students are achieving outcomes—the goal of every pundit and politician arguing for STEM for "workforce readiness."

In 2016, *US News & World Report* ranked Arizona State University—not Stanford, not MIT—as the most innovative university in the United States. ASU has taken on a leadership role in transforming higher education. Founded in 1885 as the Territorial Normal School to train teachers in the Arizona Territory, the university went through many iterations in the twentieth century and was renamed Arizona State University in 1958. ASU now is a public metropolitan research university with five campuses across the greater Phoenix area and four additional learning centers. It is leading a coalition of other regional public universities toward massive pedagogical innovation of a scope, thoroughness, and seriousness that would make Charles Eliot proud. These universities—including the University of Central Florida and the University of California at Riverside—rarely come up first in media stories about dazzling new developments in higher education. They don't have billions in endowments. In fact, Arizona State University has endured a nearly 50 percent reduction in state support since the 2008 recession. Yet faculty and administrators are committed to new ideas that bring the arts and the sciences together for palpable, measurable impact. Across the university, professors are examining the constituent requirements of their fields in light of new challenges, partnering with colleagues in other disciplines, and helping students design projects that address intractable world problems through synthesis and, sometimes, magic.

ASU president Michael Crow has dubbed his university and the others seeking to redefine their curriculums, structures, and mission "the New American University." For them, inclusion and economic equity are foundational principles, as important as pedagogical innovation, and key to it. Eliot opened the elite Ivies to those who were not simply the sons of Harvard alums (so-called legacy students). He understood that being rich is not the same as being brilliant and, to fulfill Harvard's ambitions as a "new American university" leading the way into a prosperous, technology-fueled twentieth century, it was necessary to admit the smartest people. He didn't champion what we now call diversity out of *noblesse oblige*, some sense of charity toward non-Harvard families. He wanted to admit the most capable young people and train them to be America's leaders and, indeed, to challenge the elites like himself who were from America's first families. He was hardly making Harvard egalitarian. No one would argue that. He was simply increasing the pool of those admitted to Harvard, partly to help break through institutional traditionalism and partly because he believed it would improve the university's excellence and innovation and therefore contribute to society's future.

Michael Crow wants to do something similar, but on a far broader scale. Crow defines the New American University as an institution "measured not by whom it excludes, but by whom it includes and how they succeed." This is happening at a time of significant retrenchment by the state. Arizona seems to have a death wish. It is drastically cutting its support of higher education even as it has a gigantic success story on its hands. Becoming more inclusive and more diverse, increasing graduation rates, and raising the research profile and quality of faculty, all at once, is almost unheard of. It is higher education's equivalent, President Crow insists, of a "moonshot," the term Google coined to describe the work of its secret Google X research division that explores technology so risky that few venture capitalists are bold enough to invest in it, even though its potential impact is enormous. Such innovation, in other words, is equivalent to a space program that risked putting men on the moon. Thinking quality, equity, inclusion, and innovation, Crow believes, are just as bold and equally important to future generations. "You cannot just abandon our youth—not unless you want to write off the future of the United States, of the globe, really, since we are the most powerful nation on it."

The first principle undergirding ASU's success is something Crow calls "Leverage Our Place." By grounding their studies in connection to community, to the cultural, physical, and socioeconomic conditions of Phoenix, Arizona, and the Southwest more generally, students see how their schoolwork can translate beyond the classroom. The rest of the principles are "Transform Society," "Value Entrepreneurship," "Conduct Use-Inspired Research," "Enable Student Success," "Fuse Intellectual Disciplines," "Be Socially Embedded," and "Engage Globally."

These principles point to why STEM at ASU looks quite different from Tetsuya Ishida's demoralized classrooms. Since becoming president, Crow has worked with faculty to create sixteen schools, all of which span, shuffle, recombine, and redefine traditional disciplines in innovative ways. He points, for example, to Cultural Anthropology. Not so long ago, both the number of majors and enrollments in electives were declining. Many universities, especially those faced with severe cutbacks, would have axed Cultural Anthropology. But Crow reasoned that, now more than ever, our world needs people who understand cultures other than their own. So he challenged faculty to work together to remake the department in ways that would draw a new generation of students and that would offer the broadest means of addressing human and cultural factors and from a range of methodological assumptions and histories. The resulting School of Human Evolution and Social Change is rooted in the social and life sciences and teaches one of the university's more popular majors, conjoining disciplinary areas and methods that formerly were distinct or even antagonistic.

In the Ngogo Chimpanzee Project, for example, students and faculty engage in multiple research projects to understand chimpanzee social organization and behavior and to learn more about primate evolution. At the same time, because Kibale National Park, where the project is based, is under constant assault from illegal poachers, the school's cultural anthropologists and sociologists work with local Ugandan law enforcement officers to come up with better ways of protecting the animals. They are studying the economic pressures and cultural practices of neighboring communities as well as international black markets for animal products, with the dual aim of guarding the chimpanzees and serving the local human populace.

A different research group in the School of Human Evolution and Social Change is looking at medical outcomes in partnership with the nearby Mayo Clinic. They are studying the reasons for the success or failure of patients who undergo bariatric surgery for long-term weight loss. Students and faculty use qualitative and quantitative methods across the social, cultural, and biological sciences for ethnographic and longitudinal studies designed to improve postoperative success rates.

"Design what your heart wishes" is the objective Crow has assigned to faculty. Not every faculty has gone along. The business school has been notoriously reluctant to embrace the "New American University" model, whereas other fields have been eager to see how far they can push what counts as a "major" and a "field" and a "department." The members of the Biology Department argued that they wanted a self-assembling faculty, where professors from other departments could join for specific projects and could either stay or return to their home departments after a project was finished. This meant rethinking faculty recognition and reward systems: what counts as a "contribution," as peer review, as having merit across the new and home departments. Crow approved the experiment and asked who would be the first collaborators. The first to join the new, fluid department were Philosophy and Public Policy, as it turns out. The biologists believe that they cannot do good biology—with palpable impact—without ethicists and policy advisers contributing.

Arizona State University long ago left behind a narrow-minded "skills" approach to higher education in favor of student-centered learning. Rather than cordon off the liberal arts and general education in the first two years of study, keeping them separate from a specialized major, it has integrated research, teaching, and public service as a mission at every level, from introductory courses to doctoral study. This is achieved through internships, experiential learning, project-based learning, and problem-solving competitions, all of which are woven into the fabric of the New American University.

What do ASU students do when they graduate? They find not just jobs but careers. Their range of talents makes them highly sought after throughout the for-profit and nonprofit employment sectors. In fact, they are often so versatile and multitalented, with such a keen and far-ranging perspective, that the first employer to snap them up is Arizona State University, which hires back its own graduates as educational innovators. ASU competes hard against other area employers because, says President Crow, its graduates are better prepared for the task of solving complex problems than are graduates from other universities. A generation ago, the plum jobs (at the university and in the community) would have gone to graduates from elite universities on the coasts or to ASU's chief sports and education rival, the University of Arizona.

However, ASU graduates, now, have the reputation for being bold, innovative, mature, independent thinkers. President Crow points out that booming industries are moving into the area, including several large technology firms from Silicon Valley, lured by lower costs and an exciting new talent pool of ASU graduates. Typically, public universities are the largest employer in their area, and that is still the case with ASU. It is common for a university to be the driver of local economies too, both in terms of spending and as a contributor to local culture and intellectual life. ASU now employs eleven thousand of its alums. President Crow's ambition is to increase that number to forty thousand. He is also aware of the irony that ASU now has to compete harder to employ its own graduates because the university's stellar reputation for innovation is drawing new employers to the area.

Next on the president's agenda for ASU is a Humanities Research Lab. Several scholars in the humanities are looking to team with mathematicians, engineers, and computer scientists like Xin Wei Sha as well as with the newly formed biological sciences department. "How do you free faculty to redesign their own field?" President Crow asks, and then offers the answer that defines the new world of transdisciplinary STEM education: You free faculty not by insisting they give up the standards of their traditional discipline in order to accept the standards of someone else's. Rather, you reward them and their students for constantly rethinking options, trying new programs, acting inventively and boldly, collaboratively and synthetically. In design school, this is called "iterative thinking"; as Crow puts it, "You design, you redesign, you adjust, you redesign again, you adjust—the process doesn't stop. Like learning. There's no end point, it's all a process. That's what a university is."

ASU and its cohort are not alone in imagining and realizing a new vision of higher education. Across the continent from Phoenix, in Charlottesville, the University of Virginia has engaged its entire faculty and student body in the ambitious collaborative project of designing a new course of study in the liberal arts. UVA's history is as long as ASU's is brief. Founded by Thomas Jefferson in 1819, UVA enrolls more than twenty-one thousand undergraduates and fifteen thousand graduate students and is one of the country's most distinguished research universities. In its new curriculum, students will engage with aesthetics, empirical and scientific ways of knowing, cultural differences, and ethical questions, all of which the school has deemed foundational skills needed in today's world. From mastery of a modern language to financial literacy and data analysis skills, UVA's new curriculum will turn out a new kind of graduate, one who can thrive in STEM fields or any others, really.

The new curriculum was designed during two years of dialogue among faculty, staff, and students, and in the fall of 2016 it was beta-tested by an inaugural cohort of college fellows, students, and faculty who are taking and teaching the new introductory courses in order to contribute to the next iteration of the plan. The goal is a full implementation of the new plan by the entire university in fall 2019. The students and faculty are also developing a comprehensive, capstone "Engagement" experience that will tie students' classroom learning to some real-world project, in the hopes of making a public contribution and, in the best of circumstances, making a palpable impact.

Numerous colleges and universities across the country are beta-testing new general education models now. Writing and speaking requirements are integral to many of these, including presenting and publishing for a larger public. Fulfilling these fundamental requisites is an excellent way of encouraging students to reflect on and articulate what they are learning as they are learning it ("metacognition," in educational jargon), one of the best methods for ensuring that learning will be useful in later life. Some educational institutes are partnering with local institutions: libraries, local high schools, science and research centers, civic and community organizations, and museums, as well as publishing companies, technology firms, and other corporations that might yet have roles for students that go beyond the usual unpaid-intern-at-the-copy-machine.

At Duke University, a new program called Bass Connections replaces the scattered general education requirements with a coherent focus on a complex problem that spans five broad thematic areas: brain and society; information, society, and culture; global health; education and human development; and energy. For a project on global health disparities, a student might take a literature course, but instead of reading *The Canterbury Tales* (standard fare in general ed literature courses), she'll read Boccaccio's *Decameron*, a hundred bawdy tales exchanged in the fourteenth century by young men and women who secluded themselves in a Florentine villa to escape the physical and emotional ravages of the Black Death. Or they'll read Daniel Defoe's *Journal of the Plague Year* (1665) or Albert Camus's existential *The Plague,* set against the backdrop of the bubonic plague ravaging North Africa, or Chinua Achebe's *Things Fall Apart,* with its depiction of the diseases, including leprosy and smallpox, brought to Nigeria by white colonizers, or the novel by Nobel Prize winner Gabriel García Márquez, *Love in the Time of Cholera.* From these diverse historical and international literary depictions of disease, students come to learn about the enduring superstitions, mythologies, and cultural practices embedded within our understanding of contagion and contamination. They begin to understand such recurring impediments to medical care delivery as resistance to vaccinations and antibiotics as well as larger social issues such as xenophobia.

Alongside these literary works, the students read in classical economics and in the much more recent field of behavioral economics, while also taking science, business, and management classes, in classrooms and in labs. They might devise a cost-benefit analysis and an actual, strategic business and workflow plan that embodies philosopher and economist Amartya Sen's idea that we must also account for the intangibles that enhance or cripple our lives, such as inequality, life expectancy, infant mortality, and disease. In addition to their historical, theoretical, philosophical, entrepreneurial, service-oriented, and practical work, the students will ideally spend time in another country. The result is that a general education requirement in global health disparities becomes a foundational experience for whatever a student might do after college, whether that means heading to medical school or to Ghana to work with a nongovernmental organization.

From UVA to Duke to a grand new experiment: at the 2016 South by Southwest, an annual carnival of creative technology and ideas, MIT graduate school dean Christine Ortiz, a professor of Materials Science in the Department of Engineering, unveiled her ambition to start an entirely new university on the principles of transdisciplinary inquiry.

Every academic I know has a fantasy of going off and starting their own college or university. Professor Ortiz is taking a leave of absence to create a nonprofit residential research university steeped in project-based learning. As yet unnamed, and still quite shadowy in its detail, her vision of the new education promises to be this generation's MIT Media Lab, mixing and matching all things STEM with all things otherwise.

No more lectures. No more classrooms. No more majors. Professor Ortiz is starting from scratch, getting rid of the basic pedagogical and curricular infrastructure we've inherited from Eliot's research university. Elitism, too, is an antiquated idea with which she, like Michael Crow of ASU, wishes to dispense. Why do the smartest students have to be the richest? Why do we have to compete for a handful of "diverse" students instead of recognizing the brilliance it takes to survive harsh and difficult upbringings? How can scrappy genius be channeled in higher education without it being overlooked or snuffed out? In Crow's and Ortiz's view, rethinking what we mean by *selectivity* follows from any attempt to rethink how we teach and learn.

Ortiz's methods have garnered a good deal of attention, and it remains to be seen what her new university will actually look like. She insists all learning will be learner-centered, collaborative, and project-based. Science and technology will be emphasized, with equal focus on both basic and applied research. And, again, like ASU's Michael Crow, Ortiz is endeavoring to make everything at her university work for the good of humanity and the improvement of society. As ASU and Ortiz show, we need STEM. But STEM, of course, needs the human and social sciences and the arts. Otherwise, it is good for the development of a specific skill but ultimately not terribly significant over the *longue durée* of a student's life and career.

Professor Ortiz considers her ideal student for the university of the future as someone with a vision and a mission. She explains, "We want to have an emphasis on science and technology, and, in particular, the interface of science and technology with humanities and the arts." They seek students with interdisciplinary interests "who would like to have an education that has technical depth, but also the breadth of working with that interface. Students who want to explore interdisciplinary pathways, emerging pathways, and also who sort of enjoy self-directed learning and are passionate about working on their own projects." She is in the vanguard of those rethinking standard disciplinary and graduate requirements, the merging of STEM and non-STEM fields, the different contributions of selectivity and inclusion, and other binaries established over a century ago. Crossing those divisions, she insists, is mandatory if students are to thrive in the world after they receive their degree. Her hope is that these students will go on to become the leaders we need to solve the equally vexed problems that trouble all our futures.

IF PROFESSOR ORTIZ IS SUCCESSFUL IN STARTING HER NEW UNI-versity, it will be the first institution of higher education founded in Massachusetts since Olin College in 1997. Olin is where Sara Hendren teaches. She is an artist. She is an engineer. Her projects are frequently for people who are labeled, by the able-bodied world, as "disabled." Like many of the professors at Olin, she refuses to see boundaries. She considers that strategic disciplinary transgression as her charge, her mission, her art, her design, her science.

As a designer, she works with clients—not for them, with them. She extends that same participatory goal to pedagogy. She does not teach students; she learns with them. She often poses specific problems for them to solve, and, in turn, they reach out to their clients to include them in the process of problem solving too. "Cocreation" of solutions, she insists, needs to be part of the design process.

Hendren builds these design principles into her teaching, research, and design projects in "assistive technology." For example, in collaborating with Chris Hinojosa, an engineer born with one arm, Hendren's students spent a week with him to understand his abilities and his limitations. They learned that he already could use his body, one arm, and two feet dexterously. And they learned that the last thing he wanted was the unwieldy, sci-fi-like million-dollar bionic arm contraption NASA was designing for him. Why would he want to lug around that heavy mechanical thing? However, this athletic young man longed to do what he could not do with his body or with the cumbersome bionic arm: he wanted to scale a climbing wall and, maybe someday, a cliff. He couldn't do that on his own.

So, instead of a multifunctional mechanical arm, he worked with Hendren's Olin students and, together, they fabricated a simple, lightweight device, a modular socket that allows him to switch out different, lightweight, single-use extensions, such as one that allows him to climb a wall and another that enables him to ride a bicycle. He worked with the student artists because he found their actual and visual vocabulary more imaginative and flexible than the technical jargon, blueprints, and fabrication software that seemed to limit the ingenuity of the engineers. The artists could see possible solutions that the engineers could not. At the same time, the skills of the engineers were crucial for turning artistic prototypes into strong, functional, serviceable devices. Together, everyone, including Chris Hinojosa, studied plants with tendrils to consider ways of grasping that do not require hands. They studied animals. They read and looked at art together. And they designed and built exactly the right device to do the job, one that was simple, portable, with attachments designed specifically for a particular function. The device met Hinojosa's needs perfectly.

If the students had not been trained to listen first before cocreating with a client, they never would have come up with something that was suitable. If they hadn't read widely and gone with their client to art museums, to the gym, to movies, and experienced what he could do and what he wanted to do, none of it would have been possible.

Hendren's students also worked with the eminent curator and scholar Amanda Cachia to address a problem she had in giving large public lectures. Cachia is four-foot-three. She is constantly confronted with podiums, microphones, and other stage setups designed for people far taller than she. She had plenty of experience with "disabled" podiums supposedly designed to accommodate "little people." Inevitably, the podium wires would be too short or one piece of equipment didn't interface with another in the way it should have. She wanted a device that could bring her up to the level of the existing podium, allow her the dignity to be in control of the stage on which, after all, she is the distinguished speaker, and give her the autonomy to do this efficiently without detracting from the content of what she is saying. This may sound simple enough to an able-bodied person, but it's precisely because the able-bodied take such matters for granted that there is a problem.

Hendren's students, in consultation with Cachia, experimented with various materials and settled on the high-tech carbon fiber used in racing motorcycles and spacecraft. They designed a sturdy, light-weight podium that folds, like origami, into a laptop case. They called it the AlterPodium. Cachia simply unfolds and slides the AlterPodium behind the dysfunctional (for her) existing podium and ascends to her rightful place, center stage.

These students read memoirs, literature, and disability studies in the humanities, social science, and science literature, so they understood that dignity is at least as important in Cachia's situation as are other considerations, such as weight and efficiency. They engaged with the idea of "normativity" in the abstruse, important theoretical work of philosopher Judith Butler—not typical reading for engineers, but absolutely crucial to their vocational training.

For example, in "Examined Life," a video about our different abilities, Butler and disability activist Sunaura Taylor ask: Don't we all need assistance of some kind or other? Isn't there a time in our lives when we all need others whose abilities supplement our own? Aren't we all co-learners and co-teachers? Given human frailty, aging, and mortality, isn't it inevitable that we will all need assistance at some point in our lives? Butler and Taylor emphasize that this is a fundamental question not only for the "disabled" but for everyone and for society as a whole.

Hendren notes that the theoretical questions of ability and disability, empowerment and impairment are central to the engaged form of pedagogy that she practices at Olin College. Basically, if we decide we do want to live in a world where we assist each other, we must unlearn the idea that "expertise" is a condition or an outcome, that the prof has it and the student's job is to gain it through a series of trials resulting in a diploma. We need to realize, instead, that learning is lifelong and that the conditions in which we learn can change in an instant. The human condition means we are all potentially impaired and can, in an instant, become the client, not the technology designer. This appreciation is key to how Hendren teaches. She notes that, in every space—including in the classroom—different people are experts in different things, different people need help and give it. If curator Amanda Cachia's expertise at spatial and installation art inspires the students who make the portable podium from which she can better deliver her message, who is assisting whom? Hendren would say the dependency is mutual. She believes the idea of "assistive technology" is key to good pedagogy because, in the end, as we learn we all assist one another.

Hendren argues that, in her role as the teacher, she also has to relinquish the idea that she is the expert in the room. Even as she prods her engineering students to ask harder and harder questions and produce more and more useful and sophisticated and innovative devices, she realizes that their capabilities far exceed her own knowledge and expertise. In situations where some students possess greater technical expertise than others, her students have to trust her questions and she has to trust their answers. Their ability as responsible co-learners becomes the highest standard of excellence, one that they also apply to their collective projects and problem solving.

This is not the specialized, vocational STEM learning we're accustomed to. Yet we know these students will earn entry-level jobs and, beyond that, they are destined for fulfilling careers. They are trained to address crucial challenges that graduates of most programs are not prepared to tackle. Olin's undergraduate engineering program is consistently ranked among the top five. Olin students typically start in high-paying engineering jobs. But Olin aspires to encourage its students to build their knowledge and their future on the firmest footing of all: interests and passions—exactly what is missing in the vacant eyes of Tetsuya Ishida's dazed and cowed and workforce-ready specimens.

Sara Hendren hopes each of her students aspires to become what she calls a "Public Amateur." She believes every professor should strive for that amateurism too, in the sense that, as an amateur, one is open to ideas, imagination, and change. Public amateurism is difficult for most professors—and for most professionals in the workplace. It means relinquishing expertise and status. Yet it is necessary to attain as the problems we face become increasingly contradictory and vexing. Public amateurism—receptiveness to other perspectives and other expertise—is a crucial skill to teach our students if they are to have palpable impact in the world.

I think of Sara Hendren and her students whenever I pass one of those familiar blue-and-white "handicapped" icons of the stick figure in the wheelchair. More and more often, one sees this traditional symbol replaced by one in which the stick figure leans forward, as if zooming full speed to the finish line. The zippy, racing version is part of her Accessible Icon Project, an open-source activist art endeavor that encourages anyone to download images from her website and turn them into stickers, stencils, posters, and signs that they can plaster over the usual handicapped sign, which she believes stereotypes those with impairments. The Accessible Icon signs have been showing up everywhere, from hospitals in Delhi, India, to the signs in the parking lot at the US Department of Transportation in Washington, DC. "An icon is a verb," Hendren insists; it "does things" in the world. Like all art, an icon shapes our perceptions, it expands our vision or limits it. Her goal with the Accessible Icon Project, as in everything she does, is expansiveness. This is why she teaches at Olin College, a liberal arts school of engineering. The vision of education there is far more radical, on an epistemological level, than what many think tanks and pundits insist is "revolutionary." It is also more practical and more likely to prepare students for good careers than the limited and antiquated skills training or vocational higher education movement.

All of these educators dedicated to higher education reform understand how deeply we must go in our reconsideration not just of STEM education but also of the purpose and mission of college as a whole if we are going to train students to address the scale and scope of change in the world they face. The new education isn't simply a change in curriculum or implementation of a new kind of pedagogy. It's not just a course or a program. It is all of the above, undergirded by a new epistemology, a theory of knowledge that is deep, synthetic, active, and meaningful, with real impact in the world. In the end, the new education is also a verb, one that empowers our students with better ways to live and thrive in a complicated world.

6 WHY COLLEGE COSTS SO MUCH

As I lay dying, my mind turned, as it is supposed to at such a time, to what matters most: *What happens if . . .*

It was June of 2015, and Dr. Cho, the attending ER surgeon, explained he was going to put me under anesthesia immediately, despite potential risks.

Earlier that morning, without warning or symptoms, I'd collapsed. I was in my apartment, working from home, setting up an international conference call with colleagues. And then I was on the floor. My laptop beeped, indicating that it was time for the conference call. I texted, "Fainted. Will take nap. Won't be on our call."

I was delirious and didn't realize something was drastically wrong, but, thankfully, my colleagues did. Because my husband, Ken, was away on business, they got me help. A friend and neighbor in our apartment building was suddenly at my door. In no time I was being wheeled into the Cadillac of rooms at New York University's Langone Hospital.

"I've never seen such a luxurious emergency room," I said drowsily to the admitting physician.

"It's because you are in the worst shape of anyone in the entire hospital."

They say things like that to you when you refuse to believe you are dying.

As I was being prepped and wheeled into the elevator that would take me to surgery, time slowed. I focused on essentials. What would I change in my life if I survived this emergency? Not much, in fact. I have a wonderful partner, a great family, so many loyal friends, and the best job in the world. Teaching at the nation's largest public urban university has plenty of challenges, but I've never met more hardworking, inspiring students or faculty. City University of New York is New York City's single most important engine of economic mobility—more important than Wall Street—and embodies the American dream of success through higher education. How lucky to be part of such a rich tradition, such a future!

The bustling, efficient team of eight or ten physicians, residents, interns, and nurses who surrounded me in surgery looked like my CUNY students. They were young, from different countries, international by birth or first-generation Americans.

I don't remember anything after that.

The next morning, with Ken beside me, I wanly greeted the surgery team as they crowded into my hospital room.

"You're going to be fine," Dr. Cho said. They were beaming. I could see their pride. They saved my life. They went over the diagnosis, the treatment, the recovery time, the medications. "It will take a little while, but you'll be able to return to everything that you do. You will be able to do your work again soon."

"We Googled you," another of the residents said, and the others nodded.

"Do you remember what you said to us last night, before surgery? How you talked about the tuition debt we all carry?"

I didn't.

"You told us how sorry you were that we had $250,000 in debt. You said that was the average for medical school and it was a national crisis."

Ken chuckled. "Was it before or after you asked her the questions about extreme measures?" he joked.

They all smiled.

"Actually, we talked about it later," Dr. Ali said. "None of us owes $250,000." She paused. "We all owe more. I owe over $400,000."

"It is a crime," I said.

Dr. Cho, the oldest of the group at maybe thirty-five, intervened, "Now, you really need to rest. We'll be back. You will be fine, but you were in bad shape. Please don't worry about us."

"How can I not worry about you? You saved my life. You will save many, many lives. And we have failed you." Apparently, in my pre-op delirium this was pretty much what I'd said. Ken stood up then, but he didn't need to. They were already leaving. These were doctors. They were all telling me to rest, they would be back. They were glad I was okay.

When I asked my friend Dr. Eric Manheimer, former CEO of Bellevue Hospital in New York, about the enormous tuition burden carried by young interns and residents, he responded, "No problem. They'll become cosmetic surgeons and pay that tuition back in a year."

He paused. "Actually," he said, "there *is* a problem. They can pay back their medical school debt by going into lucrative, specialized fields, but our society loses. We will soon have no general practitioners, no one in public health, no ER physicians, no one in OB/GYN, no gerontologists, no one in inner cities, no one in rural areas. So it's not just their problem. It is all of our problem—our society's very, very big problem."

As was impressed upon me during my time in the hospital, we cannot talk about transforming higher education unless we address the issues of cost and student debt. If college costs so much that it governs your choice of career, it is not preparing you for the best possible life. It is preparing you to pay off your loans. It is forcing you to make choices, throughout your college career and after, to protect your financial future and material condition, not paving the way to a fulfilling career. With $400,000 in loans, is it even possible for an aspiring doctor to be idealistic anymore?

There are equivalents in nearly every other field. The most common major now is business. A student should work toward a business degree if a career in business is what she wants. But that track can be debilitating if she follows it because she feels she doesn't have a choice as a result of her student loans. Burdened by debt, students narrow their choices. They do not explore and test options for a productive potential career that intersects with their passions and interests. Instead, the financial strain of tuition debt turns college from an aspiration for a better future, alive with possibility, into a cynical enterprise, a union card, as people used to say, on the way to the best-paying job they can wrangle, whether they like it or not.

High tuition costs not only force many students into fields and would-be career paths they wouldn't otherwise choose but also prevent many students from completing their degree. Working several hours a week or even full-time while in college has an impact on time to degree, and on the likelihood of finishing a degree. Currently, the United States ranks number one in the world in the percentage of students it sends to college—a high rank it has held for decades. However, we hover somewhere between number seventeen and nineteen in college completion rates. As Adelphi University president emeritus Robert A. Scott explains, "Of 100 high school students, about 70 will graduate from high school; 49 will enter college; and 25 of these will graduate with a four-year baccalaureate degree in six years." That low college graduation percentage makes debt even more devastating, because students must pay back tuition loans whether or not they earn a degree. The interest on student loans is also exploitative, currently 50 percent higher than on mortgages, and US student loans are structured such that they cannot be canceled through bankruptcy. There's no escape. Dropping out of college without a degree is the worst choice of all because we know what a significant difference having a degree makes in future job possibilities. The 2015 figures from the US Department of Education's National Center for Education Statistics (NCES) show that adults with a bachelor's degree earned approximately $48,500 a year, while the earnings for those with only a high school diploma averaged $23,900.

It's not as though colleges and universities are simply gouging students. In most cases, particularly at public schools and private institutions lacking large endowments, tuition has gone up out of the necessity to meet a bottom line. At the same time that costs are being passed along to students in the form of tuition, faculty are experiencing extreme cutbacks, too. Over half of all courses taught on our campuses now are taught by adjunct, part-time instructors, with no benefits and no job security. That number has risen from approximately 30 percent in 1975. These highly educated instructors teach on a course-by-course basis for wages that, if calculated hourly, are below the minimum wage. This has a direct effect on students right now, setting aside the question of revolutionizing college in the future.

For the new education, the issue of faculty funding is particularly disastrous. If full-time faculty are carrying a greater burden of work resulting from higher student-to-faculty ratio and administration, they are less likely to spend time redesigning their classrooms and their institutions for active, student-centered learning. If junior faculty feel their jobs are threatened in a precarious market where there aren't many options, they are less likely to be agents of change, agitating to make the university more relevant. In addition, part-time, adjunct faculty—typically the newest members of the profession— have almost no voice in institutional governance, so cannot be forces for change. They are paid to teach on a per class basis and typically do not attend faculty meetings; any ideas they have about transforming the institution are lost. Finally, without much hope for a future, why would anyone aspire to be a professor? If the brightest young minds are not entering the profession, there is little hope that it can be radically altered into something exciting and new.

Soaring tuition and falling funds for faculty are pernicious trends in their own right, making even a good traditional education harder to achieve. The problem is that, as we've seen, a traditional education is no longer adequate. So all of these factors compound: high tuition forces students onto narrow careerist paths, they are often taught by overworked professors, and their education does not equip them for the world beyond the academy. In other words, students today are paying more for less. It's a vicious cycle. How to escape it is one of the most important questions our society can ask.

Those young interns who cared for me so well had aspirations to careers that would be meaningful both to themselves and to others and that would enable them to lead independent, comfortable lives. That is what most of my own students want, too. With the financial stresses that face students and their universities today, change becomes harder, and sometimes a meaningful career has to take second place to one that, literally, pays off the tuition debt.

CURRENTLY, 42 MILLION AMERICANS COLLECTIVELY OWE OVER $1.3 trillion in student debt. The average 2016 college graduate carries about $40,000 in debt. And, as Eric Manheimer portends, there are consequences for all students who have to begin their quest for a productive, responsible adult life worried about paying off substantial loans. It has an impact on what they major in, what career they choose, whether they go on to advanced study, what job they take, what job they stay—or are stuck—in to pay the bills. Leaving college substantially in debt does not prepare students for the challenges of the twenty-first-century economy; it leaves them disempowered and even more vulnerable to that economy from the start. College is no longer as good as it needs to be at preparing graduates to succeed in a complex world, and its high cost is one of the contributing factors in the equation that forces students to be conservative in their aspirations. Debt stymies one's ability to soar.

If we are serious about the new education, we have to address this issue. We could revolutionize the university and succeed in providing students with the most innovative and relevant education imaginable, but if we can't alleviate the burden of cost, we are still hobbling their future. I know a brilliant young multimedia artist and theorist who is enjoying a remarkable success right now, with three exhibits in three different European cities. Jack, who earned both a bachelor's degree and a PhD from private universities, currently works as a beginning professor teaching introductory art classes at a public university in England. Older artists are urging him to do what great artists have always done—quit his job, find a cheap little studio in some tiny village in Greece or somewhere else inexpensive, and devote himself to making art while his career is hot. "Take the risk!" they admonish him. "Opportunities like this don't come again." They imply he's not a "real" artist because he won't do this. They do not understand that, having graduated from American universities, he has so much debt that he has to keep teaching to pay off steep student loans that come due each month, barely leave him enough money to pay his current bills, and prevent him from taking advantage of the chance of a lifetime.

Jack's story is familiar to current graduates in the United States. Whereas most developed nations subsidize higher education such that students pay little or even no tuition, in America even our public universities charge significant tuition. According to the College Board, the average annual cost of tuition and fees for 2015–2016 was $32,405 at private colleges and universities, where room and board averaged an additional $11,516. That's roughly $45,000 to $50,000 a year, not including books, fees, and incidental expenses. Given that the median family income in the United States is $51,000, those costs put private education out of the reach of all but the elite.

For in-state residents at public colleges and universities, the 2015–2016 average tuition was $9,410, and for out-of-state residents, $23,893. Room and board was typically $10,138 at public schools. That is a total of roughly $20,000 a year for in-state students living in dorms and $35,000 for out-of-state students. The latter number is not far off from the cost of private university tuition, which is one reason more and more public institutions look to meet their own bottom line by admitting greater numbers of high-paying out-of-state students. It's a bit bizarre, each state's public universities working to woo students from other states to meet their operating costs. One consequence is that it is often easier to be admitted to another state's public institutions than to your own.

The situation is most egregious in Southern states where governors have made lowering taxes on corporations and the wealthy and decreasing subsidies to higher education almost a litmus test for their conservative standing. Southern states top the list for greatest cutbacks to higher education, highest costs for lower-income students, highest costs for community college, lowest percentage of people with college degrees, and, not surprisingly, biggest declines in in-state university enrollment. To make up budget shortfalls, these universities charge significantly higher out-of-state tuition and recruit heavily from elsewhere. For all the talk of the importance of jobs in the poorest Southern states, these cutbacks ensure a future of poverty for the next generation of Southerners.

In inflation-adjusted dollars, tuition in the last thirty years has tripled at public universities and more than doubled at private universities. Most middle-class Americans, especially after the 2008 financial collapse, do not have the savings to front such a bill. Since the 1980s, two trend lines have been diverging: as tuitions have risen, wages and spending power for the formerly middle class have stagnated or fallen. It is likely, if you are a middle-class parent of a seventeen-year-old, that you simply do not have the ability to pay all the costs of your child's higher education. That means your child will probably go to college on a combination of grants and loans.

In her exhaustive study of three thousand students entering the University of Wisconsin public higher education system in 2008, sociologist and expert on higher education policy Sara Goldrick-Rab shows how the burden of debt makes a dramatic difference to what subject area students study in college, whether or not they finish college, and what they do in their life beyond college. She notes that, in 1981, state appropriations for higher education began to decline—from $10.18 per $1,000 of state personal income (1981) to $9.24 (in 1990), $7.52 (in 2000), $6.32 (in 2010), and $5.00 (in 2016). "Just as Americans decided that college was essential," Goldrick-Rab notes, "states began spending less on public higher education and the price of college rose." Six years after starting college, only one in two students in the Wisconsin Scholars Longitudinal Study had graduated, with 58 percent of those who started at four-year colleges and 42 percent of those at community colleges achieving a bachelor's degree.

These figures mirror the national trends. From interviews, Goldrick-Rab's research team discovered that students faced food and housing insecurity; jobs with schedules or employer demands that had to take precedence over classes, exams, or papers and other assignments; and constant anxiety over money that added psychological burdens to the material ones. These conditions are now commonplace for many students in a way that they were not for their college-going parents or grandparents. As Goldrick-Rab poignantly explains, had the students in her study started college the year they were born (1990), they would not have had to borrow any money to go to college. A simple part-time job would have covered their expenses.

Here is a sobering example of change at one private university. In 1970 a Yale student paid $2,550 a year in tuition. Working a minimum-wage job at the 1970 rate of $1.45 an hour, the student could work 4.8 hours a day to pay college tuition costs. In 2014, Yale tuition is $45,800, and that same minimum-wage job on campus pays $7.25. The Yale student today would need to work 17 hours a day to cover tuition.

As a result of rising tuitions and stagnant or falling middle-class wages, this generation of students has aptly been dubbed "Generation Debt." Although over the course of a lifetime, a person with a college education earns more than someone with no college degree—in some fields, as much as a million dollars more—starting wages in formerly middle-class occupations are lower, the jobs less plentiful, and the job insecurity greater. Not surprisingly, a third of all those with student debt are currently at least a month behind on loan payments.

Student loan debt is also the worst kind of debt to carry. Step-by-step, from 1993 to 2008, Congress passed laws that, in essence, exploited the tuition crisis by giving direct control of the student loan industry to Wall Street banks, private equity companies, and other corporations that quickly turn purchased debt over to collection agencies that are paid for bringing in the loans by any means necessary, including harassment at the workplace or through landlords. These collection agencies are profit-making ventures; they don't serve students, the government, or universities. The reason student loan debt is virtually the only form of personal debt that cannot be discharged through bankruptcy is that corporate loan institutions have lobbied successfully to make it so. Abuse is rampant, horror stories abound. Student loans can be a curse, the form of debt with the most devastating consequences on people's lives. Profiting off student suffering are many groups: bankers, private investors, and loan sharks.

And the government. Since 2009, the Obama administration worked to gain back control of this situation so that the government, not private firms, issues and recovers the debt. But this has its own problems: the Department of Education calculates that in some years the government earns an astonishing 20 percent on each loan. Senator Elizabeth Warren and others are currently working to eliminate what is, essentially, exploitation bordering on usury, but few believe that these efforts will be successful in the current administration.

WHY DOES COLLEGE COST SO MUCH TODAY? TO ANSWER THE question, we need to look back, not to 1875, but to 1975, roughly when our nation's policymakers switched direction and began thinking of higher education as a luxury rather than a public good, an item to be cut from tax rosters whenever possible instead of publicly supported.

This was a significant retreat from what has been dubbed the golden age of quality mass public higher education, the period bounded by the GI Bill (1944), the increased spending on science during the Sputnik era, and Lyndon Johnson's Great Society. For over thirty years (roughly 1945–1975), Americans put faith in democracy as the way to fight both fascism and totalitarianism, in the middle class as a key to democracy, and in higher education as the best route from the working class to the middle class. Patriotism and support for higher education went hand in hand. The Higher Education Act of 1965 marked a pinnacle in higher education in the twentieth century, extending financial assistance to the general population, including students at regional public universities, community colleges, and historically black colleges and universities. Federal spending on higher education increased exponentially, from $655 million in 1956 to $3.5 billion in 1966.

Since then, the slope of the trend line has been mostly downward. The devaluation of higher education as a public good began with California governor Ronald Reagan, motivated by political and ideological factors, including a general opposition to corporate taxes and the graduated income tax, disdain for the radical student protests at California campuses like Berkeley, and a conviction that most college professors were "liberals." He put the brakes on what was arguably the greatest boon to public education in California since the GI Bill, the California Master Plan, which was passed in 1960 and had supported the state's free, three-tier educational system of research universities, comprehensive colleges, and community colleges. As president, Reagan continued his cost-cutting agenda. He famously branded students "freeloaders" and "tax eaters." His secretary of education, William Bennett, insisted that students who defaulted on loans were "deadbeats" who spent their money on drugs, cars, and stereos. The myth of the "deadbeat welfare mother" morphed into a new post–baby boomer myth of the "deadbeat student."

There remains a racial component to the debate over public funding of higher education. Under the GI Bill, a generation of ethnic European Americans prospered after previous decades of discrimination. Irish, Italian, Greek, Polish, and Slavic Americans, largely Catholic, as well as Jews of various national origins went to college in record numbers. However, because of racial segregation in American universities in the decade before *Brown v. Board of Education,* African American GIs benefited far less than other ethnicities. Although 43 percent of black GIs said they wanted to go to college, only 12 percent enjoyed the postwar educational benefit. Now, many argue that the conservative attack on public education and reluctance to fund it, especially higher education, are at least partly based on the increasing number of nonwhite students in our nation's schools and a de facto resegregation of public education. White ethnic voters who prospered because of publicly funded higher education in the past now feel reluctant to support public education for a majority nonwhite ethnic student population. Fall 2014 became a benchmark when nonwhite students made up over 50 percent of the total population in K–12 public schools. Students of color are an increasingly large percentage of college students and are a majority at many public universities and community colleges. Whether racism is at the base of the declining funding for higher education or whether, as others argue, it really is a contest over competing social goods—higher education, Medicare, Social Security, prisons, and so on—is not easy to determine. What is easy to see is the disastrous impact this decline in support of public education has on future generations.

Ideology clearly plays a role in the cutbacks happening in many states, especially those where state government is now decisively led by those from the Tea Party and other conservative movements. Some states have not only reduced support for universities but also mandated where money should be spent in higher education—and where it should not—and often with clear ideological intent. The example of North Carolina is indicative and instructive in this regard. In 2015, the state's conservative governor, Pat McCrory, backed by the ultra-conservative John William Pope Center for Higher Education Policy, a conservative legislative branch, and a largely conservative University of North Carolina board of governors, used "austerity" and "cutting taxes" as rationales for a unanimous decision to eliminate three programs from the University of North Carolina system: a poverty center at the UNC Law School, a program dedicated to civic engagement, and a program in biodiversity. The board insisted that these cuts were not politically motivated, even though all three programs were largely supported by external grant funding and their closure would save only $6,000 annually. Hannah Gage, a former chair of the North Carolina board of governors, is adamant that the closings were about politics, not economics: "It's hard to examine the board's February action through anything other than a political lens," she insisted. Even though the governor claimed to be interested in boosting the state's economy, the programs his government cut produced graduates prepared for careers in growth areas. Nonprofits, legal advocacy, and biodiversity, according to the Bureau of Labor Statistics, all continue to be areas with increasing numbers of jobs.

Since 2008, North Carolina has cut per student state spending by 25 percent, according to the Center on Budget and Public Priorities. Over the same period, tuition has increased by nearly 35 percent. North Carolina is but one case; similar movements—cutting taxes, raising tuition, and cutting programs that are relevant, that interest students, and that promise productive careers—are happening all over the United States. Iowa, Kansas, Wisconsin, Illinois, and Florida are all notable examples.

In fact, nearly every state addressed the 2008 financial collapse by cutting social spending. Whereas most other cuts have been restored, state funding for higher education has not. In some states, including a few controlled by Democratic legislatures, higher education continues to receive less support than any other social program. Currently, forty-five of the fifty states spend less per student in 2016 than they did before the 2008 financial crisis.

The effects of cutbacks are dire. A few universities have been shuttered. At others, staff and faculty are being let go, even as tuitions rise to compensate for the retreat of state funding. Since 2008, the *average* state spending is now approximately 17 percent less per student, adjusting for inflation, than it was before the recession. That figure is higher than 30 percent in eight states: Alabama, Arizona, Idaho, Kentucky, Louisiana, New Hampshire, Pennsylvania, and South Carolina. Even though New York City and New York State enjoyed a $5 billion budget surplus in 2015, the underfunding of the City University of New York is so extreme that departments lack administrative assistants and advisers, and some courses are being cut. Dedicated faculty and staff throughout the system went seven years (2009–2016) without even cost-of-living increases. A 2016 *New York Times* exposé of CUNY described broken desk chairs, labs devoid of equipment, and plastic sheets being used to protect against leaking roofs—amid the biggest and most expensive real estate boom in the entire country. The headline read: "Dreams Stall as CUNY, New York City's Engine of Mobility, Sputters." Once again, we see how far we have fallen from the glory days of public higher education.

Elsewhere, at the University of Colorado only some 3 percent of the total operating budget is supported by the state. The rest is paid for by outside federal and nonprofit foundation grant funding, corporate deals, philanthropy, and (mostly) tuition. If you go to the fund-raising page on the University of Texas website, there is a plea to alums and supporters unambiguously labeled "Why We Need Your Support." Whereas in the 1980s the state of Texas contributed nearly half of the money for the university's operating budget, now that amount comes to only 12 percent. Increased tuition, external grants, and alumni donors have to make up the deficit.

Hand in hand with the STEM obsession goes the assumption that the sciences generate more money for universities and can make up for declining state support. Humanities, arts, and social sciences cutbacks are often justified on the grounds that the sciences "bring in" dollars through grants, corporate contracts, and other forms of what is known as "sponsored research." However, higher education analyst Christopher Newfield has calculated that, if you account for investments a university must make to sustain ongoing scientific research—new buildings, equipment, cutting-edge technology, labs, expert faculty and nonfaculty researchers, and so forth—sponsored research loses approximately twenty-four cents on every dollar it attracts. The ongoing costs amount to a discount on R&D offered by universities to funders, many of whom no longer support their own research. Universities carry financial burdens with even the most prestigious science research awards. It's another vicious cycle: the huge awards are announced with fanfare, they raise the reputation and rankings of a university, but they also add to the ongoing operating costs of that university, resulting in rising tuition costs for students. This is true at public universities as well as at major private institutions such as MIT and Stanford. Some advanced undergraduates might have opportunities to work in innovative new labs funded by sponsored research, but applying for outside funding and then working on grants mostly takes full-time faculty away from teaching. Running a lab is like owning your own small business. It typically means hiring an administrative staff to handle human resources, grants management, compliance, deliverables, and to manage the lab assistants, a changing cadre of graduate students or postdoctoral fellows who might stay in their low-paying lab jobs for six or eight years before peeling off to go into industry.

Pundits often claim "administrative bloat" is responsible for unmanageable costs at our universities. Forty years ago, there were twice as many faculty as administrators and staff at universities; today, faculty (both full-time and adjuncts) are outnumbered by administrators and staffers. One frequent claim is that, if universities were run like businesses, there would be far fewer of these administrative personnel. Yet the evidence shows that running universities more like corporations hasn't reduced operating expenses. It may even do the opposite. According to a 2012 survey by the American Council on Education, some 20 percent of college presidents now come from outside of academe, almost twice the percentage from a decade ago. Typically, presidents and other administrators who move in from the private sector are paid significantly more than those who enter leadership roles from the ranks of academics. Bringing in executives from outside also seems to correlate with increasing (not decreasing) numbers of administrators. When university presidencies or chancellor positions are filled by people who come from the corporate world, government, foundations, and the military, they typically are paid as much as they made in their previous positions, and they bring large staffs, who are also well compensated. Upon arrival, they often realize how little they understand academic governance and quickly promote academic insiders into new administrative positions, doubling central administrative staff in size and in cost.

When they're not faulting an excess of administrators for the rising costs of college, pundits often blame high faculty salaries. But this is simply, demonstrably wrong. Since 1990, faculty salaries have *decreased* by 3 percent when adjusted for inflation. The average faculty salary is currently a little over $100,000 for the university rank of full professor, $79,000 for associate professor, and $69,000 for assistant professor. These positions require professors to hold a PhD, typically a seven-year advanced degree, at a minimum. Faculty size has shrunk in proportion to the number of students, and the number of faculty on the tenure track has dwindled drastically. Only about one-third of all current professors at our colleges and universities are tenured, and less than 20 percent of new hires are even on a tenure track.

It is easy to understand why so many faculty today see the university in crisis, even in ruins—hardly the ideal position from which to dream the future of a visionary new education. Recently, Governor Scott Walker concurrently moved to minimize the guarantees to free speech of tenured professors at the University of Wisconsin, to implement a $250 million budget cut to the system, and to give that $250 million instead to a group of billionaire hedge fund managers to build a new basketball stadium for the Milwaukee Bucks. This is hardly the way to support Wisconsin's youth. He argued that the cuts to the University of Wisconsin would result in a free-market university that would save money and lead to more innovation. Instead, UW faculty became fair game, and many faculty were offered outside positions. Several left for other, less hostile climates. UW ended up paying $23.6 million in increased salaries to retain its star faculty members.

One other factor that is frequently blamed for the rising cost of tuition, especially at elite private institutions, is financial aid. In fact, financial aid does add to costs, but—as Charles Eliot knew when he instituted financial aid as a way to modernize Harvard—having the most diverse (in every way possible) cohort of students adds to the quality of the learning experience for everyone at the university and spurs innovation. This is why the nation's most elite institutions with the largest endowments often support "need-blind" admissions policies, meaning the best students are accepted on merit regardless of whether they can pay, and financial aid makes up the difference. At the top universities, this is a choice made in favor of recruiting the best talent over lowering tuition for all. To ensure a student body that is intellectually exciting, and not simply affluent and well connected, ten of the nation's top private institutions offer free tuition to all accepted students with family income of less than $60,000 or, in some cases, $125,000 a year. One negative consequence is that, increasingly, the top-ranked private universities are made up of notably wealthy students paying full tuition and then a much smaller cohort of extremely successful, competitive middle- or even working-class scholarship students.

As became palpably and, to some, shockingly evident with the release of findings from the exhaustive 2017 *Equality of Opportunity Study* of over 30 million college students, students today can no longer expect to earn more than their parents, a trend line that plummets deeper every year. One of the greatest contributing factors is the soaring tuition of our universities. Saving taxes, not supporting public higher education, and the rising costs of public higher education tuition mean that, in general, universities are no longer our society's engines of social mobility. Rather, they are increasingly training grounds for the wealthy to become even wealthier. The eye-popping headline from the *New York Times* reads: "Some Colleges Have More Students from the Top 1 Percent Than the Bottom 60."

Students today are paying more for less—for fewer services, less innovation, less opportunity. The privatizing of the university over the last several decades has not brought down costs, streamlined administrations, eliminated bureaucracy, modernized programs, or raised the quality of the faculty. It has made tuitions soar, class sizes explode, the teaching profession shrink. And it has made shell-shocked faculty and administrators quake at the word *innovation*.

Altogether, this makes it more difficult to remake Eliot's university precisely during the period when that task has become so urgent.

OF LATE, SOME OF THE HIGHEST-PRICED ELITE UNIVERSITIES HAVE been accused of becoming expensive "luxury goods" for the economic 1 percent. Critics argue that private education now costs so much because its high price tag itself conveys status. The media loves to dote on expensive frivolities such as climbing walls as signs that universities are spending wildly and inappropriately—both Chris Christie and Elizabeth Warren have attacked "lazy rivers and climbing walls" and other extravagances as the cause of tuition increases at private universities. At $50,000 or $60,000 a year, college, like jewelry, sports cars, designer fashions, and real estate, seems to convey high quality—which is surely a large part of the reason why the number of applications to the most expensive universities soars every year.

Some have compared elite private education to a "Veblen good," named for the late nineteenth-century economist Thorstein Veblen, author of *The Theory of the Leisure Class*. The Veblen effect in microeconomics is based on the idea of "conspicuous consumption" and the reality that certain goods are desired and valued precisely because they are overpriced. These goods do not follow standard models of supply and demand; rather, a spike in price increases rather than decreases demand. It may seem cynical to compare a Harvard education to the coveted Hermès Birkin bag, the unofficial diploma (starting at 11K) of any aspiring socialite, yet it is certainly the case that elite institutions have no incentive to lower their advertised fees. Each year, they reject as many as twenty times more applicants than they accept. The more exclusive and selective they become, the more applicants clamor for this rarest of the rare luxury goods. At the same time, the value—for those lucky few who can afford it—is indisputable. The graduation rate at these institutions is well over 90 percent, courses are plentiful, as are advisers, extracurricular activities, study abroad experiences, branch campuses all over the world, internships at nonprofits and corporations, and un-surpassed networking opportunities. The students are hand-chosen by admissions officers and deans of students careful to offer each cohort the most exciting peers imaginable. As the costs increase, so do the baseline expectations of these students, many if not most of whom have been educated at exclusive private high schools or su-perb public ones. Prep schools like Phillips Exeter Academy (which cost $46,900 for boarding students in 2016) not only are as expen-sive as most Ivy League universities but also raise expectations about what "school" must offer. According to Veblen's theory, if the esca-lating price of one luxury good is supported by the affluent, then the prices of other luxury goods of that social class also soar, even if they are not related to each other. Many of the goods and services of the 1 percent have seen these escalating costs—exclusive nursery schools and retirement communities, elective surgery and long-term health-care insurance, Michelin-starred restaurants and Manhattan apartments.

Given how much these schools cost, the amount of attention they receive, and their high-profile faculties, one would assume that, as in Eliot's day, they are at the leading edge of classroom innovation and modeling change for other universities. Yet this is not entirely the case. In fact, the eminence of Harvard, Stanford, and the like is precisely what can keep them in a more traditional mind-set. If you are highly ranked by *US News & World Report* and your acceptance rate hovers at 5 percent, your mandate is neither to cut costs nor to change. It would be an exceptionally brave and courageous leader who would radically alter a university so richly rewarded for doing exactly what it is doing—garnering the best students, the highest tuitions, the most distinguished faculty, and the biggest alumni do-nations year after year. At Stanford, that mission faces toward Sili-con Valley, and nearly 40 percent of Stanford students now major in computer science. Stanford keeps saying it wants to correct this lopsided student body, and it has tried to launch some exciting inter-disciplinary "CS+" majors (Computer Science + English, Computer Science + Music, and so on), but those remain small programs that do not dampen the Silicon Valley effect. At Harvard, bold presidents, year after year, try to ensure that graduates from the world's wealthiest university go into professions other than those geared to generating more wealth for the wealthy.

Yet, as the renowned Harvard cognitive neuroscientist Steven Pinker notes, his lecture halls are typically only half full, despite the fact that he's thought to be a rock star lecturer; Harvard students know that meeting other Harvard students is the most important reason to be there. A large percentage of them will go on to be wealth managers (financial advisers and fund managers) in corporations run or owned by other Harvard graduates. As Pinker notes, so many of Harvard grads "get snatched up by the big consulting and investment firms, helping to explain that 20 percent boost in their expected earnings" that comes just from graduating from Harvard. This matters for reasons aside from the obvious. If Harvard were to undergo visionary systemic change today, every other college and university in America would begin to follow suit. After all, though Harvard may no longer be the revolutionary leader of the new education that it was in Eliot's day, it remains a model for most other institutions of higher education.

And not only when it comes to thinking (or not thinking) about how to prepare graduates for the world outside the academy. The wealth of Harvard and other top private schools *does* drive change at other colleges, including excellent public universities—but it's not the sort of change that helps students themselves. In this regard, there is perhaps no clearer example of what has happened to public higher education than at the Anderson School of Management at the University of California, Los Angeles. Like all professional schools, it depends on tuition, donations, grants, external funding, and business contracts for ancillary activities (such as executive training for corporations) to make its budget. Reputation is all, and the Anderson School has to compete for its top five ranking with private institutions, in this case, with Harvard, Stanford, and Penn, elite private universities with enormous endowments. To retain its top-ranked faculty, to be competitive, to attract the best students and the best faculty and therefore the best contracts, the Anderson School went private in 2012, turning down its public support from the state, an approximately $8 million annual appropriation. The public funds come with restrictions on how much this business school can pay its faculty, how much tuition it can charge, and how and from whom it can raise funds, engage in partnerships, cut admissions deals, and so forth. The school simply could not *afford* to take the $8 million a year from the state and maintain its standing.

This move to become a privatized business school has been applauded in the business press as if Anderson should be a model for other public universities. Yet the idea has problematic implications: Is the only way to maintain a great business school to become an expensive private, or quasi-private, school? Anderson maintains all of the reputational, historical, cultural, intellectual, and sociodemographic advantages of being part of a major public school, and its faculty still engage in research with other faculty in other fields, from psychology to statistics, from all over the university. Yet, if there are no restrictions on corporate support for this public university, what will happen to independent research? Can you present objective research results about the effects of climate change on the global economy, for instance, if the study is funded by British Petroleum? Can you criticize your funders if necessary, or have we entered an endless cycle of corporate-sponsored university research findings supporting corporate interests? A public university that can maintain its reputation only by giving up its public status risks jeopardizing its commitment to the public good.

As always, when institutional and extra-institutional interests are served first, students suffer. At Anderson, one nonfaculty administrator is charged with grant or private fund-raising for every three faculty members at the school. Administrative bloat, it turns out, is the working model of this premier public business school. Privatization comes with a high price tag.

Recently, in a TSA line at the airport, I happened to overhear a well-dressed man, perhaps a businessman of some sort, say to his friend, "He got into Stanford. It's going to cost me a bundle, but he's going to be set for life." I could hear the pride in his voice; he was clearly speaking about his son.

That old expression: set for life. I thought about what this father thought his son would get from Stanford that would ensure a lifetime of success. It's highly unlikely Stanford would give him lifetime employment or even specific job training. What this father knew was that, at Stanford, his son would be well cared for and would enjoy an excellent general education. He would work closely with his teachers if he chose to take advantage of the student-faculty ratio of 4:1. And behind every faculty member at Stanford are postdoctoral and doctoral students as well as academic advisers, counselors, library and IT professionals, and on and on. The support for the young man's learning, his independent research opportunities, his curricular and extracurricular activities, his networks of alumni—all are designed to help him find his passion and define his life path. Factoring all of that in, it is surprising that Stanford costs *only* $45,729 a year.

Fifty miles away at Berkeley, the official student-to-faculty ratio is 17:1. Some say that the ratio doesn't matter, but, as a friend of mine who teaches at one of the California State University campuses likes to say, she's never seen an elite university stay silent about its small class sizes. At the publics, there are fewer ancillary advisers dedicated to ensuring students' success. Because of the defunding of higher education, acceptance to one of the top public universities in the country no longer ensures that you are "set for life." It may be almost as difficult to get into Berkeley as into an Ivy League, but it's harder to get out.

THE TASK INNOVATORS FACE TODAY IS TWOFOLD: TO KEEP COSTS down and, at the same time, to realize the new education. On the former, there have been many proposals. Most, however, simply make cuts around the edges and compromise many necessary features in the struggle to manage expenses. Or they rely on technologies like MOOCs as a solution even though, as we've seen, online learning at massive scale often costs as much as or more than face-to-face learning, with less successful results. The Center for College Affordability and Productivity offers a laundry list of some two dozen ways to cut costs. Each has benefits and drawbacks, and many institutions have tried or are working on several of these. None will result in anything approaching a return to 1980s tuitions subsidized at 1980s levels.

Some universities have tried to shorten the degree time to three years to eliminate one-quarter of the costs. Three years might work fine for some students in some programs; others might realistically require five years. Clearly, lopping off a year of study arbitrarily is unwise; it is exactly the wrong reductionist, one-size-fits-all solution to the interesting problem of how much education is sufficient in a given field or for a given student. Relaxing credit-hour limits so those who wish, including community college transfer students, can take extra courses to accelerate their time to graduation and minimize their costs seems a useful solution for those energetic students able to carry the extra load, although it also inevitably limits the cocurricular and other opportunities for those students. Similarly, dual-enrollment programs (allowing students to take a first year of college while finishing the last year of high school or permitting undergraduates to simultaneously work toward master's degrees) are great in the right circumstances, self-defeating in others. Some reformers advocate jettisoning general education and heading directly into the major. Others suggest that skills-based certification based on mastery or competency tests can replace a year or even two of courses. Once again, managed thoughtfully and strategically, these might be useful ways to reduce costs, or they can turn out to seriously diminish a student's future career possibilities. As we've seen, innovative general education programs can provide exactly the analytical and crosscutting interdisciplinary thinking and communication skills that are most in demand in a complex workplace.

Technology can help reduce costs in some situations. The ever resourceful Arizona State University president Michael Crow has repeatedly experimented with new money-saving methods in the face of constant state cutbacks. Some technologies have worked, others have faltered. He is currently enthusiastic about eAdvisor, an online advising system that is less expensive than face-to-face advising and that turns out to appeal to this generation of students, who would rather gain advice from online software than by going to office hours with the advising staff. President Crow even credits eAdvisor with helping to increase graduation rates because it offers students suggestions for courses and majors, with clear pathways to careers, that factor in students' interests, skills, and personalities. "I just took it, pretending I was my daughter," Crow jokes. "It said I needed to run things and maybe should be a movie producer."

Community college remains the most economical way to go to college, and more and more middle-class Americans are taking advantage of this affordable solution. There, expenses are managed by being largely nonresidential, with none of the million-dollar costs of Division I collegiate athletics, and without extensive research facilities. Community colleges emphasize teaching over research and tend to hire dedicated faculty who teach many courses for lower wages than at research universities. Indeed, some argue that faculty salaries at four-year institutions could be controlled by following this model of increased teaching loads and diminished research responsibilities, a solution that works only if faculty-reward structures and university-ranking criteria change as well—and only if industry and government take up the mission of basic research that is now primarily the province of higher education. For community college students, the tuition savings only pertains if four-year colleges readily accept transfer credits.

Other ways of lowering expenses and cutting costs include eliminating regulation and red tape (estimated to potentially save as much as 3 to 11 percent of current university operating costs) and combining programs to minimize duplication of faculty and administration. Again, there are wise and foolish ways of making such cuts. And some can even lead to innovation. A few years ago, for example, New York University sought to minimize administrative costs by combining a number of small programs on the language, history, and cultures of different ancient civilizations into one Study of the Ancient World program. Faculty were rightly angered at the top-down approach. However, when the next year came around and program applications not only increased but proved to be intellectually exciting, including applications from international students who brought entirely new non-Western areas of expertise beyond the usual Greek and Roman, the faculty began to reconsider. The program is too new to tell whether graduates from this new global ancient world program will be successful at obtaining jobs as professors, curators, translators, or in other occupations, but there are examples in every field where bold new ideas can also lead to economic efficiencies.

All of these are useful efforts, if modest in scope. In the end, though, remedying the problem of high costs at our public universities requires championing public higher education at the level that was commonplace in America between 1945 and 1975. We need to focus on our values, reconsider shortsighted policy decisions that affect public education, and rethink the decisions made over the past decades about how the public money should be spent—for instance, as tax rebates to huge corporations or as subsidies, at a fraction of the cost, that support public higher education. We, as a society, made different decisions during the golden age of public education.

We all know that college has never mattered more. It also has never cost more. Tragically, our public universities today cost as much as our elite private universities cost a generation or two ago. Despite frantic fund-raising by administrators and faculty, the decline in per student state support for higher education has been passed along to the individual, tuition-paying student. The situation grows worse every year and will continue to disintegrate unless the public understands how much higher costs hurt us all, not just the next generation on whom we force the tremendous debt burden.

The United States has ended its era of strategic investment in its youth. Not to put too fine a point on it, we have given up on the one national business that has worked best for us for 150 years: higher education. Despite the system's unparalleled success, we are no longer investing in our human capital. This is in contrast to Sweden,

Brazil, Germany, Finland, France, Norway, Luxembourg, Slovenia, and Iceland, where higher education is radically subsidized to the extent that tuition is free.

Short of free tuition, we could work on improving the terms of debt disbursal. One of the most interesting income-based student loan repayment ideas comes from Australia. It was enacted in 1989 partly to address the outcry when the country began charging tuition for its public universities. In this plan, students pay differential tuitions: those entering high-paying fields pay higher tuition than those entering the arts, nursing, elementary education, philosophy, or theoretical math (to give a few examples). Students can then opt to pay the tuition up-front at a 10 percent discount rate or to borrow tuition at the full rate on an income-based repayment plan under the Australian government's Higher Education Loan Program (which goes by the not too subtle acronym HELP). Those who earn more than the equivalent of about $40,000 a year have approximately 4 to 8 percent of their income (depending on their take-home pay) deducted automatically by the Australian Taxation Office to repay their loans. If a graduate runs into unemployment or illness, payments cease until they start earning an income again. At the same time, if a student has a windfall, he or she can pay the whole debt back earlier. The United States government offers a version of income-based student loans but at higher interest and repayment rates and with a number of requirements that make these loans far less attractive as an alternative.

If nothing else, the enemies of public education and proponents of privatization need to understand that public education *is* a good investment. Every economic study of higher education shows it is the best investment a country can make, both for its own collective productivity and for the individual productivity of its graduates. It's penny-wise and pound-foolish to cut taxes by cutting higher education. A college degree confers a mean $365,000 lifetime benefit for the average American man (after subtracting all its direct and indirect costs over a lifetime) and an average $185,000 for women. Federal, state, and municipal governments all make a profit of $231,000 on each American who graduates from college, mostly through higher income taxes and lower unemployment benefits paid over the course of a lifetime.

There are signs that the public in general is coming to understand that the cost of higher education is a social problem and one not just for students but for all of society. We may even be at a tipping point, coming to see that the forty-year defunding of higher education is robbing American society of its greatest asset: an educated younger generation prepared to tackle the problems of a turbulent future. In the 2016 presidential campaign, Senator Bernie Sanders's passionate advocacy of free tuition captured national attention, especially from youth. His campaign platform was then taken up by Secretary of State Hillary Clinton in her bid for the presidency. Subsequently, the states of Kentucky, Minnesota, Oregon, and Tennessee announced plans to offer free or subsidized tuitions at community colleges, and, in San Francisco, Mayor Ed Lee announced a partnership with the City College of San Francisco, a community college, to offer free tuition to any city resident.

An ambitious proposal was announced in January 2017 by New York governor Andrew Cuomo in a press conference with Senator Sanders. The governor announced a proposed Excelsior Scholarship that would make all the two-year and four-year colleges in the City University of New York and the State University of New York systems tuition-free for all New York residents whose families earn less than $125,000 a year. Governor Cuomo argued that over 70 percent of all new jobs in the state now require a college degree and that it hampers our students if, in order to attend college, they must graduate with tuition debt. "It's like starting a race with an anchor tied to your leg," Cuomo said.

Of course, to prepare our students for their future, we need to make college not only free but also better. It makes no sense to offer free tuition to students in a system that has been hamstrung by decades of state-level funding cuts. In order for Governor Cuomo's plan to reach its full potential and move beyond politics to a true enhancement of our students' futures, it needs to be supported with concrete measures for increasing support to the state's impoverished college and university system. New York's public universities already have one of the lowest tuition rates in the United States. In 2016, six schools in the CUNY system were in the top ten on the collegiate "social mobility index," which charts the disparity between the low family income level of entering students and their higher level of earned income when they graduate. At some of the city's community colleges, over half of the students come from families that earn less than $25,000 a year (not $125,000 a year), and they attend college for free through a combination of federal, state, and city grants. The Excelsior Scholarship would extend that same benefit of free tuition to middle-class families in the state.

It's a thrilling proposal—but only if it were to be matched with increased public investment in CUNY and SUNY. Free or reduced tuition means nothing if the system is so starved for funding that it cannot offer even the most basic courses required for graduation, has decaying facilities, and uses technology from the last century. Over the last decades, CUNY's full-time faculty has decreased by 33 percent at the same time that its student body has increased by 15 percent. That said, the governor's proposal, if accompanied by significant reinvestment in public education, could mark the beginning of the new education and set an example for other states to consider. "Here's my prediction," Senator Sanders said. "If New York State does it this year, mark my words, state after state will follow."

Such a statement would have been a pipe dream only a few years ago, but there are other signs, too, of a changing attitude toward refunding higher education. In the November 2016 election, California voters reversed a "tax revolt" that began with the 1978 passage of Proposition 13, an amendment to the California constitution that decreased property taxes and included language that required a two-thirds majority in both legislative houses to increase future income or state sales taxes. Instead, voters supported all three education-related initiatives on the ballot, including one that increased taxes on high-income earners to fund a variety of initiatives supporting public education, from preschool to higher education.

The cost of ensuring excellence in public higher education, if shared by all, is within reach. According to Keep California's Promise, a data and advocacy project run by two University of California professors, the state of California could cut tuition in half for every student in the University of California and California State University systems (over 700,000 students) if only it resumed state contributions equal to the 2000–2001 per capita student spending levels. How much would that cost the median California taxpayer each year? Thirty-one dollars per person. Thirty-one more dollars each would make a tremendous difference: the public contributing to higher education as a public good, the commonweal growing richer, and students starting their future without debt—set for life.

As I DISCOVERED AS I LAY DYING, DEBT SHAPES EVERYTHING. THE interns who owed $400,000 on their medical education faced a choice between the kind of medicine they wanted to practice and the more lucrative specializations that would pay off those towering loans. Their decisions would be driven by necessity, contingent on the consequences of a society that has abdicated its responsibility to its youth.

Many people reading this book grew up knowing that if they studied hard, they had a good shot at going to college. If they worked for it, college was within their grasp because an older generation had made a collective contribution to their education, to their future. Middle-class parents had enough money to save for their kids' college education and knew that they would be helped along by their own tax contributions being spent by their states on college.

The dream of affordable higher education for all (or, at least, most) Americans was once the American dream, a dream of the middle class, a dream of democracy. Such a dream prompted the creation of the land-grant universities and inspired Charles Eliot's vision of innovative university transformation, not just at Harvard but throughout higher education. It continued to motivate America in the era of the GI Bill and the Great Society. It may seem idealistic to think we are on the verge of such renewal again given the downward trend line in so many states. But we are also, elsewhere, seeing a different trend in response to the growing debt crisis our students and higher education face.

The problems of traditional education and cost compound each other. Renewed support for higher education is needed and a new vision is required, one that remakes the university of 1865—and the university of 1965—for our time. The world is more complex and terrifying than ever before. We must reinvest in education, our main bulwark against the forces of disorder and ruin. It's the best investment we can make as a nation, not only for the sake of younger generations of students but also for all of us facing an unsettling and unsettled future.

7 THE MEASURE OF A STUDENT

"You give a dog a treat when he performs well and he's happy. He doesn't remember that the treat came with a price tag, that it's for performing something up to expectation. It's all jumbled—the warm fuzzy feeling, how good the treat tasted, the affection, approval, the pat on the head, 'Good boy!' the connection, the bond. He's a happy dog."

Professor Alexander Coward once again runs his fingers through his sandy hair. The look is tousled, the gesture anxious.

A boyish smile dimples his right cheek, as if he is remembering some beloved, faraway family pet. Momentarily, his sadness dissipates. It's easy to see the charisma and empathy that made the four-hundred-seat lecture hall at University of California, Berkeley, overflow with students clamoring for a spot in Math 1A.

Students rarely clamor for Math 1A. It's the introductory course, the one that's required for several competitive majors. It's known as a flunk-out course. Coward is lost in his thoughts. He's comfortable

193

there, residing in silence. When he speaks again, sadness has returned. "Humans aren't like dogs. If there's both encouragement *and* a reward, it becomes a disincentive. You wouldn't think it would work that way, but it does. Instead of a warm fuzzy feeling, we get cross and cynical if we think we're not learning for our own good but for some external reward. We start thinking we deserve the reward and feel cheated or demoralized if we don't get it. Maybe it's because we keep having to take tests from an early age. We're always being graded, compared with everyone else, overtested so that we grow to resent it. Pretty soon the grade is what we strive for, not the learning. It becomes what counts—even *all* that counts. We're not learning to improve ourselves. It's not both/and the way it is for dogs. If you try to give both, it's less than either."

Coward is a math professor at Berkeley. Or was. In 2016, his contract wasn't renewed. Before that, when he was still teaching Math 1A, he worked hard to apply the best pedagogical principles of active, engaged, motivated learning to help students master math. His Math 1A was no standard, dry lecture class but rather an intellectually engaged course that inspired curiosity and encouraged students to stick with the subject. His sections filled up fast. Whereas some Math 1A professors had a hundred students, his sections swelled to overcapacity with four hundred students. He didn't give quizzes to ensure the students were doing the homework. He didn't give homework in the conventional sense. Instead, he inspired his students with ever more difficult problems and excited a love of math several didn't know they had. In the end, when they were tested, his students did great, exceeding the demands of the course set by the department.

He should have been a hero. As he came to see it, though, there was only one problem. His students started enjoying math a little too much. They started learning the math for its own sake, not simply to pass an often-dreaded prerequisite for highly selective majors such as electrical engineering, computer science, physics, biology, economics, or even the technology-focused undergraduate bachelor of science degree offered by the Haas School of Business. Students who couldn't enroll in his course registered for math classes with other profs but then came to sit in on his course for no credit. Even when a departmental adviser warned him that his exam was too difficult, Coward was confident his students would do well—and they did, without any class time devoted to how to game the test to earn the best scores. Coward adamantly refuses to "teach to the test." He teaches for the love of math, and inspires that love in his students.

Coward's ideas on how to teach run in the opposite direction of much contemporary education practice, where test scores have become a stand-in for actual mastery or knowledge. In K–12, teachers today can be denied merit raises if their students fail to obtain high enough scores on high-stakes standardized tests. High schools, like colleges and universities, boast about the average SAT scores of their students. Universities are ranked partly on the average SAT scores of entering students and on Graduate Record Exam scores of graduates. It's fair to say that we have become a test-obsessed culture on every level. At a top school like Berkeley, students need superb grades and test scores to get in and equally top grades to be admitted to the most selective majors. Much current education is geared toward improving test scores. By contrast, Coward bases his pedagogy on the work of researchers who have found that tests and grades can actually undermine learning and even performance. He is interested in the research on what makes for optimal learning, especially comprehension and an ability to apply the math principles one learns to other areas of one's education and one's life.

Coward is most influenced by the classic studies conducted by British psychologist Ruth Butler and published in the late 1980s. Butler investigated how over 130 seventh graders in twelve classes at four schools responded to feedback they were given on tests requiring complex thinking tasks. Each day, the students' work was collected and independent markers would give the exercises one of three different kinds of feedback. Some students received formative feedback designed to help them in the future (for instance, "You thought of quite a few interesting ideas. Next time, why not try to add a few more examples, maybe drawing from personal experience."). Others received only a numerical score ranging from 40 to

99 (called "summative" feedback); they received no comments or explanations or guidance about the future. A third group received both formative and summative feedback, a helpful suggestion and a score.

Everyone assumed the more thorough response—the formative feedback plus the summative score—would be the best way to encourage students to learn and to do better on future assignments, but no one had actually tested the notion before. There were some surprises.

Those who had received only formative feedback showed the biggest gains, with a dramatic 30 percent improved score on a second exercise. This was not surprising in itself because formative feedback has long been shown to be the best way to improve learning. It's similar to how we encourage learners everywhere except in school. If I'm teaching my son how to throw a fast ball, I might give him encouragement along with some feedback on the biomechanics of his windup or the placement of his fingers on the seams of the ball. I do not give him a summative grade, say, a B–, as he's learning to pitch.

Those who had received summative scores did better on the second exercise *only* if they had done well on the first. This confirms extensive research on the limitations of summative feedback. If given only a number, students tend to assume they are "bad" at the skill or subject being tested, and so the low score tends to be a disincentive to learning. Students who do poorly don't just feel they have failed. They feel that they are *failures*. Having a low opinion of one's abilities does not often inspire one to pursue further learning.

There was another important insight from the high-scoring students who received summative feedback. Although they did better on the second exercise than they had on the first, they also quickly forgot what they had learned for the test. Unlike those who had received formative feedback, the students who had achieved high numerical scores had only short-term gains. In other words, even the ones who did best had simply "learned to the test."

The biggest surprise for learning experts came from the blended third group. Those who had received the written comments (formative feedback) as well as the test score (summative feedback) showed no benefits from the formative help. The very presence of a grade canceled out the advantages of formative feedback.

Professor Coward throws up both hands again. He rubs his face. "We are not dogs. If we want to learn, we need feedback. Grades interfere with the process." Coward challenged his students with problem sets all semester. He didn't assign a textbook. He never told them what would or wouldn't be on the final exam. He empowered them to learn, to gain mastery over the subject, to think like mathematicians. He tantalized them with thorny problems and seeming contradictions, and rewarded their ability to think through the most challenging mathematical conundrums. He honored them by assuming they wanted to learn for their own good, for their future. There were no pop quizzes for surveillance purposes, to make sure they were doing all the homework. Instead, he treated them like adult, autonomous learners, who were taking the class not to earn a grade but to understand the basic fundamentals of math and how those principles could be applied to the rest of their learning. He used time-honored, student-centered learning principles that go back at least as far as John Dewey: grant your students control over their own learning process; have them work in teams or groups; encourage them to assess the validity of what they know; have them reflect on what they have learned and why it is important in other situations; have them teach one another; assist strategically when they are flailing; step out of the way when they are progressing again; and recognize their achievements.

He was reprimanded for his unconventional methods. No one had seen so many students flock to Math 1A. Aspersions were cast on the rigor and content of his teaching, as if students couldn't possibly be that excited by a truly demanding course. But it's math. When the students in his courses scored just as high or higher than students in other sections of Math 1A on departmental finals, his popularity could not be dismissed on the grounds that the course was "easy." Instead of the department being curious and even admiring about his methods, it warned him about deviating too much from departmental "norms." He responded to the criticism by working even harder to ensure his students were learning. He gave out his cell phone number and invited students to call if they ran into problems. He carefully explained fundamental principles and, even more, encouraged them to learn the principles themselves, including by teaching one another, challenging themselves with ever harder problems. The next time when he taught the introductory course, even more students signed up for his class. Many who couldn't get in officially just came anyway in order to learn.

"What does it mean to adhere to department norms if one has the highest student evaluation scores in the department, students performing statistically better in subsequent courses, and faculty observations universally reporting 'extraordinary skills at lecturing, presentation, and engaging students'?" Coward summarizes the problem the Math Department had with his teaching: "In a nutshell: stop making us look bad. If you don't, we'll fire you."

Only two images decorate the walls of Coward's spare, modest study, with its functional Ikea-style furniture. One is of Muhammad Ali from his fighting-trim days, in boxing trunks practicing in front of a mirror. Above the mirror are posters from Ali's previous fights. "Champions are made from something they have deep inside them, a desire, a dream, a vision," the legend says. "They have to have the skill and the will. But the will must be stronger than the skill."

On another wall is a poster of Steve Jobs. There are words on it from his famous commencement address at Stanford, shortly before his death, the one that begins, "Your time is limited." It ends with the admonition: "Stay hungry. Stay foolish."

"I went on a bit of a shopping spree a few months ago because I decided I wanted some inspiring posters for my students, but as it turned out I needed them for myself," Professor Coward says, almost in a whisper.

2016 was a tough year. In the month after Math 1A ended, his students received their final grades for the course, and he received a figurative pink slip. His time as a math instructor at Berkeley is over. On his Facebook page, students leave him warm and fuzzy goodbyes, tinged with sorrow that he won't be returning to Berkeley.

We constantly hear the lament that the United States has a STEM crisis. Nationwide, less than a quarter of high school graduates who say they want to study STEM fields in college make it. Most transfer into non-STEM disciplines by sophomore year. Nationally, a poor grade in an introductory math class is what is most likely to prevent a student from pursuing a STEM dream, whether it is to become a doctor, a nurse, or an engineer. Our major universities are structured to limit the number of students who do well enough in introductory courses in math or organic chemistry to pursue future STEM careers. It's hard, in such a structure, to even know what to do with a superstar teacher like Alexander Coward, who takes the big introductory course—typically known as a flunk-out course—and turns it into an intellectually exciting, inspiring course for hundreds of students.

This brings us, once again, back to the origins of the research university and its infrastructure that was carefully designed to provide a path toward professionalization and credentialing for a range of new or evolving fields. We see this in the pyramid structure of most colleges and universities today, a wide base tapering to increasingly specialized, disciplinary, and preprofessional knowledge. To earn a spot in some specialized majors (electrical engineering or molecular biology, for example) requires earning a top grade in an introductory course. Flunking out, so far as a future career in one of the sciences might be concerned, might be earning a B+ instead of an A. At large universities, the general introductory courses tend to be lecture courses taught by beginning professors, low-paid instructors on one-year contracts, or adjunct professors teaching part-time. Or they are taught in weekly lectures by famous professors, with many smaller discussion sections (including the grading of papers and exams) run by graduate students. These courses typically sort the best students from the rest and determine who will go on to be admitted to upper-division, specialized, disciplinary, preprofessional work in a major. Upper-division courses are often far smaller, sometimes even offered as tutorials and independent studies with senior members of the department. The top students graduating in that field might then decide to go on to the even more specialized work in graduate school or professional school, often pursuing the specialization of their adviser.

Often the big introductory lecture courses have departmental final exams, with the percentage of passing or A grades fixed by a departmental consensus. If too many students are taking and doing well in math, it changes enrollments in other STEM majors throughout the university. That means, if too many students are doing well on a standardized test, a department can either make the test harder or change the grading curve. If the objective is to work toward increasing specialization and professionalism, this system works. If the objective is to expand a field or to address the shortage in STEM training, this system is counterproductive.

It is also unproductive if one's mission is to actually teach each and every student to understand a subject better than they did when they entered the course. That was Alexander Coward's predicament. He was not particularly concerned with the institutional or historical reasons behind the design of the large introductory courses like Math 1A. He is passionate about math and its importance to anyone who wants to survive in school and outside of school. During his time teaching Math 1A, he worked hard at his teaching and was unstinting of the time he was willing to spend with students. He really didn't care about their grades (although, in fact, his students did very well on their final exams). He was dedicated to making sure that each and every student who wanted to learn the basics of mathematics did so. He wanted them to learn to think like mathematicians. If his students also earned an A at the end of the process, he would applaud that, but for him, good grades were secondary to the purpose of teaching math to students—lots of students.

No one reading this book will be surprised to learn that the apparatus of grading and judging, assessing and failing students—including bell curves, grades, and standardized testing—were fully developed in the nineteenth century. All of these innovative and supposedly scientific assessment methods were quickly absorbed into the new education of Charles Eliot and his colleagues. These were yet another creation of the industrial age, designed to remake the long traditions of formative feedback (admittedly, sometimes meted out with a switch). The methods we still use for evaluating student achievement were adopted from quantifiable measures of productivity developed for factories and the brand-new assembly lines.

It was a nineteenth-century scientist, Sir Francis Galton, who invented the modern science of statistics, developing the now familiar ideas of standard deviation and deviation from the norm. When applied to grading students, the model allows teachers to place each student on a curve relative to the others, such that there is a specific percentage of top students, middling students, and failures. It was a new way of grading—and eminently *scientific*, it was claimed at the time. The bell curve is a prime example of institution-centered learning because it does not base assessment on how much an individual student has actually learned. Rather, a different number of students might be permitted to receive the top grade depending on institutional goals. For example, one year a department might want to award the highest honors (say, an A) to the top 10 percent of students. Then, if there is less funding or too many applicants the following year, that department might set the bell curve so that only the top 2 percent receive honors. It's not that students know more one year than another but that the "cutoff" for excellence or for passing or for failure varies depending on preset criteria as determined by institution-centered needs. In this case, assessment is not designed to help the student but to control the number of students passing through the system. One year, for example, several faculty might be away on sabbatical and the department might not want too many A+ or honors students going on to the advanced, specialized courses. Another year, the opposite might be the case. Before these "scientific" measures came into play, instructors wrote out comments or rendered verdicts based on an oral exam, recitation, or performance. Teaching and learning were by rote, of course, and students still could fail to pass a course, but failure was not preset (what's called "norm referenced") according to the predetermined percentage of students who should or should not be allowed to succeed relative to one another.

To demonstrate the efficacy of his bell curve, in the 1890s Francis Galton invented what he called the "bean machine," a device in which little balls drop into a grid with interleaved rows. The balls fall down the chutes and are collected in compartments—the fewest at the pinnacle, more at the sides, and then few again at the lowest point, with all of them falling into a pattern known as the bell (or Gaussian) curve. In Galton's bean machine, moving the levers one way or another adjusts the curve, determining how many balls fit into the top bin. The student ends up with a "mark" or a "grade" that seems to be objective, but of course it allows the person or institution setting standards to determine how open or closed the curve will be.

Galton's bean counting (literally) may seem neutral and scientific—until one learns that, among other things, Sir Galton was a passionate eugenicist. He believed British aristocrats were genetically superior to everyone else and that the British government should subsidize procreation among the upper classes and sterilize the poor and working classes. One motivation for his bell curve and his bean machine was to be able to rate intelligence scientifically in order to bolster his theories of who would or would not improve the human curve.

The bell curve can also serve constructive purposes. It can be a tool an institution uses to see how well its students and its professors are performing. If used well, a bell curve can help an institution see, at a glance, who is succeeding and who is failing and compare instructors easily. If every instructor gives the same test to students from the same demographic and the standard is the same for all, then the institution can clearly see whether any one professor's students are disproportionately achieving the pinnacle. Such students change the distribution; they visually, literally, spoil the curve. The bell curve can also become an end in itself, as if the objective is to achieve high scores rather than the excellence that those scores represent. The bell curve can easily be turned into a tool for wielding bias. Because we know performance correlates with training and because public education in the United States is funded locally and varies greatly depending on the wealth of a municipality, it is easy to think the top scorers are the most brilliant students, not those who are lucky enough to attend schools in the wealthiest districts. The bell curve is not inherently sinister, but it is important to recognize that even seemingly objective systems for assessment come with assumptions about values, worth, and humanity built in along with other ideas about the definition of intelligence, its innate character, and an individual's ability to change, learn, or improve through education.

The rise of grading—as distinct from evaluation—is another improbable story with some strange components. We don't have a precise record of who, what, when, where, why, or how the earliest examples of letter and numerical grading came into being; quite a lot of folk legends surround this history. The term *grade* seems to have come from the idea that students wouldn't "make the grade" in the same way that an imperfectly manufactured product would "fail to make the grade" by falling off a sloped conveyor belt in an assembly process.

As for the first prophet of grades, some point to a British don at Cambridge, William Farish, who in 1792—the story goes—decided to issue points or numerical grades to the students who wrote out commentary followed by oratory. Others give the credit to Yale president Ezra Stiles, a notably learned scholar who delivered his inaugural address to the student body in Hebrew, Arabic, and Aramaic. In 1785, Stiles personally graded the fifty-eight seniors at Yale: "Twenty *Optimi*, sixteen second *Optimi*, twelve *Inferiores* (*Boni*), ten *Pejores*."

The term *grade* had another early educational usage. "Graded," "age-graded," or "grade" schools arose in the third decade of the nineteenth century, as uniformity began to be praised as an educational objective. More and more schools placed children in grades according to their chronological age, and compulsory public school laws began to designate the age at which a child had to begin school. At the time, it was almost a fad to group like things together. Eggs, for example, began to be arranged, graded, and sold by uniform size ("Grade A" eggs). Kids aren't eggs, though. So they were sorted by age, not height or weight. Sorting by a cutoff birth date reduced to one measure the constellation of factors that might otherwise determine whether a child was ready to start school. Kids were sorted not by ability, interest, or emotional maturity. A child entered school with other students who had passed an arbitrary threshold.

By the last decades of the nineteenth century, educators began experimenting with letter grades to represent educational achievement. The first institution of higher education to create and implement a system of letter grades was Mount Holyoke, in 1897. America's first women's college adopted them as part of its effort to move to the forefront of modernizing education for modern women. Yale, Harvard, William and Mary, and several other colleges in the late nineteenth century also experimented with different ways to "standardize" written evaluation and commentary through a single metric that stood for everything a student had learned in a given term. Harvard tried a twenty-point system and, later, a hundred-point scale. William and Mary had four groupings, from excellent to failure.

A controversy arose in response to Mount Holyoke's decision. Interestingly, it was not about whether it was wise or desirable to reduce the complexity of handwritten, discursive feedback to something as simple as a summative letter grade. The controversy was over *E* as the failing grade. Although A, B, C, and D had no referential value, the fear was that students would fail their courses but somehow palm off their E grades as designating either "Excellent" or "Effort." It was important to have a clearly marked failing grade, with no room for ambiguity. So Mount Holyoke adopted the *F,* justified by the Anglo-Norman *failer,* meaning nullification, nonoccurrence, or failure. Other schools soon followed suit.

Apparently, University of Illinois professor of agriculture Herbert Mumford introduced the idea of grades to the American Meatpackers Association soon after Mount Holyoke adopted them. The meatpackers worried, though, that it was difficult to reduce something as complex as the quality of sirloin or chuck to an A, B, C, D, or F. So, from the beginning, they insisted that, along with the grade, the written comments of the meat inspector be tied to each and every piece of meat. What we would now call the "metadata" traveled with each piece of graded meat.

Strangely, educators were less skeptical about applying grades to student learning. They were quick to take on a variety of standardized measurements that reduced the complexities of intelligence, aptitude, and achievement to a single alphabetic or numerical score.

The different forms of testing have a history as complex as that of bell curves and grades, and also have unsavory elements. The development of IQ (intelligence quotient) testing is typical in certain respects, although also the most troubling. In 1904, psychologists Alfred Binet and Théodore Simon were commissioned by the Ministry of Public Education in France to design tests to identify and diagnose children who were struggling with the French academic curriculum. They used the word *intelligence* to describe what they were testing for and were careful to define the term according to the older sense, meaning understanding; the ability to grasp a concept; sagacity; or aptitude. The Binet-Simon test was not intended to measure some fixed biological attribute but, rather, was supposed to be a diagnostic aid that could help teachers improve student outcomes.

Binet's views were disregarded. Within a year of his death in 1911, other psychologists had devised equations that calculated scores on the Binet-Simon test against age to yield an "intelligence quotient." In World War I, Robert Yerkes, president of the American Psychological Association, and Edward Lee "Ted" Thorndike, an eminent behavioral psychologist, used the new IQ tests on more than a million recruits to determine who possessed enough intelligence to serve as officers. Both were eugenicists and believed ethnic groups had particular genetically programmed intellectual abilities. They believed the IQ tests supported the conviction that Jews, Italians, Irish, eastern Europeans, and African Americans were intellectually inferior to native-born, English-speaking, Anglo-Saxon Americans. The tests were also adopted by the US immigration service and contributed to the passage of the exclusionary Immigration Restriction Act of 1924. Oddly enough, the same tests that were deemed objective and scientific for categorizing race and ethnicity had to be recalibrated and weighted by gender. Women, who were assumed to be less intelligent than men, inexplicably did just as well on the IQ tests as men.

In 1913, educator I. E. Finkelstein grew alarmed that thoughtful, expository evaluations of whole people were being reduced to test scores, letter grades, numbers, and statistical averages. He wrote an unsparing critique of these new practices. His criticism foreshadows virtually all modern denunciations of the reductive nature of grades, including Ruth Butler's and Alexander Coward's. Finkelstein argued that standardized grading deludes us into thinking it represents something real, important, objective, comprehensive, scientific, and true. As he put it, "Whether numbers or letters . . . we can but be astonished at the blind faith that has been felt in the reliability of the marking system." Finkelstein wondered how human thought— messy, impartial, nuanced, inconsistent, changing, and, above all, complex—could be reduced to a single number or a letter, just like eggs or sirloin or automobile parts moving along on a conveyor belt. He protested that all these forms of summative assessment made knowledge a score, not a process that you would continue to develop and improve lifelong. How can grades, Finkelstein wondered, possibly be meaningful or equitable—or an inspiration to further understanding?

Charles Eliot was not immune to the lure of the supposedly "scientific" letter grading system. As a young chemistry teacher, he had departed from the recitation and oratorical mode of teaching to pioneer labs and deductive and inductive scientific methods, and he was among the first Harvard instructors to give up traditional oral exams in favor of written ones. The reforms he put in place as president of Harvard, designed for specialization, professionalization, and credentialing, were of a piece with the various grading and standardized testing impulses of the era. In the 1870s, during his presidency, Harvard experimented with a hundred-point scoring system for classifying students, in the 1880s there seems to have been a brief and incomplete experiment to use a letter grading system, and in the 1890s percentile rankings were adopted with a special classification for "merit with distinction." Eliot was nothing if not a modernizer, and these changes grew out of his ambition to turn Taylorist scientific labor management theory, designed for mass production and the assembly line, into scientific learning theory for the new, modern university.

Standardized college entrance exams have a less controversial history than IQ tests, but their legacy is just as influential, especially as evidenced in the movement known as "accountability-based" standards or, sometimes, "outcomes-oriented" education. Because high school teachers are implicitly preparing their students for college, and grade school teachers are preparing students for high school, the test that would become the Scholastic Aptitude Test in 1925 has had a profound influence on all of contemporary education, not only in the United States but also worldwide.

As we've seen, in 1914 when Frederick J. Kelly wrote his dissertation "Teachers' Marks, Their Variability and Standardization" at Kansas State Teachers' College, he advocated standardized achievement testing in the form of one-best-answer, multiple-choice testing. He developed this method, first, because there was a teacher shortage and it allowed for efficient grading by the untrained, who could simply put a grade sheet over the test sheet and mark off the right answers, thus freeing up the teachers' time. Second, he believed a standardized test could be diagnostic of basic skills. It would end "variability" (subjective judgment) because every test question would yield one and only one exact right answer and serve as a measure of how well schools and teachers were improving what he called the "lower-order thinking" of those who were from, in the terminology of the day, "the lower orders."

As secondary education was becoming commonplace and as immigrants flooded into the United States, Kelly's Kansas Silent Reading Test was used to speed up the grading process at a time when there was a teacher shortage. Less than a decade later, the College Entrance Examination Board adopted Kelly's efficient but reductive form of testing as the basis for the SATs. Like the production of the Model Ts of the era, knowledge was standardized, grading was automated, evaluation was summative. Throughout contemporary education, preschool to graduate and professional school, it still is. We might call it high standards, but it is, more properly, standardization, a legacy of an era when standardization was scientific, exciting, and new.

ALEXANDER COWARD IS THE RARE EDUCATOR WHO HAS LITTLE USE for bell curves, grades, standardized measures, or teaching to the test. He cares about his students and he cares about math. An eloquent explainer, he likes to emphasize that the logic behind mathematics applies to all the areas of life. Calculus is the study of change, geometry the study of shapes, and algebra (the basis of all mathematics) the study of symbols and how to manipulate them. Having clarity on such fundamental principles is necessary in any contemporary occupation, whether a factory worker reporting on robotic productivity, a middle manager analyzing sales reports, an X-ray technician reading a CT scan, or an ordinary citizen trying to understand the welter of data visualizations, statistics, and polls cited by authorities on just about any topic. Coward believes that his heresy at arguably the greatest public university in the world is that he thought the essential job of a professor in a top math department was to help brilliant students learn. He thought it was a public good to keep the highest possible standards in an introductory math class required for many majors and to use formative feedback so that students truly learned the subject matter. Far beyond that, he was creating the conditions in which they could learn to think like mathematicians, learn to *be* mathematicians.

Berkeley is a great public university, arguably the greatest. It is extremely difficult to get into Berkeley. It is a notoriously demanding university and it has an impressive retention and graduation rate of over 90 percent, close to that of the exclusive, elite Ivy League universities. Berkeley's commitment to excellence is legendary. In this extraordinary setting, the inspiring teaching happening in Coward's Math 1A lecture hall still stood out as exceptional.

Coward reports that, in 2014, he was warned by senior department members to moderate his methods. He says he was advised to conform more to the ways that other profs taught. His students weren't just taking the class because it was fun or easy, a "gut" course, in student parlance. They did well on departmental exams and retained and applied what they learned in his class. The Mathematics Department tracked the students who took Coward's Math 1A class and measured their performance the following semester in Math 1B and compared it to the performance of students who had taken Math 1A with another professor. It turned out that Coward's students achieved more in the second class by a small but statistically measurable margin than the other professors' students. One will recall that, in the learning theories of Ruth Butler, formative feedback was shown to increase long-term results. Coward is certainly convinced that his careful, encouraging feedback had an impact on students' ability to retain math beyond his courses.

If students are excited to be taking an introductory course that, at most universities, is greeted with dread, especially one as important as basic math, don't we all want to know the secret? What was Coward doing that others weren't? What can others learn from his pedagogical methods? Is his way of teaching math a one-off or is it a model that others might emulate? Given Coward's success, one might think that there would be great curiosity about his methods within his department and within the broader institution. That does not appear to have been the case. Coward claims his department chair asked him, "If you had a job at McDonald's and came along with all these new ideas, how long do you think you'd carry on working there?" Coward did not find this to be a helpful question, and continues to find it insulting and depressing that teaching in a stellar fashion would be compared to working at McDonald's. (The Math Department maintains that, for privacy reasons, it cannot address Alexander Coward's allegations about why he was let go.)

As Coward contemplates his bid to be reinstated at Berkeley, he is considering other potential career choices. Several of his friends in the field have left academe entirely for Silicon Valley opportunities that are incomparably more lucrative. These friends tend to think higher education is so hopeless that it cannot be salvaged. It's obsolete, out-of-date, not in tune with the kinds of computational thinking students gifted in math need these days. Math is important in every field where data are relevant, but it is still taught as if its only function is to train future math professors, with rigid and partitioned specializations and subspecializations and antiquated distinctions between theoretical and applied fields that no longer pertain unless you are a math professor conducting and publishing research for other math professors. Even the academic disciplinary distinctions among math, statistics, computer science, and engineering are archaic outside the academy and constantly blurred in real-world practice. Yet, in the modern research university, these are not only separate fields but sometimes antagonist divisions, with highest prestige going to the most theoretical and abstract mathematics and a general academic condescension to the applied. Peer-reviewed publishing in these highly specialized fields is crucial to the reputation of scholars, departments, and the university as a whole.

At this point, Coward isn't sure whether the university is worth fighting for. Perhaps there are simply too many obstacles to real teaching and learning. He's not sure how some distinguished full professors, many of whom made their reputations in their twenties or early thirties, still pull their weight as scholars or as teachers. It's not clear where students and student success fit into the larger disciplinary reputational system of a distinguished department.

Are those tenured, full professors the problem? Is it the fault of this increasingly rare breed that is so concerned about its own research agendas that they want only a handful of the very best, most persistent, most independent students so they can focus on the highest level of mathematics, on more publications and, where feasible, more grants? Is it the fault of the institution? The answer to these questions is both yes and no. Of course there are problems everywhere within inherited and legacy systems, including with stodgy professors, who are loath to change their ways. But material factors contribute to these problems. Specifically, the necessity of maintaining high rankings exerts a tremendously conservative pressure on any institution. If an institution tries something new that isn't recognized yet in the field, or (heaven forbid!) if it attempts an experiment that fails, its rankings can plummet.

Rankings of a department and an institution are precious and costly. According to a study in *Research in Higher Education,* if a university were to try to rise significantly in the rankings in *US News & World Report,* it might have to spend millions or even tens of millions of dollars to compete with top twenty universities. Berkeley's Math Department, in its enviable top five position, dares not lose its place; trying to crawl back to the top could prove financially disastrous or even impossible in a university that has suffered forty years of per capita cutbacks. The pass rate of students in introductory courses doesn't factor in to prestigious ratings. Limited funds make it all the more imperative to have large lecture courses like Math 1A that serve as flunk-out courses so that only a few students make it into the far smaller, more selective advanced math classes taught by full professors. This funneling frees those full professors to publish articles, fulfill professional duties, and obtain grants for highly specialized research that keeps the rankings elevated. Only 12 percent of the University of California, Berkeley's total operating expenses are covered by state support. The rest must be covered by tuition and external sources—typically, by sponsored research or grants earned, in rigorous competitions in the sciences and often with less than a 5 or 6 percent acceptance rate. The professors working toward those grants might defend themselves by noting that the Math Department at Berkeley is in the top five because they work day and night to produce peer-reviewed research.

They would not be exaggerating. Contrary to the image of the lazy professor who only teaches four or six hours a week and has summers off, every study of professorial labor shows they are among the hardest working of any profession. Every time a new study is undertaken, the reported workload increases. Currently, faculty work on average sixty-one hours per week annually. They work ten hours a day per workday and then ten hours every weekend, including summers.

Full professors work longer hours than either associate or assistant professors. About 40 percent of that time is spent on teaching, in the classroom or preparing for class. That means teaching is pretty close to a full-time job in itself, without the other required components of research and university service. And it's a solitary profession: most of what faculty members do they do alone, on campus or at home. An anthropologist conducting one study of faculty labor titles his findings "The Long, Lonely Job of *Homo academicus.*"

Even if professors are actually teaching a lot and spending a good portion of their time in that effort, the overall ecosystem of higher education does not reward good teaching in the same way it rewards (and requires) measurable "outputs"—peer-reviewed articles, books, professional papers, and grants as well as "citations" of their work in articles by their peers. These outputs are measured and documented by universities, another example of reducing intellectual merit to a standardized metric. Talk about a deterrent to innovation! From the beginnings of the modern American research university in Eliot's day, teaching and student learning were not the central mission. Teaching more students to understand and even love math is, in a structural sense, not the objective of a world-renowned math department. Standards setting, measuring, assessing, and ranking are important to maintain not only top students but also top faculty. Measurable standards are connected to reputation, ranking, and accreditation. This approach is also about the replication of expertise. Full professors at elite universities such as Berkeley typically view their highest calling as preparing their students to become full professors at elite universities such as Berkeley. Rankings don't track the students who flunk Math 1A, but they do encompass how many math majors go to graduate school and where.

As of this writing, Alexander Coward holds informal math office hours at the Free Speech Movement Café in the center of the Berkeley campus, where he continues to teach math for free. He's begun signing up student mentors to help other students with their math and, so far, nearly fifty students have expressed interest. He has also taken a number of online programming courses from Udacity and is now programming every day, working on his own start-up company, an accreditation system that will help students validate what they learn outside of formal education. His approach in his new company, as in his tutoring at the Free Speech Movement Café, is to guide people through what they know, give them suggestions about what might have value in the world, and offer a platform from which others can then judge that work themselves. "No grades," he insists.

EVERYTHING IN HIGHER EDUCATION IS GRADED AND RANKED: students, professors, departments, institutions. If the bane of would-be innovators and risk takers in corporate America is the quarterly shareholders' meeting, where one must constantly show an upward-trending balance and short-term gains, then the bane of like-minded individuals in higher education is accreditation, including rankings. The Carnegie Classification of Institutions of Higher Education, the framework with which every US college and institution is classified within comparable groups for educational and research purposes, both ensures quality and can stymie experimentation. All the data relevant to accreditation, certification, and ranking are available in the National Center for Education Statistics Integrated Postsecondary Education Data System, the dreaded "IPEDS." Any slip in status is recorded there, for all to see, on a public website.

Grades rank individual students within an institution. Test scores rank individual students outside of and across institutions, ostensibly to give a clear measure of excellence on a national scale. Institutions themselves are ranked relative to other institutions, on many different kinds of criteria, including research productivity (mostly, peer-reviewed publications) of the faculty, grants obtained by the faculty and postdoctoral fellows, professional prizes, and placement of graduate students in tenure-track jobs. Each part of this process is overseen by accreditation bodies, most of which were established in Eliot's day as part of the professionalization of higher education.

One criterion underlies all of the others: selectivity. And, for most institutions, selectivity is based on grades and test scores of individual students. To get into the best schools, a student has to do best on tests. To be considered a top school, colleges select the students who test best.

The circularity of the current regime of assessment promotes specialization. Scholarly experts decide which fields and subfields should be tested. Test-making experts design tests on those subjects. K–12 teachers base their instruction on high-stakes, end-of-grade standardized tests that feed into national testing standards like the SATs. Admissions officers select the students who perform best on those tests. It's selectivity all the way down, in other words, and a selectivity that makes innovation, in a very literal as well as metaphoric sense, extracurricular: if it is not on the big standardized tests, it is not likely to be a core curricular requirement.

If your institutional reputation is based, directly and indirectly, on how well students do on summative tests, then it is important to shape what you teach and how you teach to meet the parameters of the test in order that your students achieve the highest scores possible. Yet we know this results in an impoverished and ineffective form of learning. If you want students to retain knowledge in an applicable, useful form that serves them beyond the test, then teaching them simply so that they can ace a standardized test is the worst way for them to learn. Conversely, teaching to the test hones the educational process to reductionist perfection.

Fortunately, there are institution-wide alternatives. Consider Hampshire College. In 2014, Hampshire did the seemingly unthinkable: it did away with grades and standardized tests altogether. Faculty and administrators decided that, instead, they wanted to select students based on a variety of holistic factors that would promote an atmosphere in which everyone could learn, innovate, and thrive together.

The decision was historic. Hampshire College is the first institution of higher education to *refuse* to accept SAT or ACT scores. It didn't just make them optional. It banned them. It won't look at them. It doesn't record them. The test scores are not in any way part of the admissions process.

Hampshire College is located in Amherst, Massachusetts, in an education-rich corner of New England, near Amherst College, Smith College, Mount Holyoke, and the public University of Massachusetts, Amherst. It was founded in 1970 as one of the "five colleges" and, from the start, it was an experimental alternative to the other schools. Hampshire faculty don't grade students in their courses but instead give them long narrative evaluations. Students there graduate without GPAs, yet employers, graduate schools, and professional schools still eagerly pursue them.

Hampshire often sets trends. Opting out of SAT/ACT for admissions has consequences, though. As Hampshire president Jonathan Lash wrote in a public statement a month after Hampshire banned SAT and ACT scores from prospective students' applications, "You won't find our college in the *US News & World Report* 'Best Colleges' rankings released this month. . . . That got us kicked off the rankings, disqualified us, per *US News* rankings criteria. That's OK with us."

What happened when Hampshire jumped off the rankings treadmill? An increase in "yield" (percentage of students who accept the offer to attend Hampshire) from 18 to 26 percent was the first, eye-popping result. That surprised everyone. President Lash believes Hampshire is reaching more effectively the very special kind of student it wants by making it harder to apply, requiring more essays, not substituting one reproducible standardized test score for actual quality. So, applications have declined, quality has increased, and so has yield—making the application process itself less expensive to administer.

Not only that, but diversity (as measured by standard educational reporting rubrics) has increased by 21 percent, as has the percentage of first-generation students and low-income students. Hampshire educators theorize that, unlike SAT scores that correlate with expensive test preparation (either in affluent school districts or Kaplan-like after-school programs), it is possible that when students represent themselves without benefit of SAT scores, other highly desirable talents, skills, and accomplishments emerge that may not be about affluence but about originality and what's been termed "grit."

Hampshire's admissions officers are also convinced that the new system is a better match for the kind of independent, self-motivated student the college seeks. When Hampshire surveyed its past and present students, before eliminating standardized entrance exams, it discovered that not one of them had considered the *US News & World Report* rankings before deciding to attend.

A couple of years after the decision, President Lash and the faculty and students at Hampshire remain pleased with the results. A survey of recent applicants shows that they believe Hampshire has the most humane and interesting application system in the country. (Obviously there is some self-selection at work.) It is designed so students reflect on their purpose in going to college in the process of applying. It becomes a learning experience in itself. President Lash insists that Hampshire remains "deeply committed" to its strategy and often hears from students and their families who admire its stand on SATs. He is certain that they have better applicants who are "more committed to Hampshire because of what it uniquely offers."

And Hampshire is certainly committed to its students. With only fourteen hundred undergraduates, it is nonetheless in the top 1 percent of all colleges for placing its graduates in doctoral programs. More than 50 percent of its graduates go on to earn at least one graduate degree.

We should all hope Hampshire's bold experiment isn't just a one-off but a trend or, better, the beginning of a new and better way. At the very least, the school has lived up to its motto: "To Know Is Not Enough."

HOWEVER BOLD ITS INNOVATIONS, IT'S NOT SURPRISING THAT A small, young, private, alternative institution would be leading change in higher education. It's simply easier for a school like Hampshire to implement large-scale change, in part because everything it does is inevitably on a small scale. But what if the tyranny of grades and standardization could be resisted at even the largest public schools?

That is the question being asked at the Meadowlark Retirement Community in Manhattan, Kansas.

Today happens to be Taco Day. "Your party will be down as soon as class is over," the receptionist tells me. She points to a large round table with crisp white table linens at the opposite end of the dining room, beyond the buffet line. "The students usually sit with the other residents, but today they reserved a table for your visit."

A number of people in the Meadowlark dining room wear purple. Pretty much everyone in Manhattan does. It's the school color of the Kansas State Wildcats. The university dominates the town, and the residents embrace it fully. Almost all of them attended K-State themselves or are related to someone who did. Even residents who went to rival institutions express admiration. Social, intellectual, and cultural life—everything down to the traffic patterns in this town— is shaped by what's happening at the university.

I'm here to interview students in a class called "The Anthropology of Aging: Digital Anthropology." I'm looking for alternatives to massive lectures that function as failure mills, to grading-obsessed departments, to institutions so determined to cut costs that they've forgotten their mission of preparing the next generation to be responsible, independent-minded, dedicated, and wise inheritors of a complex and sometimes baffling future.

That's a big job. It cannot be left to small, dedicated institutions like Hampshire College—founded fifty years ago on principles of student-centered learning—to shoulder the entire future.

That's why I visited K-State, a very different institution from Hampshire—and from a distinguished, highly selective massive public institution like the University of California, Berkeley. K-State is effectively open admissions, accepting 97 percent of those who apply. There are more than twenty-one thousand undergraduates, mostly in-state, and the tuition is under $10,000 a year for these students, low compared to many state universities, but higher than it's ever been. Manhattan, Kansas, has a village feel; an exuberant, almost aggressive friendliness obtains. The graduation rate at KSU is about the same as at most CUNY colleges, around 25 percent in four years. That may seem dismal until you realize that the typical student at KSU, as at many other large public universities, holds down at least one full-time or several part-time jobs while attending.

"The Anthropology of Aging: Digital Anthropology" is taught by Michael Wesch, one of the most famous profs at K-State, or anywhere, for that matter. He was the 2008 Professor of the Year, an award given by the Carnegie Foundation for the Advancement of Teaching. It's the Pulitzer Prize of academe, awarded to inspiring undergraduate teachers. Wesch is known for his courses as well as for influential YouTube videos about higher education that have been viewed well over 10 million times.

My personal favorite, "A Vision of Students Today," has had more than 5 million views. The video begins with a grainy, slightly sinister shot taken from the entrance to an empty lecture hall, all noirish black and white. A quote from Marshall McLuhan appears: "Today's child is bewildered when he enters the nineteenth century environment that still characterizes the educational establishment where information is scarce but ordered and structured by fragmented, classified patterns, subjects, and schedules."

This is the university we've inherited from Charles Eliot's time. McLuhan knew what a poor fit it was for his world—in 1967. Obviously, much has changed since then. Except in formal education. Youth are still being graded into passivity and a state of fear by standardized classes that deliver standardized answers that can yield good results on standardized exams that have only marginal applicability to their lives beyond school.

In an age when even our toasters collect our data, in formal education, of all places, we still gather data on student learning and achievement as if it were 1914. Students today are lucky their skulls aren't measured with calipers, the bumps on their heads counted and diagnosed. Someday our current, standardized ways of assessing learning will be relegated to the dust heap of pseudoscience history, just like phrenology.

The two hundred students in Prof Mike Wesch's lecture course didn't just view "A Vision of Students Today." They made it. Instead of taking exams and writing term papers, they worked together on this one semester-long collaborative class project. In this video, the camera pans to a traditional, lifeless lecture hall. Now there are students in the seats, facing forward, looking toward the blackboard on which is written a question: "If these walls could talk, what would they say?" Silently, the students supply the answers, each one holding up a piece of notebook paper on which is scrawled a response. Their faces are grim. "18% of my teachers know my name," one piece of paper says. "I complete 49% of the readings assigned," says another. "I buy hundreds of dollars of textbooks I never read." "My neighbor paid for class but never comes." These bleak statements together offer a rough approximation of the state of higher education today. Far more encouraging is the backstory of how this video was made. Prof Wesch challenged his students to work collectively, to turn the large lecture class into a video production company. They pursued research in many different forms, finding answers in books and articles, archives, through data analysis, and through social science survey methods and ethnographic interviews. They used digital tools to host and share their data sets, and they learned how to collectively write a script, shoot a video, edit, and then release and advertise it to the public.

What kind of class is this? Anthropology? Business? Data analysis? Research methods? A filmmaking class? A digital literacy course? All of the above. It takes all of these skills to learn how to work together, to manage a project from an idea through implementation and share research in a way that makes a compelling story, to produce it, edit it, publish it, and get it out there in the world where it can have an impact, a *palpable* impact. A note held up by one of the students informs us that the students made 367 edits to the evolving script of "A Vision of Students Today."

What jobs will these students have when they graduate? They don't know. But the experience prepares them for whatever they do in ways far more significant and lasting than what they might learn in a more traditional lecture course.

One of Wesch's students, Jordan Thomas, finished his course, took a gap year from K-State, and rode his bicycle from Kansas to Colombia. Most people he told about his plan to tour South America alone, on a bike and by hitchhiking, thought he was crazy.

"I'm not crazy. I just have questions," he likes to say. When he returned home, he coproduced a video about his experience, "To Live in This World," that was shown at an international film festival in Paris. He went to live in Taos, New Mexico, for a time, living and studying traditional agricultural practices in the Taos Pueblo Native American community. Then he came back to K-State to finish his degree, and applied for a Marshall Scholarship to study alternative food systems and sustainability at Oxford. He won this extremely selective and internationally renowned scholarship in 2015. The gap year paid off in the form of a highly coveted scholarship and in a range of skills that will take Jordan Thomas far.

Jordan is Mike Wesch's student. But, as Wesch tells me, beaming with pride: "Jordan's *my* teacher." Student as teacher, teacher as student, in the famous terminology of Paulo Freire, the fountainhead of student-centered learning.

I fill my plate at the taco bar and wait at the dining table for the students taking Wesch's "Anthropology of Aging" class.

This year, Wesch's students plan to make a video game together. But unlike most games, this one has a serious purpose: to teach people who play it about end-of-life decision making. It is an ambitious class, given that developing and engineering a video game is difficult and only a few of these students are computer science majors. But that's by no means the greatest test these students have to pass. To enroll in this course, they must commit to doing something highly unusual. They have to move out of their dorm rooms and live for a semester at Meadowlark Retirement Community.

Professional anthropologists would call this participant observation. The students have apartments among those of the other residents. They have moved out of their comfortable dorms where the

Purple Pride football and basketball talk never stops and into a place where cribbage and NPR are social currency. They are giving up their student lives to study aging, living day in and day out among senior citizens negotiating life with dignity and independence in the face of pain, loss, tragedy, sickness, fear, death.

By the time I arrive midway through the semester, the students have made close friendships with the other Meadowlark residents. They are also totally absorbed in their research. They are conducting ethnographic interviews with the residents to learn more about life as a senior citizen. They are also taking classes and pursuing independent research in a number of areas that, together, constitute their "general education" across the curriculum at K-State: gerontology, pathology, psychology, neuroscience, public policy, law, demographics, neuropharmacology, and the business of modern American health care. "The Anthropology of Aging: Digital Anthropology" is about the furthest thing imaginable from Eliot's vision of specialized, disciplinary, professionalized higher education.

Meadowlark Retirement Community is the right institution to teach them. It is as radical in its world as Wesch's courses are in higher education. Annie Peace, director of Health Services at Meadowlark, tells me that Meadowlark is part of the "Household" movement in senior citizen living. The movement champions elder-centered living that focuses on autonomy, on independence, and on every resident being able to live as fully as possible within the limits of their abilities and desires. Its approach is not so different, in a broad sense, from student-centered learning. She likes having the students in residence and feels Wesch and his students are kindred spirits. "We're fighting the same battle," she tells me, "just at different points along the life cycle."

It turns out that the typical retirement community, like the modern university, has nineteenth-century origins. Retirement communities derive from asylums for older adults and those who were destitute, mentally infirm, or dying—"shut ins," they were often called. Just as compulsory public education evolved out of the factory workhouses, retirement homes evolved out of the old poorhouses, which were home to those (mostly women) who had become wards of the state once they were no longer "productive" and lacked offspring to care for them. As with most institutions, it's hard to shake those dismal origins. "We've got our work cut out for us. We're trying to change an institutional design that's been in place for a long time," Peace says.

At the end of the course, Wesch will file an official grade for each student, but their most meaningful assessment is a letter he writes to the entire class, reflecting on each student's contribution—to one another, to their professor, to their school, to Meadowlark, and to the world beyond. No grade or multiple-choice exam could begin to cover all that these students will learn this semester. He knows they will have spent more hours on this course than probably any other of their college careers, and will have read deeply in new subject areas, researched topics afield from their particular major, and learned skills they never considered before (from statistics to programming).

At lunch, Chuck, one of the students, tells me about how Annie Peace sometimes invites them to weigh in on the problems she faces. He relates a story that starts with the state passing a new regulation that required a heavy fire door between the residents' apartments and the shared entertainment areas at Meadowlark, where there's a theater, game rooms, a library, and a tavern that resembles the set of *Cheers*. The problem arose because two men, both in wheelchairs, loved to come down to the bar after games to have a drink and talk sports together. With the new fire doors, they'd be forced to call a night nurse or watchman to let them into the bar. They were insulted. They wanted the obstacle removed. But the new safety regulation wouldn't allow it.

Peace invited the students to share in devising a solution. They read the state regulations carefully. They looked at the pathway from the apartments to the tavern. They talked to the two men involved and learned about their sense of indignity and hurt pride from the new rules as they examined the construction of the men's wheelchairs. And then they met with the resident engineers and contributed to the design of a system in which the wheelchairs could be fitted with remotes, the heavy fire doors with sensors. The men could have their autonomy, the state could maintain its safety standards, and Meadowlark could keep its accreditation.

"Boss fight," Chuck smiles. "We're putting it in our video game—it's the kind of problem that we want players to confront and solve." Because I know a little about game design and have sat in on design sprints with professional game developers, he tells me about the interface they are planning. What Chuck is aspiring to is complicated even for a pro. Their game will have to include multiple and malleable avatars with evolving role-playing scripts. Someone might play as a resident or a family member or a prospective resident or a doctor, nurse, administrator—or maybe a state regulator. That regulator might suffer a stroke and end up a resident at Meadowlark. An elderly resident could lose a younger family member to cancer. As a player, you would learn empathy for others but also experience vulnerability for your own avatar. Like life. Unpredictable. And very difficult to script and program.

After lunch, we go to the apartment of Robert, another of the students in "Anthropology of Aging." The rest of the class is there. Robert is one of three students who pulled an all-nighter to draft the latest iteration of the storyboards for their game. The students are chattering about the progress they've made. It's clear some are already experienced at programming code and markup language, while others are struggling to master HTML5 or are working hard on their digital animation skills using a suite of software tools. Despite their varying skill levels, all are helping one another even as they talk about gerontology research and report on some story a resident just told that would be perfect to build into the narrative of the game.

"So here's the thing," Robert says, "no matter what your condition, you still have to make life-and-death decisions. Even if you are losing your short-term memory, you have to understand rules and medicines and insurance forms on top of that. Last night, we argued a lot about whether people should get extra points if their avatar has cognitive limitations, is making life decisions without the capacity to make clear decisions. We thought they should, then wondered if that was fair. What if someone is losing abilities but was a lawyer before they retired? How do you balance those things?"

"We plan to put everything difficult that we've seen here into our video game," Karl, who also worked through the night, says. "We want to put players into situations that require ingenuity and empathy. You need both to win the Game of Life."

At least two of the students in Wesch's class hope to work at professional video game companies when they graduate. They both have part-time jobs as coders and speak computerese like a second language: HTML5, JavaScript, C++, BrowserQuest, Unreal Engine 4. One of the computer science students wants to be sure that, if you play the game, your own data can be secure and private. He's concerned with how they need to customize the software to ensure this. Others in the class hope to enter health professions, and they want to make sure everything in the game is data-driven, based on actual, sound research. Two students tell me they aren't sure yet what they want to do after graduation, but they are confident that, because of this class, they'll be ready for whatever they decide to pursue.

Professor Wesch, in the corner, has a smile at the edges of his lips. His students huddle over the coffee table, drawing pathways, crossroads, vectors, all talking at once, working out the game play, as he holds back, lets them talk it all through together. It is from his restraint, his appreciation of his students' autonomy, that one appreciates his pedagogy's power. Like Alexander Coward and other great profs, he teaches by inspiring confidence in his students. He has set the conditions for an unparalleled educational experience here at Meadowlark, where these students are learning more than they ever could from a seminar or a lecture class where he performed the role of the professor in all the conventional, authoritative ways. They will draw from the knowledge and experience they gain in this course for the rest of their lives.

It is ironic—tragic, even—that Wesch's impressive course is offered here in Kansas, where the assault against all of public education is relentless. State funding per college student is now 21 percent below what it was in 2008. Students at Kansas State pay $1,500 a year more in tuition than their older brothers and sisters who graduated from K-State in 2008. Faculty face new financial burdens and political pressures. In 2016, the governor and legislators aggressively cut corporate taxes and personal income tax for the wealthy, resulting in a massive budget shortfall. To make up the difference, another $19 million is coming out of the higher education allocation in 2017. This means more cutbacks to services, to faculty. It is positively heroic for a university and its faculty and students to innovate against such odds.

It's not easy to remake higher education these days. In the cases of Alexander Coward, Hampshire College, and "The Anthropology of Aging," we see different ways to work around the inherited structures of the university. In each instance, the mission is active, student-centered learning. Whether the obstacle is assessment methods, grading systems, external ranking systems, disciplinary division, the physical space of the classroom, or state-level cutbacks, Coward, Hampshire, and Wesch have moved away from the standardization and rigid professionalism designed for the needs of a society that no longer exists. Not everyone can succeed against the weight of a 150-year tradition. In Coward's case, the obstacles were simply too great.

Several weeks after I leave Manhattan, Kansas, Mike Wesch sends me a copy of the letter he has written to the class. The students have given him permission to share it with me. It's twelve single-spaced pages and recognizes each student, singling out something unique that each contributed. Wesch praises one student for a singular ability to inspire collaboration. Another keeps the group going with his generous sense of humor; another has discovered a talent she didn't know she had: she began creating a visual diary to capture the intense dialogues in class and everyone learned from these "mind maps." Professor Wesch also offers feedback on areas each student might work on.

"Somehow like any great group, we are more than the sum of our parts," Wesch writes toward the end of his evaluation, in the section addressed to the class as a whole. "We needed each and every one of you. Working alone, we would have come away with individual 'assignments'—videos, photo essays, maybe a simple game—most of them forgettable. Together, we created something worth remembering."

What these students learned at Meadowlark is far removed from the nineteenth-century university. This class won't help K-State top the rankings in *US News & World Report,* but it's not rankings or GPAs or even majors and minors that truly matter in the end. Professor Wesch has provided a platform for learning. It's been a "boss fight," as the gamers would say. The students have grown and they have explored, challenged one another, sometimes failed, and then succeeded, memorably, all of them, together.

8 THE FUTURE OF LEARNING

THE RED HOUSE IS EXACTLY WHAT ITS NAME SUGGESTS, BUT DON'T let the humble frame edifice fool you. Inside, a revolution is brewing. "The Red House may just be the most valuable piece of real estate in higher education," insists Dr. John (Jack) DeGioia, president of Georgetown University.

The epicenter of change at Georgetown and well beyond, The Red House is where students, faculty, and administrators gather to plot what comes next for higher education. No idea is too big, none is too small, and nothing that happens at The Red House stays at The Red House. When The Red House tries something that works, they let the world know so the rest of us can try it out and improve upon it. In partnership with Arizona State University, Georgetown hosts a leadership conference each year. In blogs, articles, and books, proponents of the new education network ideas, exchange success and failure stories, and plot what to tackle next.

I pause outside the gate, unsure whether I'm at the right place. Except for the color, this could be any ordinary dwelling. It's perched at the edge of campus, where gown meets town, at a remove from

227

the austere Gothic spires of Healy Hall, the National Historic Monument that marks the main entrance to the nation's oldest Catholic university. "Come in!" a student beckons, opening the gate. He's one of two students living in The Red House this year, serving as a "student leader." Another eight student leaders are on the payroll and work as peer mentors and connectors with students, faculty, community members, and advisers. It's a network model, with The Red House as a central node, spreading outward from this core to events, lecture series, projects, programs, courses, studios, internships, initiatives, challenges, competitions, and myriad cocurricular activities connecting ideas originating in this modest frame house with nearly every part of campus, to the District of Columbia, and beyond to the larger world.

I feel the buzz the minute I step inside. Half a dozen students, staff, and faculty invite me to have a seat at a large square table that occupies much of the first floor. Everywhere around us are mind maps, white boards covered with arrows and circles and boxes, and multicolored sticky notes with words like *iterate* and *remix* and *rebundle*. Over the mantel, a large sign urges: *Yes, a University Can Reinvent Itself!* Nearby, pinned to the wall, a T-shirt enjoins: *Create the Future.*

Professor Randall (Randy) Bass, vice provost for education, presides over The Red House with the physical grace one associates with an athletic coach. In a fashionably wrinkled white shirt open an extra button and a neatly trimmed beard and silver earring, his manner is friendly and laid-back. His job is to ask, "What if?" What if the teaching and curricular structures of the university were not chained to credit hours, semesters, academic calendars? What if a schedule could be as flexible as the subject matter? What if students could gain certification in part or all of a field of study based on competency, not test scores or coursework? What if some courses or majors were blended with mentored, immersive learning experiences and independent or collaborative projects, including internships? What if in four years of school students could work on a BA and an MA at the same time, through a combination of online learning, self-paced learning, traditional coursework, and experiential learning?

Each and every "what if?" questions the status quo of the modern university. For every aspect of higher education, Bass wants us to ask whether it is useful, important, and supportive of students' future choices—or simply a legacy of a university designed for social exigencies that have since changed. "What forms of higher education are possible now?" he asks rhetorically, then revises his question: "What forms of higher education are *only* possible now?" By demanding that we think in the "now," he moves from an abstract vision of how things might be to an action plan.

Radical leadership of higher education change is not what one normally associates with a 225-year-old Jesuit institution known for training some of the most influential Beltway minds. President De-Gioia is an unlikely hero of new ideas, exactly the opposite of the corporate tech honchos who proclaim the end of college and insist we need to give away our beloved alma maters to the highest bidders promising disruption. Disrupt for what purpose, to what end, for whose profit? Jack DeGioia is the consummate insider. With a BA and a PhD in philosophy from Georgetown, he spent his entire teaching career at Georgetown before moving into administration and becoming the university's forty-eighth president. He is the first non-Jesuit to assume the office and is the longest-serving president in the university's history.

A latter-day Charles Eliot, Jack DeGioia wants the university he loves to lead a much larger transformation of colleges and universities across the country. He directs, among other initiatives, the Forum for the Future of Higher Education. "We're not striving to merely keep up with the changes that are happening around us," President DeGioia insists. "We want to define that change, continue to lead, and make each new class of students the best they can be."

"Rebundling" is an important concept at The Red House. The term takes on the "unbundling" movement that started in several think tanks and has been influential with state legislators justifying their cutbacks to public higher education. The American Enterprise Institute, for example, has distributed a white paper arguing that students should not be going to expensive colleges but, rather, should acquire skills training from online colleges that don't come "bundled" with the "frills" of brick-and-mortar campuses. Educational technology, they argue, can turn your alma mater into a purveyor of online courses, created by centralized high-tech for-profit companies that offer certification and credentials removed from all the expensive, energy-draining "ideology" of college. To modernize, the unbundling argument goes, we should get rid of everything from the research mission to athletics, from the philosophy and anthropology departments to the PhD programs, from advisers to a general liberal arts education.

The Red House philosophy opposes unbundling at nearly every turn. The Red House "rebundles." Its goal is to keep what is great about a modern research university while shedding the inherited features and practices that make it difficult to prepare students for their futures. Research experiences are put at the very core of learning and teaching because a directed, guided research project—pursued alone or as part of a team—is the best way for students to learn how to define and explore a topic, sift through available data, determine what is or is not credible information (from misleading statistics to "fake news"), analyze it, and then reshape what currently exists into something original and informed that contributes to the current state of knowledge. In the contemporary world, research is a survival skill.

US universities now contribute over 50 percent of the nation's total basic research across fields, from philosophy to astrophysics. Rather than disavow this core feature of the intellectual enterprise, one that has been at the heart of the university's purpose since Eliot's day, The Red House emphasizes research even more, making it a key part of student-centered learning. As a skill, research demands that you find a path where there is no road map; it is both an analytical process and a process of discovery. It requires rigor, tenacity, originality, and confidence.

Three other principles animate The Red House's quest for innovation. The first is that radical, successful change has to be embraced by those inside, not outside, the institution and those who are most dedicated to the mission of preparing students, not those finding ways to profit from them. Second, technology alone cannot be a solution to education's problems. You can spend a whole day at The Red House without hearing the word itself, even though it's hard to think of any educational technology that Bass, whose previous position was heading one of the university's technology programs, hasn't pioneered, evaluated, and integrated into the fabric of Georgetown's teaching and learning. He knows that technology is everywhere, like the air we breathe. The purpose of The Red House is to redesign higher education, which means using the best technology relevant to the goals at hand. And it means understanding fully its limitations and liabilities.

The third principle, and the one perhaps most contrary to expectation, is that elite universities like Georgetown must partner with institutions with different demographics and traditions. This isn't *noblesse oblige* but a necessity if the goal is to educate students for life after graduation. Georgetown's partnerships with Arizona State and LaGuardia Community College, two underfunded and yet progressive and innovative institutions, mean that everyone gains a different perspective on what is or isn't possible and within what limits. The world beyond college is more complex and diverse than our elite forms of higher education can be. You simply miss vital parts of an education if you learn for four years amid students from elite backgrounds at an elite university trained by elite professors. The world you find in such a setting is not a simulacrum of the real one beyond campus. That is also true, in a different way, for students at a regional public university or a community college, who are often remote from sources of power and affluence. Partnerships work in all directions, enabling those from varied backgrounds and institutions to see horizons that they wouldn't otherwise know were there.

One the central concerns of Randy Bass and his colleagues is automation. According to the World Economic Forum, 7.1 million more human jobs will be automated by 2020. What will that mean for the job market—and for the jobs humans will still be doing? One answer that The Red House proposes is that higher education move away from its legacy definitions of what constitutes a "field" and what counts as mastery or excellence in a specialized, traditional discipline (say, English or biology). Instead, institutions should foster deep, integrated learning, synthesis, and analysis across the borders of disciplines, including by cultivating the difficult and increasingly necessary skill of collaborating with those whose expertise and cultural background may be radically different from one's own. These human skills are vital and necessary, especially in a world powered by robots, where possibilities for misunderstanding can multiply.

Take, for example, a recent focus at The Red House in a project called "Principles and Challenges of Childhood and Society." To understand such a vast subject requires more than just taking a course in a particular department. It requires getting rid of the one-size-fits-all fixed idea of a course—3 credits, 15 weeks, 3 hour-long class sessions a week. It requires learning across the campus in just about every field, and then going beyond the campus's borders. To understand the scary parts of childhood (hunger, school violence, educational insecurity, cyber-bullying, and developmental disabilities) as well as the rich possibilities (play, imagination, learning, and creativity), the "classroom" must expand to include every department and professional school, plus K–12 schools, policy think tanks, archives and data repositories, community organizations, video games, and playgrounds.

"Students regularly report being transformed by these learning contexts where they learn that both creativity and critical thinking are key to problem solving," Prof Bass tells me. "They develop capacities for collaboration, empathy, resilience, working on unscripted problems and in conditions of uncertainty. They become comfortable with taking risks as a condition for innovation. Many report that these courses were among their only opportunities to truly own the problem they were working on, and to do so over a sustained period of time."

The Red House's rebundling is the antithesis of narrow, vocational skills training. So we have to ask: Does it outfit students for a vocation? Put bluntly: Do students who've been through The Red House get jobs?

Absolutely. Graduates have been remarkably successful not only at finding jobs but also at finding the particular jobs they dream of. They've gone on to a wide variety of careers in fields such as counseling, nutrition, policy, legal aid, nonprofit start-ups, and for-profit technology companies. They're working in government, education, and research labs. Some are continuing their education in professional programs—graduate school, medical school, law school, engineering school, or public health school programs. The Red House advising team knows, from talking with present and potential employers, that they are especially interested in their students' breadth and their risk-taking abilities.

How easy is it to remake the university to allow for this kind of expansive and relevant approach to pedagogy, one that traverses disciplinary divides among departments, institutes, undergraduate colleges, and professional schools? That's another question. For now, The Red House concentrates on inventing new courses, programs, and interdisciplinary pathways, while also working on the much slower process of changing the infrastructure of higher education. As Randy Bass jokes, if you want to take on big challenges, start with world peace. Then, once you have that accomplishment under your belt, you can tackle the truly intractable problems of academic and financial bureaucracies, like "how you transfer undergraduate tuition into the medical school cost centers."

FOR THE LAST FOUR YEARS, THE RED HOUSE HAS CHALLENGED students to be leaders in the new education revolution. Each year a small group of students, led by visiting architect and learning designer Ann Pendleton-Jullian, tackles "The University as a Design Problem," a course sponsored by the President's Office, and from which DeGioia himself actually hopes to learn. The course empowers students to rethink their role at the university and to propose solutions to problems that they identify at Georgetown, solutions the university can implement.

In a tailored navy suit and an ivory scarf tossed over her shoulder with an insouciance that could make a Parisian green with envy, Professor Pendleton-Jullian certainly has the look of an architect. She challenges students to see insurmountable problems as susceptible to solution. She calls her pedagogical method "pragmatic imagination" and describes it with terminology and metaphors from the world of architecture, computer science, philosophy, music, dance, and astronomy. Here, in this room, she is mostly quiet. It's the students' turn to present their work. This is the Formal Critique (Crit) session of what the students lovingly call "Wicked Problems 101." They have divided into three teams, each member contributing a unique set of skills and aptitudes to a problem they are defining, researching, and working to solve. The term "wicked problem" was coined in the 1970s by global planners to describe challenges so complex that any solution necessarily creates a subsequent wicked problem to be solved. Wicked problems include AIDS, hunger, the raging forest fire in the Alberta, Canada, tar sands, ISIS, the collapse of global political systems, world demographic disruptions, demagoguery, terrorism, racism. The mismatch of archaic education systems and the demands students face in their future is a wicked problem, too.

Prof Pendleton-Jullian is respectful of what is called "design thinking" but also points out its limits and where her approach deviates from it. Design thinking is a methodology best defined by two of its most popular teachers, Bill Burnett and Dave Evans at Stanford: "Designers don't *think* their way forward. Designers *build* their way forward." What they mean is that design thinkers proceed by setting a goal, prototyping a specific solution, testing that, and then improving on the feedback they receive. For even the most abstract and seemingly insoluble problems, they often draw blueprints and plot cause and effects. A practicing architect as well as a learning theorist, Pendleton-Jullian is somewhat skeptical of reducing complex processes to causalities and resists the distinction between thinking and building. Sometimes the solutions you can build and prototype miss the deeper core values, ideas, prejudices, histories, cultural norms, and insights that may be invisible and impossible to build, but shape everything else and have a tremendous impact on the solution you attempt to implement. She challenges students to go deep, not simply to forge ahead.

There are too many of us to all fit into The Red House, so today's Crit has been moved to Healy Hall, the center of campus. The fifteen students are already there, setting up their white boards, flip boards, and PowerPoints, and talking with the videographers at the back of the room. Bass and Pendleton-Jullian welcome the judges: Dr. Donald Harward, president emeritus of Bates College and director of the nonprofit Bringing Theory to Practice project; Professor Anthony E. Cook, an eminent constitutional, business, and civil rights lawyer who teaches at Georgetown's Law School; and John Seely Brown, the legendary former chief scientist at Xerox Corporation and director of its Palo Alto Research Center, proponent of radical innovation, who calls himself "part scientist, part artist, part strategist—and 100 percent motorcycle enthusiast."

I'm the fourth of the invited judges. We've received no information in advance. There's no program. The students are in charge.

The seminar has been modeled on a classic architecture studio, with three different kinds of critique sessions during the term. The "Desk Critique" happened at the idea stage, where the students and the profs wrestled with shaping concepts. Next there was a "Pin Up," where all the teams presented their progress to one another. In a "Formal Critique," you bring in judges from outside who have not been privy to any of the discussions and who may not even know the problem.

The first group calls itself "Agency and Purpose." They are endeavoring to redesign higher education to address the flood of negativity directed at Millennials. A recent study has shown that Millennials have received more criticism than any other generation since World War II, including a 2014 best seller that writes off the generation as "excellent sheep." The author argues that those born after 1985 are a different breed than past generations. Whether from obsession with their video games and iPhones, or rendered docile and other-directed by a regime of standardized, high-stakes testing, these Millennials are said by employers to be passive, picky, and overly sensitive.

The Agency and Purpose team has undertaken its own qualitative and quantitative research, including survey data, to track the life goals, values, and character of Georgetown students. Through various charts, they substantiate their claim that, when judged by rubrics and metrics applied equally across generations of Georgetown graduates, Millennials are more innovative and committed to change, not less, than previous generations, and they actually aren't sheep-like at all. However, because the Agency and Purpose group's goal is change, not critique, they move quickly from this perceptual correction to a plan. They argue that, if this is what the world believes, perhaps one way of revolutionizing Georgetown would be to counter the prejudice with a curriculum that distinguishes Georgetown as an institution that champions self-determination, risk taking, and independence. The team's proposals to President DeGioia lend concreteness to these goals by suggesting how the work of The Red House might be developed into a full curriculum available to all students.

The second group, "Stress and Resilience," also begins with a defensive comment about how they are not "excellent sheep." Theirs is an ambitious program to enlarge the concept and methodology of "resilience" being bandied about in contemporary risk management literature in order to address the dropout rate for "high-stakes" (not "high-risk," as they make clear) students at Georgetown and beyond. They are complicating the idea that resilience can be objectively measured as a differentiator of stakeholder and shareholder value. They propose an ingenious new conceptualization of risk modeling that factors in personal, individual, cultural, economic, and familial demographics. They statistically model nonparallel social factors, including prejudice. They complicate standard resiliency theory with the engineer's knowledge of how stress actually operates on a mechanical level. Too much stress doesn't make structures stronger. It breaks them. If resiliency were a simple matter of being stronger as a result of stress, it would be easier to build on fault lines or in war zones. The Stress and Resilience group proposes a suite of new programs, courses, and collaborative peer study groups designed to address risk and support resilience. They argue that their institutional modeling has great implications far beyond Georgetown and higher education more broadly.

We judges are blown away by the depth, seriousness, and originality of the first two groups' proposals. They will later pitch these directly to President DeGioia, who, unlike in previous years, can't be here for this final Crit session.

It's the third group, called "Ideals in Contradiction," that surprises me the most. The group addresses perhaps the most shameful event in Georgetown's history, one that has put the university in the national headlines all year. In 2015, it was revealed that in 1838 some of Georgetown College's early leaders addressed a financial crisis by selling 272 of its slaves to a Maryland planter. They did so even knowing that families within this group of slaves would be split apart and many of the slaves would be sold again into the most heinous conditions in the Deep South. Many in 1838 condemned the action as anti-Christian, including the Vatican, and the university president was removed from office.

The 2015 revelation exacerbated existing racial tensions on campus. The *New York Times* published a number of exposés, often with as much attention to the student protests as to the historical events that occasioned them. The Ideals in Contradiction team addresses both the past and present hypocrisy of a Jesuit institution that espouses social justice yet has owned and sold slaves in the past. The team frames its problem in these terms: "How can a competitive research-driven institution live up to its Jesuit social ideals? How can an institution own its past and move forward?"

At any prestigious university, and especially a private one dependent on tuition and donors to thrive, reputation is everything. It is highly unusual for a university to put its institutional credibility in the hands of students. One of the judges expresses surprise that

The Red House students would take up such a sensitive issue at the height of its volatility and notoriety.

"Why not?" Ann Pendleton-Jullian responds. "Our point is that a university is all of it—what is inside the classes, what you bring into the classes from outside, what you bring from the classes out into the world again. It's artificial to cordon the university from the world. Those barriers are what we're dismantling."

Another judge asks the students if they know the protestors. There are smiles all around and one of them politely answers, yes, of course they do—and then indicates that at least one of their team is regularly among them.

"The distinctions between research and activism, between objective and invested research are other concepts we're examining," Professor Pendleton-Jullian says. "No one is *outside* a wicked problem—even if you aren't protesting it, trying to solve it, you are part of the problem. If you don't think it's your problem too, then it's either not truly wicked or you are naive and not thinking deeply enough. If you aren't in the thick of the wicked problem, there is little hope that the solution you propose will be relevant or significant. That's key to designing an intervention into a wicked problem."

The students in Ideals in Contradiction once again reference the negative depiction of Millennials in the media. If you only read the news, you would believe the protestors were spoiled, privileged, and trivial in their complaints. If you have the opportunity to listen to the students themselves, you see how carefully they have drawn a connection between the slave past and the structural inequality in higher education in the present. Supposedly, professors are all liberals, yet if over 80 percent of full-time full professors are white and over 65 percent are male, some kind of inequality or bias is being perpetuated through the rankings, selection, curriculum, and pedagogy. The Georgetown student body, including those in graduate and professional school, is much more diverse than the faculty.

"There's a problem in the past and in the present. So, what should Georgetown do?" another judge presses. The group's list of solutions is impressive. The team has been engaged in proposing, organizing, or analyzing the efficacy of initiatives throughout the semester. One question they ask is what a research university might be able to contribute positively in the present, given this deplorable incident in the past. Georgetown University can work with descendants to provide genealogical information as descendant family connections are discovered. Another committee of faculty, administrators, and students has voted to rename two buildings on campus that commemorated those responsible for the decision in Georgetown's slaveholding past, a recommendation enacted by the university. The university is developing a new research center to study the enduring impact of racism and segregation and a new department of African American Studies. The students as a group sit on committees working on a range of cocurricular internships and community-based experiential learning partnerships. They are proposing a number of "reverse mentorships," where students and faculty, who are usually isolated from community issues, listen and learn from the community. This continuum of changes and additions addresses the past and will have ethical and material impacts on the university's future and help to restore and reaffirm some of its most deeply held values.

The Ideals in Contradiction team resists calling these actions reparations, but says they constitute a good start and can serve as a model for other universities. Almost all of the Ivies and most Southern universities have similar histories as well as the same persistent structural forms of inequality. "You take a problem this big, and it's real and it isn't just history, it's now," one student says. "The only way to go forward is by at least fully acknowledging the problem. That's Square One. It's not an end place. It's only a start."

Randy Bass's "What ifs?" have been turned, in this room, into plans, proposals, and realistic solutions—temporary and partial to be sure, but nonetheless honest in their grappling with recognition, reconciliation, and a start toward reparation.

Like the students of mathematician Derek Bruff at Vanderbilt, these students have used agile design principles to arrive at solutions. Like anthropologist Michael Wesch's class at Kansas State University, they have used immersive, experiential learning and some game-based principles to understand problems from the inside. Like students of Sha Xin Wei at Arizona State University and Sara Hendren at Olin College, they have worked across disciplines, using both abstract thinking and design pragmatics to address significant, pressing real-world problems. Like those taking classes from Andrea Lunsford at Stanford and Juana Maria Rodriguez at Berkeley, they are using a variety of traditional and social media to ensure that their research has impact in the world. Like the students in a global MOOC on "The History and Future of Higher Education," they have used technology strategically and wisely, integrating it into their research and their mission. And like Tressie Cottom McMillan's students in Digital Sociology, they are tackling urgent and controversial issues with serious research, sound methods, foundational principles, and plans for future action.

The topics taken up by the students at The Red House don't fit comfortably into conventional majors and minors. They don't look like vocational skills training. Isn't this a problem for the future of the students involved?

Apparently not. Whether turning their research project at The Red House into a for-profit or nonprofit company (as different graduates have done) or going to work for nongovernmental organizations or corporations from Peru to Silicon Valley, graduates leave confident in their abilities and employers have responded enthusiastically. There is no formula for what they do or where. There is no one-size-fits-all, no single "skill" that makes them "workforce ready," but they are prepared for a full range of future occupations. These young people are succeeding now, and they will continue finding success if their job disappears out from under them, or if they simply wake up one morning and realize they have chosen the wrong career path and need to find something better suited to their needs, their desires, or their mission in life.

"Don't you wish we could find a way for every student to experience something like The Red House as part of their college education?" I ask.

"Now *that's* a wicked problem!" Ann Pendleton-Jullian laughs.

WHAT WOULD CHARLES ELIOT BE DOING TODAY IF HE WERE around to reform higher education for the post-Internet age? He well might be working to redesign elite American universities such as Georgetown. Or he might set his sights on emerging countries. That, after all, is what the United States was in 1869, when it was recovering from the Civil War and a series of catastrophic financial crises.

In 2002, an American-educated Ghanaian, Patrick Awuah, returned home to Africa, determined to take the best of what he had learned as an undergraduate at Swarthmore College, in his MBA program at Berkeley, and from his position as an executive at Microsoft, all combined with the best ideas he could glean in Ghana. His ambition was to design his own university from scratch. He could have made far more money continuing to climb the corporate ladder at Microsoft, but he knew he had an opportunity to make a palpable impact in his own country.

"I wanted to create a university where everything about it was deeply rooted in values and mission—the mission of the transformation of Africa, the success of Africa," he says. He created Ashesi University.

In Ghana, higher education tends to be for the elite, and both the polytechnics and the universities are strictly preprofessional in orientation. Awuah, drawing on his experiences in the United States, wanted to counter both tendencies by establishing a more egalitarian institution and one that combined a liberal arts school and a professional school. He wanted to draw upon the best features of the quite different American institutions he had gone to: a highly selective, private, progressive liberal arts college with Quaker roots and a business school of a massive public university. He sought to create a university that would both embody values and prepare Ghanaians for the future. He especially strived for an antidote to what he saw as cronyism and narrowness in higher education in his country, which he believed led directly to political corruption. At the same time, he engaged in many conversations with Ghanaians as well as with other intellectuals, entrepreneurs, and educators throughout Africa in order to transform what he had learned in the

United States into a unique university that would help Ghana realize its future potential.

He chose the name "Ashesi" to represent this unique hybrid of Africa and the West. It means "beginning" in Akan, one of the native languages of Ghana, and is inspired by a quote from Johann Wolfgang von Goethe: "If there is anything you can do, or dream you can do, begin it. Boldness has genius, power, and magic in it. Begin it now." Unlike many universities in Ghana, Ashesi prides itself on its unique ethnic, economic, and gender diversity. It is the first school of engineering in Africa to admit equal numbers of women and men. Its goal is to teach students how to "learn and think analytically in different domains." Ashesi's logo is a hand-drawn stool representing the three pillars of the university: *scholarship, leadership,* and *citizenship.*

Like Charles Eliot before him, Awuah believes a better system of higher education can cure the crisis of leadership in his country. Eliot went to Europe in the 1860s to learn from the European research universities, in the hopes of revolutionizing the Puritan college in America. Awuah left his executive position at Microsoft to enroll in the MBA program at Berkeley specifically to learn what he needed to create a sustainable university in Africa. He explained his ambitions to his professors at Berkeley and was delighted at their eagerness and generosity in working to help him succeed. Drawing up the original plans for Ashesi University essentially became his two-year MBA project. "No matter what was assigned," he says, "I always had another case running in my head. Everything I did, everything I learned, was useful to my mission to start a university in Ghana."

The founding of Ashesi University in Africa helps us see what is possible here. Patrick Awuah's appreciation of his education in the United States also comes with a clear-eyed sense of what is obsolete in America's legacy institutions. The new education he envisions for Ghana need not be governed by these American traditions. Like The Red House, his university rebundles the university, choosing what works best for Ghana and reshaping it in better ways. For example, instead of the final capstone experience common at American universities, Ashesi students take on a special project and attempt to design a solution in their first year, just when they enter the university. They might study autism and launch an autism awareness campaign. Or they might pose solutions for a bumper pineapple crop rotting in farmers' fields amid starvation elsewhere. "They try to solve a problem and make it work early," President Awuah says. "That way, they can see, from all the courses that come later, what they could have done better. They actually see how their college education is useful to solving the problems." This inverts the legacy American model of required, low-status general education or introductory courses that students dispense with as quickly as possible on the way to their major. At Ashesi, students' independent, research-based projects, with their ideas that succeed and hypotheses that fail, set the foundation upon which they subsequently build all of their learning.

Ashesi turns upside down the usual American pyramid structure of higher education that goes from the broad general education base to narrower, more specialized courses leading to independent studies and capstone projects. Beginning with the research project requires realigning other key facets of the traditional university: curriculum, disciplines, and the very notions of specialization and expertise. By starting with an intensive, significant research project with real-world impact, students inevitably see that, without attending to social, religious, economic, and cultural conditions, they are able to accomplish little. Through this experience, they learn that implementing their vision requires more than engineering and technology solutions. Subsequent general education courses take on the intensity of boot camps, imparting crucial survival skills for those trying to understand the best ways to implement their vision and providing invaluable workforce training too. Students read historical and philosophical texts to understand more about different points of view, including some that make them reconsider their early and enthusiastic, but still inchoate, opinions. In a year-long course called "Texts and Meaning," students read difficult literature and learn the skills of interpretation and critical analysis, and then apply those methods to everything else they read—the day's newspapers, pharmaceutical advertisements, terms of service agreements. "With each course they take, they see how education is helping them to think better, to be better citizens and parents and educators. They see that theory and philosophy exist in textbooks—and in problems in the world. You need theory and philosophy to find better solutions."

President Awuah believes that to train leaders of a nation of 27 million people that has been plagued by corruption, you need sustained, ethical entrepreneurship. At Ashesi, students learn about the history of European colonialism and exploitation in Ghana and come to understand that the ingrained culture of what we in the West consider corruption was, for many centuries, the only way for an ambitious Ghanaian to ascend the ranks in colonial society. Awuah insists that no study of ethics today can proceed without a grounding in a rich West African precolonial heritage that goes back at least to the eleventh-century Kingdom of Ashanti.

Writing, critical thinking, cultural and religious history, and languages are part of Ashesi's core vocational curriculum. Students major in computer science, business, management information systems, or engineering and take yearlong seminars on leadership, ethics, and collaboration. Required service learning is also woven into the training in entrepreneurship. We might call this "social entrepreneurship" in America, but Patrick Awuah insists that all entrepreneurship that is ethical is social entrepreneurship.

As at The Red House, Ashesi students are engaged participants in shaping the university itself. In 2008, they were handed the challenge of debating, drafting, and establishing an honor code for themselves and future Ashesi students, an idea inspired by the Quaker principles of Swarthmore. Ashesi became the first African university to create and implement an honor code. The students designed it themselves and insisted that being an Ashesi graduate meant that the code had to be part of their identity, not just in school but also for the rest of their lives. Since then, Ashesi has presented every first-year class the challenge of taking several months to draft and argue over their own honor code. Two-thirds of the class has to agree in order for the university to accept the new code. "There were a few years when it wasn't clear that they would design and sign on to an honor code. They kept us wondering." Awuah laughs. "But in the end, they did. They all did."

In the dozen years since Ashesi University has opened its doors in Accra, it has been recognized as one of the finest universities in West Africa. Its graduates are highly sought after and are often offered multiple positions upon graduation. Nearly all have accepted desirable jobs, mostly in Africa, and with an emphasis on giving back to Ghana and the continent more broadly. As with The Red House students, Ashesi graduates are heavily sought after by their country's government, corporations, nonprofits, NGOs, schools, universities, and beyond. They graduate as programmers and engineers and, almost immediately, advance into leadership positions. They are becoming the faces of a new Ghana.

In September 2015, Patrick Awuah was named a MacArthur Fellow, honored with what is commonly known as a "Genius Award." With all the press from this coveted award, he has remained humble, noting that his new university in Africa was inspired by the best of two US universities. At the same time, he is grateful for the award because he believes that his brand-new university, created from scratch and designed to help students toward a better future, has something important to offer to its older American prototypes. He hopes that Ashesi might inspire a learning revolution in the United States, too. It's time. Having influenced the rest of the world with some of the finest institutions of higher learning, America now should take its own measure, think about where it needs to go next, and remake itself for its own future and that of the planet.

Patrick Awuah would be the first person to admit that his challenge is minor in comparison to the gigantic task of remaking all of higher education in the United States. Yet what he is accomplishing in Ghana—and what so many innovators are making happen in higher education throughout the United States—helps anyone, at any college or university, to imagine their own new possibilities.

What happens if we turn the American university inside out or upside down? How does infrastructure change affect intellectual change? What are the relationships among curriculum, assessment, technology, cocurricular activity, access, equity, entrepreneurship, and social justice? How do we think about each of these things, perhaps starting with one change and building upon it? If Ashesi University can remix the best elements of the American university for the particular urgencies of its time and place, so can any US college or university rethink and remix itself. Because the United States does not have one overarching and uniform national educational system, it is, in one sense, easier for an individual college or university to experiment with bold ideas, to see what makes the most sense and offers the best opportunities for its students, faculty, institution, and community. We can and should glean great ideas from everywhere, including Ghana.

In 1869, Charles Eliot wrote "The New Education" following his sojourn among the universities of Europe. He took what he learned, cherry-picking what worked best for a young, changing nation leading a vast, global industrial transformation. The modern American university he and his colleagues created has had a good run, and continues to offer abundant benefits. But a hundred and fifty years is a long time for all institutions, and especially ones dedicated to training a new generation for its future. It is time now for America's own *ashesi*, a new beginning for higher education.

ON EVERY CAMPUS IN THE UNITED STATES, PEOPLE ARE TRYING, like Patrick Awuah and his colleagues in Ghana or at The Red House at Georgetown, to rethink higher education. To be sure, plenty of people in academe would rather preserve the status quo. However, I believe we are approaching a tipping point, with those dedicated to changing higher education gaining an increasingly prominent voice.

There are obstacles. The American Association of University Professors reports that now over half of the new positions in higher education are filled by part-time workers; in the 1990s, the AAUP was alarmed when that number was 30 percent. Who exactly will lead the necessary transformations in higher education if there are no jobs for innovative, young professors?

There is also the problem of outside interference, of investors calling for change who do not necessarily have students' best interests at heart. We've been burned too many times by the logic of modernizing higher education, which too often really means defunding. When "edupreneurs" look at higher education as a multibillion- or even multitrillion-dollar cash cow, "scholarship, leadership, and citizenship"—Ashesi's three goals—are not their objectives. And as we saw with MOOCs, if the endgame is profit for a few, not a better form of education for all, we don't have a technological solution to an education problem but a technological problem that exacerbates an education problem.

In this book, I have looked beyond the shiniest examples of high-end, abundantly resourced innovation such as the Media Lab at MIT and the design school at Stanford. Most media look to these places for new ideas in higher education. These programs do cutting-edge work, without question, but can they really offer models for 99.5 percent of the 21 million students who do not go to MIT and Stanford? Selectivity limits rather than expands the solutions we can consider and the problems to be solved.

Recently, I was at a board of directors' meeting for Mozilla, the foundation that supports the open-source Firefox browser used by some 500 million people worldwide. On the bedside table in my hotel room in Palo Alto, the epicenter of Stanford University and of Silicon Valley, was a crystal-clear, magnificently minimalist bottle of water. It was called "drink." Its label proclaimed it to be a thousand times cleaner than tap, bottled, or filtered water: "The cleanest water in the world." It cost twenty dollars.

I couldn't help but think of the question posed to the students at Arizona State University: "What will life be like in Phoenix when there is no more water?" The answer to such a question is never going to be a sleek twenty-dollar bottle of "drink."

Silicon Valley thinks it can revolutionize higher education, but it is not clear whether its solutions will actually address the urgent crises we face, either the creeping obsolescence of our institutions of higher education or the broader issues of a changing job market and economy. Silicon Valley has helped create—indeed, consists of—offshoring, automating (and non-taxpaying) global supercorporations and has done little to identify this development as a looming social catastrophe or to propose real solutions to it. Those solutions must address higher education reform, but they also must start *within* higher education. We who are dedicated to meaningful change and who know our institutions best—faculty, students, administrators, staff, parents, alums—need to be working together to design a new education for the treacherous world we live in now.

We need educators and administrators themselves committed to redesigning an ethical, democratic, pragmatic, forward-looking education, one that not only uses technology wisely and creatively but also understands its limits and its impacts and addresses its failings. We need individuals and institutions to work together to rejuvenate an antiquated system for our accelerating times and to ensure that the solutions we craft address the real problems rather than just generating new ones.

The lecture is broken, and so we must think of better ways to incorporate active learning into the classroom.

High-stakes end-of-semester summative, standardized testing is broken, and so we must design challenges that help students to build on what they know and learn from what they don't, growing stronger from each test instead of feeling defeated by an exam score that cannot capture growth or change.

Cost is prohibitive, and so we must adopt new models of credit, such as the Australian graduated repayment model, and far better models of support, including renewed public faith in the importance of supporting higher education for the sake of all our futures—including, for the skeptics, on purely economic grounds.

The traditional professorial and apprentice models don't teach students how to be experts, and so we must look to peer learning and peer mentoring, rich cocurricular experiences, and research to put the student, not the professor or the institution, at the center.

The major in a traditional discipline no longer maps to the complex ways students encounter the world or the jobs and careers of the present and the future, and so we must champion relevant interdisciplinary projects, missions, programs, and goals, across departments and silos of knowledge and expertise.

The exclusivity of more and more of our universities increasingly buffers them from the world beyond, and so we must encourage more partnerships and resource sharing across elite and non-elite institutions, including community and regional colleges, HBCUs, and other minority-serving institutions.

Increasing numbers of students now attend community college, and so we must find better ways to support faculty and advisers there. We must improve systems of credit transfer and course alignment to ensure that students with associate's degrees can go on easily and smoothly to earn bachelor's degrees at four-year institutions.

The situation of adjunct and contingent labor threatens the future of the university, and so we must insist that full-time positions be replaced with full-time faculty.

All of this is doable. Different kinds and levels of intervention are necessary at different institutions, but there are beginnings everywhere. Any ambitious student, at any college or university, can right now find programs and professors who are already charting new frontiers of higher education. We need to champion those leaders, use them as models, and accelerate the change that—often against obstacles—they have launched.

Ultimately, all of these changes serve a larger goal: we must help students toward independent, productive, responsible lives. In the famous words of inventor R. Buckminster Fuller, "We are called to be architects of the future, not its victims."

I've been fortunate to enjoy a long and varied career as a college professor. My first year out of graduate school, I worked three jobs: teaching at night at a liberal arts college where my students, all a decade or two older than me, were professionals returning for a coveted bachelor's degree; teaching newly released prisoners at a community college; and teaching Great Books to Russian and American high-energy physicists, who refused to speak to one another, at Fermi National Accelerator Laboratory. I've taught nuns and priests studying for PhDs in a Franciscan monastery, and I've taught at universities in Japan, Spain, and England. I've taught at a massive public state university and in the Ivy League. I spent most of my career as a faculty member and administrator at Duke University, and now I help teach the next generation of college professors at the nation's largest public institution of graduate training, the Graduate Center at the City University of New York.

Over the course of nearly thirty years in the classroom, I've come to see that students' aspirations don't change all that much, not from place to place, or year to year. They are in college to help prepare for their future life's path, whatever that may be. I've also come to see how, every year, the way we structure and rank higher education is increasingly out of step with the demands of the world they have inherited, the world beyond graduation. So many of the features Charles Eliot and his peers helped design in the wake of the Panic of 1857 and the Civil War, amid the upheavals of industrialization, urbanization, and globalization, have become impediments to learning in our age.

In a moving seven-minute video, "I Am Going to College Because . . . ," thirty students answer the simple question "Why are you in college?" The videographer posing these questions is a student in a leadership program I supervise at CUNY. After finishing her associate's degree, Estefany transferred to Baruch College, one of the most competitive colleges in the CUNY system, where she is completing her double major in business and multimedia design.

Like Estefany, a majority of the two-year and four-year CUNY college students she interviews were born outside the United States and are the first members of their family ever to go to college. During the opening credits of the video, Frank Sinatra croons "New York, New York" and an American flag appears. Then small flags appear designating the birthplace of each speaker: China, Ecuador, Bangladesh, Mexico, South Korea, Dominican Republic, Indonesia, Puerto Rico, Pakistan, Colombia, Yemen, Myanmar, Peru. Some of the students seem to be traditional college age, others look to be in their thirties or forties.

Why do they go to college? "I go to college because . . . I want to do something I love; I want to help others; I seek equality and social justice; I care about people and want to serve others; I am a woman and want to see more women in STEM fields; I am the first person in my family to be able to write my own name and I want to write it proudly and for good; I want to be useful to myself and everyone else; I want to help children; I want to contribute to my community; I want to make my family proud; I want a more successful future."

The goals of achieving a better, engaged, responsible future are shared by many students, at every institution, at every level of society. Nathaniel, Harvard Class of 2015, is currently working at a nonprofit and applying to combined law and graduate school (JD-PhD) programs. I ask him the same question that Estefany asked her classmates: Why go to college? "Everyone spends a lifetime embedded in a world that they invariably shape by the fact of their existence," Nathaniel says. "We should be given the tools we need to shape it responsibly and to recognize the beauty surrounding us." He hopes, in his career, to contribute to that goal. "I'm interested in how we create political-economic institutions that are resilient to political shocks, how we can structure economic and political life so people are able to pursue their aims in life."

When I ask him what at Harvard most prepared him for the kind of life he hopes to lead, he singles out three things: his debate team, a "community of friends who are intellectually engaged and willing to challenge my beliefs," and writing a senior research thesis. "I love digging through archival material to craft something that is both art and argument," he says. At Harvard, he earned a degree in Social Studies, a small, interdisciplinary concentration that allowed him to design his own major around a research agenda of his choosing. He loved it. When I ask him whether there is anything he would change about his education, he says there isn't a lot he would change, but he regrets that, because of the rigidity of the GPA on which his JD-PhD application partly depends, he wasn't able to take many courses in other fields, where he would have had to compete with students who were specialists in those fields. It's a valid critique. Why not allow students to explore more widely, perhaps taking some courses as Pass/Fail? It would hardly take a revolution at Eliot's university to make a simple structural change that would support the best students in their boldest choices.

At a recent family dinner, I had the pleasure of talking with six students, all either in college or just starting at graduate or medical school. Together they represent eight different colleges and universities: Dickinson, Drexel, Hampshire, University of Maryland, University of Pittsburgh, Rutgers, Skidmore, and the Philadelphia University of the Sciences. They were eager to talk about what college means to them and what they know has to change.

"The first thing I'd change is how much college costs," Claire says emphatically, "and maybe I'd have them guarantee me a job after college that pays $40,000 a year or more so I can pay off my loans." She quickly adds that she hopes to have a career that is satisfying and contributes to society, but that's a vague goal compared to the pressure she feels from mounting bills. Having taken a gap year before college to work as an au pair in Germany, she's seen the freedom, idealism, and sense of life mission of German students whose higher education is almost entirely free. "It's harder to have dreams when you're worrying about debt," she says. The other students agree. They all hold jobs, including Ethan, who works part-time at a local restaurant even during his notoriously challenging first semester of medical school.

When I ask what, other than the high cost, they would like to change about college, they are unanimous in wishing there was more choice and flexibility. "There are so many courses I'd like to take in the humanities," Kaitlin, a mechanical-engineering major, laments, "but my program makes that almost impossible." As a workaround, she enrolled in a special program, the Maryland Scholars, that allows her to pick a track complementary to her major. She chose the arts track; she is living mostly with arts students, attending a host of cocurricular arts events, has built a website on which she charts and reviews her activities, and is able to stretch herself considerably beyond the more limited world she previously inhabited.

Every one of the science students expresses a similar wish for more courses in the humanities. At Pitt, Ethan took on extra courses each semester so he could finish his pre-med major early and spend senior year taking philosophy, comparative religion, ethics, and other humanities courses outside pre-med. Connie, who is studying to be a physician's assistant at the University of the Sciences, eloquently expresses the same urgent need. "I work in the medical field because I want to help people," Connie says. "But almost all my courses are about scientific 'subject matter' in the abstract. They barely mention how people's lives and cultures influence their health. I'd like more '*people* matter.'"

Alyssa, a major in animation, film, and production design at Hampshire College, says she wishes "there were more opportunities to connect the theory I'm learning with actual practice in different kinds of jobs." Her goal is to be an "imagineer," an animator or designer in the entertainment industry. Like the other students, she's found a workaround through internships and online courses that she takes over the summer, filling in what she isn't able to fit into her regular curriculum.

"I wish college did a better job of helping us to prepare for life," Kaitlin adds. When I ask what she means by that, all of the students chime in. They'd love more support connecting the abstract academic subjects in their majors to everyday life. They want their science programs to connect more directly to the problems science is supposed to solve. They wish there was somewhere in college where you could address actual life issues.

"You can get an A in microeconomics and not know how to balance a checkbook. Or you can major in political science and be unprepared for the ways your neighbors voted in the last election," Claire says.

"It would be good if there were more support for surviving school," Youki says. Many of his classes have collaborative projects, but no one shows you how to collaborate successfully. Too often, one person ends up doing most of the work. "Or how to manage roommates," Alyssa chimes in. I laugh; of course effective collaboration and living with others are two of the hardest skills to learn at any point in one's life and work.

"Basically, we all want to take 'How to Be an Adult 101,'" Claire quips.

As beginning college students or adults returning to school, at various economic levels, and at vastly different institutions—from LaGuardia Community College to Harvard—students are all asking for the same thing: a new education designed to prepare them to lead a meaningful life in the years after college. Not a single one of them clamors for the kind of higher education revolution touted in the *New York Times* or the *Wall Street Journal* by higher education's great "disrupters." In an evening of energetic conversation, these supposedly revolutionary technological innovations in higher education don't even come up—no MOOCs, no content management systems, no learning measured "keystroke by keystroke," and definitely no "skills" education if that means vocational skills without context. They want a flexible, expansive curriculum that allows more opportunities for intellectual exploration and personal growth and that prepares them not just for jobs but for consequential careers and for what they all know will be a bumpy road ahead.

All of these possibilities exist, in ways big and small, at our institutions. Like the great and bold education revolutionaries of the late nineteenth century, we need to use the best models we have and build on those. We can't just leave it for our most industrious students to find the most innovative programs and courses. We need to lead and support change. We need to revolutionize our universities, vigorously support them as a public good, and redesign them so that they are also good for the public.

The new education must prepare our students to thrive in a world of flux, to be ready no matter what comes next. It must empower them to be leaders of innovation and to be able not only to adapt to a changing world but also to change the world. That is the core requirement of the new education.

All the rest is merely elective.

TEN TIPS FOR GETTING THE MOST OUT OF YOUR COLLEGE EXPERIENCE

You can get a great college education almost anywhere. And the same is true for a bad one. With a little research and planning, you can make the most of college while preserving your sanity and making progress toward your degree. Here's how.

1. *Diversify.* College is one of the most varied worlds you are likely to inhabit. The rest of life, before and after college, tends to come presorted. Even a small college likes to admit students from as many backgrounds as possible and offer the widest possible range of courses and cocurricular activities. Treat college like a foreign country, an amusement park, or a museum. Indulge! Take chances! You may come up with your life's passion (or partner) where you least expect it.

2. *Mitigate risk while taking risks.* Find out ways that your college supports experimentation. If your university offers pass/no pass courses,

use those for your boldest choices. If you are an engineer, use that one precious elective (engineering schools are notoriously heavy on requirements) on a studio art class simply for the opportunity to spend a semester with creative students who solve problems with an entirely different set of assumptions and tools than you do. Conversely, if you are an artist, why not take a programming course? Learning how to learn requires being exposed to different ways of knowing and working with those with different skills and visions than your own.

3. *Find a great prof and take advantage of all they offer.* Great profs don't just lecture well—they challenge you to think in new ways about new things. They don't give answers; they ask deep questions. Visit their office hours, even if you are in a lecture class with four hundred other students (you would be surprised how few students do this). And if a favorite prof offers a quirky seminar, take it—even if it doesn't fit your major and your requirements. It may be what nourishes you during a dreary term of required courses when you're checking off too many boring boxes. (Note: This has a practical side, too. A professor who knows you well is far more likely to write you a good letter of recommendation.)

4. *Shop around for the right adviser—and use them. Often.* A great prof helps you to think boldly and ask new questions. A great adviser answers questions and helps you navigate bureaucracies and requirements that can undermine your success. (Rarely is a great prof also a great adviser. Each is an expert in a different realm.) Sometimes you get lucky and the adviser assigned to you is great—stick with them. Other times, you need to ask around, check out the campus Teaching and Learning Center, the dean of students, and the mentors or live-in faculty in the dorms. Ask other students who helped them the most, and see whether that person works for you. Or ask the departmental administrative assistant—often this person can steer you to the adviser who is magic at cutting red tape.

5. *Start an evolving, personal résumé as soon as you get to college and use it as your personal guide on your life path.* If you literally write out your life goals at the beginning of your college career, you can then update your résumé each semester, revisit your goals, and track the ways you are changing and growing. An evolving, personal résumé gives you a good baseline for seeing the variance between what you hoped to achieve and what you are doing. You can add in cocurricular events, internships, workshops, and other experiences that were meaningful to you and delete the ones that you felt wasted your time. You get to decide what does or does not belong on your personal résumé. Far better than filling in the requirements for a major, your evolving résumé helps you think about what you require to lead a good life—in college and beyond—and what you still need to do to get there.

6. *Make your major minor.* Look for a major in the field you think you might want to pursue as a career, but also look for one with the fewest requirements so, structurally, you can keep your options open, explore other fields and interests, and take all the electives you want in your major in the areas you want. Majors are designed by specialists in an academic field; they rarely map to what an actual job in the field requires (unless you are planning to be a college professor in that field). Even then, graduate schools like to see evidence of independent thinking, and so do employers. See whether your college offers a self-designed or topical major that crosses disciplinary boundaries. Most college students graduate without finding their life's passion (80 percent, according to one recent survey). Expanding your options might help you find something you never considered before.

7. *Form a study group.* The best research on college success—whether at a top ten university or in a remedial class at a community college—indicates that being in a study group is the single most significant way to improve your performance, sustain your motivation, and keep you on track to success. As with an adviser, you may need

to try out a few before you find the right group, but it makes every aspect of college easier and even offers a support network for after you graduate, too.

8. *Know when to find a tutor.* If you are required to take a course in an area where you feel shaky or face an important exam (LSAT, GRE, and so forth), be as efficient as possible. Many a student has dropped out of college because of one soulless requirement. Don't let something cynical defeat you. Find a tutor or a testing service— don't even think about it as an intellectual exercise. "Teaching to the test" is an intellectual waste. You won't change that. So do it as quickly and painlessly as possible so that it doesn't undermine all the exciting things you are doing elsewhere in college.

9. *Learn beyond the classroom.* Internships and classes with experiential components are ideal ways to see how the field you are studying translates into jobs in the real world. So many questions about careers never come up in a classroom. Do you like to work alone or in groups? Do you like to spend time at a screen (reading, writing, calculating, coding) or doing things (meetings, sales)? Do you like speaking in public? Do you prefer to work inside or outside in nature? Dressed up in business clothes or casual? Do you like people to be clear about what you need to do or would you rather blaze your own course? Do you like cities or want to live in a small town, in the United States or abroad? Do you like to travel or hate getting on planes? What level of material wealth makes you happy? How many hours a week do you want to work? What kind of social role do you like? Are you an activist or do you prefer to go by the rules, whoever makes them? These questions are rarely asked in school. They make a difference to your future success.

10. *When it's time to submit an actual, professional résumé, remember your first reader may be an algorithm.* All of the exciting things you have learned and mastered and accomplished in college will impress your second reader—the human one. Getting past the machine that

does the first sort can be tricky. Take advantage of the career center at your school to find out the best models for résumés and cover letters (two difficult genres to master). You can find out how to customize your résumé and job application to accurately reflect your skills while matching the exact key words in a job description. You can also find out how to balance that D in Calc with the prize you won at the city hackathon. The humans who have to wade through the résumés selected by algorithms will be just as impressed by strong interests and skills supplemented by bold experiences and curiosity as by grades. All the extras you gather in college add up to a picture of you as the inquisitive, fearless, and ambitious person you are. Congratulations! You are gaining an education that will serve you for life.

TEN TIPS FOR TRANSFORMING
ANY CLASSROOM FOR ACTIVE,
STUDENT-CENTERED LEARNING

WHETHER YOU TEACH IN A RADICALLY INNOVATIVE PROGRAM OR AT a traditional institution in a course with a prescribed syllabus, you can immediately transform your classroom into an active, student-centered learning space where your students learn how to learn. These methods are all designed to offer students the opportunity to take responsibility for and creative leadership of their own learning. (Note: All these techniques work in meetings, too. I've done several in team-building workshops with CEOs of Fortune 100 companies.)

1. *Think-Pair-Share.* This works best with index cards (optional) and a timer. I like to do T-P-S in a formal way to ensure that everyone has a chance to speak and everyone has a chance to sit quietly and listen. (a) *Think:* Set a timer for 90 seconds. Each student jots out a quick, low-stakes answer to an open-ended question the prof asks (ex: What was the single most provocative/disagreeable/brilliant/inspiring

comment you read in this week's assignment?). (b) *Pair:* Everyone, even the introverts, should have a chance to be heard in the classroom. When the timer sounds, set it for another 90 seconds and, this time, have the students pair up and take turns reading and listening to one another's answers. Then they can discuss and come up with one synthesized item to read to the class. (c) *Share:* Go around the room (if less than forty students) and have one person from each pair share their pair's comment with the group. Whatever you do next in class, this method ensures that everyone is involved, alert, and already thinking across a range of ideas. If you have more than forty students, use an online collaborative tool (such as Google Docs) and have pairs record their comments. You can project and start your lecture from the list students compiled. (d) *Communicate:* I like to add a public component and have students share these comments on a public blog.

2. *Question Stacking.* Ask students to raise their hands in response to a question and write down the name of everyone with a hand up. Have everyone put their hands down and call on people in order. No one asks a second question until each person responds or withdraws the question because someone else answered it already. We know seminars can replicate inequality even more than lectures, by seeming to be open but privileging those who are best at mimicking or mirroring the intellectual style, language, or even demographic characteristics (race, gender, sexuality, region, religion, etc.) of the professor. (Admit it: we've all been to a lecture where we know in advance who will be waving a hand and dominating the Q and A. That happens in class too.)

3. *Everybody Raise Your Hand.* This is the method used by the polymath, self-taught speculative fiction writer Samuel Delany. Whenever you ask a question, have every student raise a hand. You call on anyone. They can answer or say, "I don't understand the question" (in which case you ask "Why?" and start a discussion there) or say, "I don't know the answer—but I bet Derek/Dahlia does." This simple technique asserts that "I don't know" is a starting place, not a source

of shame. (Your students will also prepare more if they know they are responsible for every question, every class, even if they don't know the answer.)

4. *Interview.* Have students work in pairs and interview one another. I like to have them ask, "What three things are you most worried will be hard about this class?" and "What three things can you contribute to our class that we don't know about?" and do a skill pairing on the first day of class. You can also use the technique throughout the semester to ask about the assignment or problem sets or whatever is on the syllabus for the day. Example: "What did you find hardest to understand about the assignment for today? What are you sure you have down cold and can teach someone else about today's assignment?" Have them together prepare what they think will be an interesting question, challenge, or problem to present to the whole class to address or solve. In a large lecture, you can sort out the kinds of questions by groups and have them work in a group on the topic.

5. *Class Constitution.* On the first day of class, set up a collaborative online tool and have students write a collective "class constitution" and "terms of service" agreement for the class. This is ideal in a class of fewer than fifty, but we did it for eighteen thousand in our MOOC. I typically get students started by offering a document written by others that they can edit or by putting up bullet points of all the minimal class requirements and letting them determine everything else. I encourage students to begin with their loftiest principles ("life, liberty, and the pursuit of happiness" is one model) and then think about how they want one another to participate and contribute to those goals. I even have students create assessment systems, such as contract grading and student peer review and analysis of one another's work.

6. *Collective Syllabus Design.* Also on the first day, I like to leave the room and have the students design all or part of a syllabus. I've done this for entering freshmen and for doctoral students, with equal

success, in a range of courses across the humanities, social sciences, and computational sciences. Sometimes I create the first half of the syllabus and challenge the students to create the last half; other times, I might have one required text in each unit and have them add the rest. Students have consistently been ambitious and rigorous—sometimes more than I would want to be. One time, in Mapping the Futures of Higher Education (https://futuresinitiative.org/about-mapping-futures/), my co-teacher and I literally left the room on the first day of class and had students structure, organize, and design the course. We were not disappointed.

7. *Collaborative Note Taking.* Set up a Google Doc or other collaborative tool and have students take notes together in class, including with a back channel for conversation during class, where they also add links and other items they find in web searches. This puts a twist on the "laptop or no laptop" question. You can also create extra-credit reward systems for those who contribute most, require that everyone contribute something, have students vote up and down ideas, and find other ways that the laptop becomes an instrument of learning, not—like the school newspaper of old—a form of diversion and escape.

8. *Collaborative Projects with Peer Assessment.* It is now commonplace to assign group collaborative projects. Almost everyone hates them because the diligent end up doing the work for the whole group. (Note: This is also true in the business world.) I begin collaborative projects by having the group come up with a list of six to ten contributions that need to happen for the collaboration to work. These can be "fire starter" (coming up with great ideas), "implementer," "budget master," "technology maven," "design guru," or anything else deemed central to the success of the project. Before each class session, students work privately, read over the list, and award no more than one peer badge in each category to one member of their team. The group reassembles and everyone looks at the list. The prof circulates and looks at these too. It's easy to see who is and isn't collaborating, what needs to happen next to rectify any problems, and how.

9. *Exit Tickets.* Whether for six or six hundred students, at the end of each class have students write out one thing that they don't understand/want to discuss more/disagree with, and the like. Have students sign their cards. It's a substitute for taking roll or giving pop quizzes, allows for reflection (the single most important element of learning), and is a great way to start the next class.

10. *Public Contribution to Knowledge.* Students work best when they know their work is for their future beyond school, not just for the test, and when they realize their work contributes. For the last decade, I've refused to assign students any term or research project that they do only for me for the purpose of a grade. I ask students to find a way for their work to have a bigger impact and value beyond the course, whether that is posting on a class blog or editing or augmenting Wikipedia entries or tutoring local kids (or first-year students) in what they have mastered or in actually using their knowledge to effect some kind of change in the world.

The best part of student-centered learning designed to prepare students for a complex world outside the classroom and after graduation is that, once you let students begin, they will lead you to many different ideas, solutions, and applications. *Let's get started!*

TEN TIPS FOR TRANSFORMING YOUR INSTITUTION

ANY INSTITUTION LOOKING TO BETTER SERVE STUDENTS CAN SIM-
ply run through the list of reforms institutionalized between 1865
and 1925; given the history from which they emerged, any of these
should be up for serious reconsideration. We cannot change structural inequality or ineffectiveness with goodwill alone. We need to
design new structures with equality and effectiveness at their core.
Here are ten places where we might start thinking about making
structural change:

1. *Change the faculty reward system.* Effective change in higher ed
requires faculty willing to work with university administrators to approve, support, and implement change. It's a lengthy and tedious
process. Given the current academic reward system—where raises
and promotion depend on publication of a university press book or
peer-reviewed journal articles—faculty have little incentive to dedi-
cate their time to institutional change (or to teaching, for that matter).

Let's change that! First, we need to rename "service" as "institutional leadership" or another respectful title. (We know how badly our society treats service workers.) Instead of a rigid, one-dimensional reward system, faculty could have the equivalent of contract grading while they undertake institutional duties. If someone pledges to work hard for five years to contribute to a change that benefits an institution, that work should be rewarded. If publication is the sole, unbendable criterion for recognition, an analysis of their work (process and product) published on a university website or in a professional publication should count as interdisciplinary research. If you want serious institutional change, you need to take seriously the ways you reward your faculty for dedicating themselves to that effort.

2. *Eliminate the diversity tax.* The current faculty reward system contributes to faculty inequality. By gender and by race, the workload of unrecognized, unremunerated actual and affective labor is not equally shared. Currently, about 45 percent of students in higher ed are students of color; only about 25 percent of faculty are. If your institution trumpets diversity and calls forth the same scholars of color for every photo op, for every committee assignment, for heading every new initiative for diversifying the institution, and for advising and recruiting your growing cohort of students of color, you are taxing, not encouraging, diversity. Change that. Offer the equivalent of extra course credit or time off or monetary compensation for extra labor. Period.

3. *Adopt Equitable Admission and Support Systems, and create a new, combined office of "Admissions and Career Placement."* Making the SATs, ACTs, and GREs optional is a step toward equity. Recruit the best students from all secondary schools—not just from affluent "college prep" public school districts and private schools. And make sure every student receives the level of support, tutoring, and advising that affluent students routinely receive and expect. Advising is especially important to help first-generation college students navigate what Philip W. Jackson long ago dubbed the "hidden cur-

riculum" of higher ed, the unspoken values, expectations, habits, and norms that govern interactions among students, faculty, staff, and administrators and that can be unfamiliar to students who do not come from white-collar backgrounds. By combining "Admissions and Career Placement," institutions can put the same energy, values, and mission that are espoused for admissions into career placement. Success should not just be judged by who is recruited but by who succeeds—who graduates, where they go after graduation, and how they progress in their careers. For student success, the beginning and the end of the process should match, which requires dedicated support to each and every student along the way.

4. *End distinctions between "full-time" and "part-time" students.* Now, most states and most schools require full-time status for scholarships, athletics, awards, and honors. Forty percent of today's students work thirty or more hours a week at paid jobs. Many older students also have childcare and other family duties. It's punitive to make a scholarship depend on full-time status, especially as tuition and other costs rise. It's also institutionally punitive to make "graduation rates"—a measure calculated by first-time, full-time students—the metric. Those institutions with the most diverse (in all ways) student body will appear to be failing, rather than flexible, by that metric. Completion rate is a more accurate and fairer measure.

5. *Fix transfer.* Right now, students pay a penalty when they try to gain credit for their community college courses at a four-year college or university. Although some systems (notably, the University of California and the California State University systems) do a good job at making transfer equitable, on average, community college students lose 20 percent of their credits when they move on to a four-year institution. Students also lose credits when they transfer from one college to another. Stop it!

6. *Redesign general education that matters.* If general education at your institution is a confusing smorgasbord of disconnected

disciplinary areas (pick one from Column A, two from Column B), you are losing your one chance to show students (and faculty) how knowledge is connected. After material conditions, the second most common reason students drop out of college is they don't know why they are there. An incoherent introduction to college exacerbates a sense of purposelessness. General education should be the ideal place for students (and faculty) to make intellectual connections. The pandemic wasn't just a health crisis but an economic, social, racial, gender, geographical, political, and media crisis. Most big events ripple across academic, disciplinary boundaries. General education should give students the intellectual tools for applying the specific knowledge they gain in their major to the world beyond. Include experiential learning early to show students why and how their learning connects to their communities and the world. Emphasize higher-order skills (communication, critical thinking, collaboration, project management, and so forth) that will serve them for a lifetime. Follow the example of Ashesi University in Ghana and have the general ed sequence include an ambitious capstone project, including a list of questions students don't yet have the knowledge to answer. Finally, desegregate and decolonize the curriculum: make sure what students learn in general education is diverse, current, and socially engaged in every way.

7. *Reevaluate "seat time" as the metric for measuring competence.* When I began an #AcademicTwitter discussion of "seat time" as a measure of achievement or competence, one witty person responded: "If we're measuring the amount of time a learner's butt is in a seat, we're measuring the wrong end of the learner!" An airplane pilot, brain surgeon, or dancer may need to log a certain number of hours to hone their reflexes. In most fields, time spent in a classroom has zero correlation with achievement. Some courses work best in one-month intensive chunks; others are best spread out over a year—or three years. It's also ludicrous to measure faculty workload exclusively by the Carnegie credit hour. Micro-credentials, intensive courses, certificates, and digital badging are all options. Find a better, more

equitable way that works for your institution—and possibly also has dividends for how you use your own resources (classroom space, weekends and vacation times, international plans, collaborations with other institutions, team teaching, lab sharing, peer mentoring structures, studio space, etc.).

8. *Engage in serious faculty development in pedagogy theory and practice so faculty can understand and master the most effective, equitable, active, engaged learning and teaching methods.* We have over a thousand studies now about the effectiveness of active learning, but it's rare for any college instructor to have read these or anything else about pedagogy. Most of us teach the way we were taught. We have abundant research on the effectiveness of active learning for every student at every level. We know a great lecture, like a great sermon, can inspire us and stir our emotions. But it doesn't actually teach students how to become experts themselves. A lecture doesn't help us with the deep learning required to retain or apply key insights, information, methods, or skills to later intellectual or personal situations. Lectures need to be translated into active, participatory learning opportunities. We need "pedagogy research leaves" and other ways of supporting faculty willing to spend their time understanding better ways to teach.

9. *Rank institutions by social mobility, not just average income earned upon graduation.* The work of Raj Chetty and others has shown that most of higher education exacerbates income inequality. Princeton, for example, was long lauded as the university whose graduates earned the highest salaries; Chetty's team calculated that the families of Princeton students were also among the nation's wealthiest. By contrast, most of the schools at City University of New York rank very high in moving students from the lowest income quartile to the highest. If social mobility is our goal, we should be celebrating those schools that achieve it. However, this, like all other issues, is structural. Without proper funding of higher education, social mobility will always be more ideal than reality and, for private institutions,

seeking wealthy future donors will always be a priority. The whole system is connected—from public funding to admissions to rankings to donor relations and endowment investments—and needs serious rethinking.

10. *Do what we say we do—aspire to be our best selves.* Everyone: Go read your institution's mission statement! If we examine our institutional structures against our own expressed mission, we will see the mismatch. No student has ever gone to college because of a citation index or because of "academic analytics." We know our values. We know what attracts students to our campus. All we need to do is do what we say we do.

Bonus: *Re-fund higher education.* Right now, we're seeing various proposals, initiatives, and programs around the country designed to make tuition free or affordable and to minimize (or erase) student tuition debt. Equally, colleges and universities are becoming aware of student poverty. An estimated quarter of all current students face food or housing insecurity. We need to reinvest in our children's futures—in our society's future. *Now.*

ACKNOWLEDGMENTS

I'M CONVINCED BAD STUDENTS MAKE GOOD TEACHERS. ONCE, AT A meeting of some of higher education's top innovators, we were all surprised by a warm-up exercise that revealed that most of us had been suspended at least once from high school. Those of us who struggled through school often understand that college can be a second chance. Perhaps because we were not destined to be academics, we don't view college as an apprenticeship for the purpose of creating future college professors but as a place of options and challenges that can help each and every student find a productive, responsible path beyond college.

On my pathway to being a good teacher, I must first thank my ever patient father, Paul C. Notari, who stuck by his rebellious and dyslexic teenager long after others would have given up. If my father had not been willing to make the extra ninety-minute detour every day on his way to and from work to drive me to the high school at which I had been accepted after getting kicked out of my own, this book would not exist. A son of immigrants, a World War II veteran, my father believes that his life was transformed by the GI Bill and an opportunity to go to college to become an engineer. My second appreciation goes to Mrs. Lipman, the teacher who believed in me when I was driving my other teachers mad. She sponsored me at the prestigious high school to which she had moved, then took the risk of nominating me for a National Council of Teachers of English Award, over more appropriate students, one of the national awards that ensured I would go to college.

At Duke University, where I taught for most of my academic career, my official, professional journey toward reimagining higher education began in earnest with a brief letter in my fax machine (it was 1998). I was at a crossroads in my career, contemplating leaving Duke to take a chaired professorship in constitutional-era history and culture when Duke president Nannerl Keohane and the late John Strohbehn, the provost, presented me with a tantalizing alternative: stay at Duke and become the first vice provost for Interdisciplinary Studies at Duke or anywhere. It was the most creative, innovative opportunity imaginable, working with faculty and students from every part of the university to create new programs that spanned the usual divides and silos of the undergraduate departments and professional schools, as well as helping to launch a new art museum, a science and technology center, a humanities institute, and a performing arts center that spanned town and gown. After a particularly challenging meeting, Nan once jokingly described my job description as "breaking things and making things." I've never looked back, and my gratitude to her, as a model of bold dignity and excellence, remains enormous.

I also thank Duke alumna Melinda French Gates, who decided to move from her leadership role in technology innovation to philanthropy the same month that I became vice provost. Her financial support—as well as her intellectual rigor and commitment to higher education—was inestimable and inspiring in every way. Thanks also go to Peter Lange, the provost with whom I worked for seven years, and Dick Brodhead, the president with whom I worked in my final two years of administration, as well as all the faculty, students, and administrative colleagues who worked hard to make good, important things happen. All of you have convinced me that change is possible. Sometimes, it's not nearly as hard as we think it will be.

I moved from Duke University to the Graduate Center, City University of New York, in August 2014, mainly because of my conviction that no society can flourish without a profound investment in public higher education. One cannot champion higher education as a public good from within what a friend calls the "velvet walls" of a handsomely funded and expensive private university. CUNY sends six times more students from the lower to the middle class than the combined "Ivies Plus" (the eight Ivy League schools plus MIT, Stanford, Chicago, and Duke). Since coming to CUNY, I have come to admire, deeply, the commitments of faculty, administrators, and students who work to deliver and to gain the best and most innovative education possible against financial restrictions that those at well-funded institutions cannot conceive. CUNY's can-do spirit is at the core of this book. For making this inspiring move possible, I thank President Emeritus William Kelly (now Mellon Director of the New York Public Library), President Chase Robinson, and Interim Provost Louise Lennihan. Chancellor J. B. Milliken has been unfailingly supportive. I also thank Provost Joy Connolly and all my great CUNY colleagues and students, including David Olan, Mario DiGangi, as well as colleagues Matt Gold, Steve Brier, Herman Bennett, Robert Reid-Pharr, Ruth Wilson Gilmore, David Joselit, Kandice Chuh, Ofelia Garcia, Duncan Faherty, Tony Picciano, and Eric Lott.

Thanks to the Internet and social media, I have had thousands of partners in writing this book. Almost everything here has been learned, tried, experimented with, modified, discussed, or implemented via online discussions and collaborations with a multitude of faculty members, administrators, students, technology innovators, and the public at large.

In 2002, I joined a cadre of dedicated scholars and technology innovators to found an open, online network dedicated to education innovation (it turns out, the world's first and now oldest academic social network), the Humanities, Arts, Science, and Technology Alliance and Collaboratory (hastac.org, or "haystack"). Now, with over fifteen thousand network members and untold numbers of users, HASTAC has inspired every word of this book. We have never collected dues or had a corporate sponsor or even an ad, and we continue through the enormous goodwill and ideas of vast numbers of intellectual contributors plus the financial support of several institutions of higher education (Stanford briefly, then Duke University for well over a decade, and, since 2014, the Graduate Center at the City College of New York) and nonprofit funding agencies (Digital Promise, the National Science Foundation, and, through administering the annual Digital Media and Learning Competition, the John D. and Catherine T. MacArthur Foundation). Over twelve hundred graduate and undergraduate student HASTAC Scholars have informed my thinking about the future of higher education with literally hundreds of blogs and forum posts each month dedicated to "Changing the Way We Teach and Learn." Special thanks go to the graduate student directors Erin Gentry Lamb, Fiona Barnett (our leader for several years), Kalle Westerling, and Allison Guess.

Mandy Dailey, Sheryl Grant, and Demos Orphanides have been daily companions in the writing of this book, as they worked to keep HASTAC's busy human network and cutting-edge Drupal-powered website functioning. They have taught me the power of collaboration and the way to transform bold ideas into effective, if virtual, realities. Dozens of scholars, artists, and scientists have served on HASTAC's steering committee, and I cannot think of a single idea in this book that was not deepened and enriched by my interactions with all of them.

At the Futures Initiative, at the Graduate Center, CUNY, thanks go to my colleagues and partners in academic transformation, Katina Rogers, Lauren Melendez, Kaysi Holman, Celi Cuello Lebron, Kitana Ananda, and all of the Futures Initiative graduate student fellows and faculty fellows, as well as the faculty, administrators, mentors, and students in the groundbreaking CUNY Humanities Alliance, a partnership between the Graduate Center and LaGuardia Community College funded with insight and originality by the Andrew W. Mellon Foundation. Day in and day out, you all amaze me with your ideas and commitments.

One reason I am optimistic that change is possible in higher education is the warmth with which my contrarian ideas have been received over the last decade. I cannot even begin to thank individually all the people, institutions, professional associations, nonprofits, think tanks, and corporations, in the United States and around the world, who have invited me to give keynote addresses, workshops, or plenaries. I have learned something crucial at each stop. I have learned from the dozens of people I interviewed in the course of writing this book, only a handful of whom are presented in the book. And my greatest debt, always, is to the thousands of students who have taught me pretty much everything that I know about learning. Again, my thanks to all of you. In this book, you are anonymous or pseudonymous for your privacy. You are indelibly and forever named in my heart.

I have also learned immeasurably from all of the colleagues at the John D. and Catherine T. MacArthur Foundation, especially those who designed and developed the Digital Media and Learning Initiative, including President Julia Stasch, Connie Yowell, my partner at the Digital Media and Learning Competition David Theo Goldberg, and dozens of colleagues, competition winners, and others exploring the boundaries of the new education. My board colleagues at Mozilla, including Chair Mitchell Baker and Executive Director Mark Surman, continue to inspire me in every way. I cannot begin to say how much I have learned from their commitment to a better, more open Internet and greater web literacy for all. At Data and Society, under the fearless leadership of danah boyd, we tackle complex topics, such as privacy and automation, with an aim of contributing to a better society. On the National Council for the Humanities, under the leadership first of Jim Leach and then William "Bro" Adams, I continue to be inspired by my colleagues in the humanities whose ideas give context, depth, and richness to our society. Although I cannot name you all here, I thank you deeply for all you do and all you give.

Futures Initiative fellow and English doctoral student Danica Savonick has been a superb research assistant and an insightful and knowledgeable colleague at every stage of this book. I have also learned much from her own original research on CUNY's open admissions programs in the 1970s. Lisa Tagliaferri and Jessica Murray helped with technical support, and Elizabeth Goetz lent invaluable professionalism during the copyediting and proofreading of the final manuscript.

My agent, Deirdre Mullane, is as creative, brilliant, dedicated, and feisty as any agent could possibly be. My editor, Dan Gerstle of Basic Books, has been a constant interlocutor and guiding hand. In an era when it is thought that editors don't really edit anymore, he has been as wise and supportive a spirit as any author could dream of. From Basic Books, I also thank Nicole Caputo, Betsy DeJesu, Allie Finkel, Ann Kirchner, Linda Mark, Carrie Napolitano, Courtney Nobile, Christina Palaia, Liz Tzetzo, Elisa Rivlin, and Melissa Veronesi who helped make this book a reality.

Many friends and colleagues offered sustained and specific contributions to this book and its author: Anne Allison, the late Srinivas Aravamudan, Dan Ariely, Anne Balsamo, Lauren Berlant, Jackie Brown, John Seely Brown, Simone Browne, Constance Carroll, Ann Marie Cauce, Barbara Claypole-White, Tressie McMillan Cottom, Jade Davis, Petra Dierkes-Thrun, David Eng, Steve Fagin, Caitlin Fisher, Michael Gillespie, Inderpal Grewal, Macarena Gomez-Barris, Larry Grossberg, Jack Halberstam, Jessamyn Hatcher, Sharon Holland, Annie Howell, Kellie Jones, Caren Kaplan, Ranji Khanna, Ann Kirschner, Julie Thompson Klein, Adeline Koh, the late Celeste Castillo Lee, Liz Losh, Lisa Lowe, Eric Manheimer, Richard Marciano, Tara McPherson, Sean Michael Morris, Tim Murray, Lisa Nakamura, Alondra Nelson, Chris Newfield, Charlie Piot, Guthrie Ramsey, Teemu Ruskola, Robert A. Scott, Nishant Shah, Jesse Stommel, Diana Taylor, Terry Vance, Priscilla Wald, Laura Wexler, and Kathy Woodward. I also thank all those who helped or hosted me on two international research trips, to Finland and Japan. I thank especially Rebecca Jennison, Aki Kinjo, Seiki Kinjo, Shin Mizukoshi, Ichiro Okamoto, Maryvonne Okamoto, and Naomo Okamoto, and, in Finland, Saku Tuominen and Mikko Tolonen. I fear that in trying to list these contributors I will have left out many who have inspired my thinking over the last decades, so generous have hundreds of educators been with their thoughts and feedback over the years. That said, in the end, only I am responsible for the ideas in this book, some of which are sure to rankle even the best of friends and colleagues.

The first draft of this book was written during a brilliant month at the incomparable Bogliasco Foundation, in Liguria, Italy, when I was recovering from a catastrophic illness. The gracious staff, the exquisite scenery, the healthy and delicious food, and the wonderful congeniality of the fellows in residence restored me and set this book on its path again. I thank Laura Harrison, Ivana Folle, and Alessandra Natale and fellows Alberto Caruso, Kia Corthron, Ramona Diaz, Julia Jacquette, Helen Lochhead, Dina Nayeri, and Renata Shepherd.

My loving thanks, as always, goes to Charles R. Davidson and Susan Brown and Gavin and Morag, to Karina Davidson, to Sharon, Mary Lou, Kris, Sage, and Christina Notari, and Paul and Marlene Notari, and to all of my beloved and (of course) brilliant nieces and nephews in or about to be in college and who are rooting for the new education. Finally, my constant thanks and love go to the best editor, interlocutor, and loving partner that anyone could have, Ken Wissoker, my everything.

IN ADDITION TO ALL OF THE MANY FRIENDS, FAMILY MEMBERS, COLleagues, and institutions thanked in the 2017 edition of *The New Education*, I would like to thank Christina Katopodis, a fantastic coauthor with whom I'm writing *The New College Classroom,* a practical guide to active learning (forthcoming, Harvard University Press). Christina is the executive director of our Transformative Learning in the Humanities grant supported by the Andrew W. Mellon Foundation. I codirect this faculty peer-learning program with my brilliant colleague Shelly Eversley (Interim Chair of Black and Latinx Studies at Baruch College). I thank her along with Annemarie Nicols-Grinenko, Jessica Murray, Khanh Le, and Boya Wang—and the hundreds of CUNY faculty and students participating in this initiative. TLH is part of a visionary Innovative Teaching Academy that spans all twenty-five of CUNY's two-year, four-year, graduate, and professional schools, under the leadership of Chancellor Félix V. Matos Rodriguez. I thank my colleagues at the Futures Initiative (especially Adashima Oyo and Lauren Melendez, my fellow leaders, and Jackie Cahill, who stepped in at a difficult time). Finally, enormous thanks go to HASTAC's Co-Director, Jacqueline Wernimont (Distinguished Chair of Digital Humanities and Social Engagement in the Program in Film and Media Studies) and Brinker

Ferguson and Nikki Stevens, the team at Dartmouth College that has generously co-supported HASTAC.

I also wish to thank the literally thousands of colleagues and their students from all over the world for hosting me at events, for inviting me to conduct seminars and workshops, for asking me to consult with them on change at their institutions, and for sharing their own ideas and success stories. These individuals and institutions are far too many to name, so I simply thank you for all you do on behalf of improving higher education. I also am deeply honored to have received the 2021 Arts and Sciences Advocacy Award by the nineteen hundred deans of the Council of Colleges of Arts and Sciences. It's quite humbling to receive an award most recently bestowed on Phi Beta Kappa and the American Academy of Arts and Sciences. I'm also humbled that *The New Education* received the Frederic W. Ness Book Award for 2019, and I thank the Nobel Prize Committee's Forum on Education for inviting me to be one of the keynote speakers at their convenings in Santiago, Chile, and Stockholm (virtually). I thank my wonderful colleagues at the Andrew W. Mellon Foundation, where I served as a Senior Fellow in Residence during 2019–2020. President Elizabeth Alexander could not have been more welcoming. I had especially memorable conversations with the officers in the higher learning division, including Armando Bengochea and my friend and coauthor Dianne Harris (now Dean of Arts and Sciences at the University of Washington). I look forward to writing more together in the future. I also thank Pratt University President Frances Bronet, for our many walks, dinners, and talks about the future of higher education, and University of Washington president Ana Mari Cauce, for continuing interaction, including via email and, of course, social media.

Finally, thanks to my new editor at Basic Books, Claire Potter, and everyone there who has worked to see this current edition of *The New Education* reach a wider audience.

NOTES

PREFACE TO THE 2022 EDITION

x **women in the US labor market plummeted:** Claire Ewing-Nelson, *Another 275,000 Women Left the Labor Force in January* (Washington, DC: National Women's Law Center, February 2021), https://nwlc.org /wp-content/uploads/2021/02/January-Jobs-Day-FS.pdf.

xiii **nation's elite private universities:** Raj Chetty, John N. Friedman, Emmanuel Saez, Nicholas Turner, and Danny Yagan, "Income Segregation and Intergenerational Mobility Across Colleges in the United States," *Quarterly Journal of Economics* 135, no. 3 (February 2020): 1567–1633, https://doi.org/10.1093/qje/qjaa005; "Some Colleges Have More Students from the Top 1 Percent than Bottom 60," *New York Times*, January 18, 2017, www.nytimes.com /interactive/2017/01/18/upshot/some-colleges-have-more-students -from-the-top-1-percent-than-the-bottom-60.html.

xiii **higher incomes have higher test scores:** Linda K. Wertheimer, "Colleges Are Making the SAT and ACT Optional Now. Will That

Stick?"*Boston Globe*, May 1, 2020, www.bostonglobe.com/2020/05/01/opinion/colleges-are-making-sat-act-optional-now-will-that-stick/.

xiv **pandemic exacerbated income inequality:** Ashley Robinson, "The 4 Trends in 2021 College Admissions You Need to Know," PrepScholar, June 1, 2020, https://blog.prepscholar.com/college-admissions-2021-trends.

xvi **Eliot worked on America's first sterilization law:** Adam S. Cohen, "Harvard's Eugenics Era," *Harvard Magazine*, March–April 2016. https://www.harvardmagazine.com/2016/03/harvards-eugenics-era.

xvii **faculty are from more affluent backgrounds:** Allison Morgan, Aaron Clauset, Daniel Larremore, Nicholas LaBerge, and Mirta Galesic, "Socioeconomic Roots of Academic Faculty," SocArXiv Papers, March 24, 2021, https://doi.org/10.31235/osf.io/6wjxc.

xvii **traditional education would be taken off the market:** Scott Freeman, Sarah L. Eddy, Miles McDonough, Michelle K. Smith, Nnadozie Okoroafor, Hannah Jordt, and Mary Pat Wenderoth, "Active Learning Increases Student Performance in Science, Engineering, and Mathematics," *Proceedings of the National Academy of Sciences* 111, no. 23 (2014): 8410–8415, https://doi.org/10.1073/pnas.1319030111.

xviii **easily found using online sources:** William Littmann, "How I Found the Courage to Decolonize My Syllabus," *Platform*, March 1, 2021.

xix **what they wanted to take with them:** Farah Jasmine Griffin, "Teaching African American Literature During COVID-19," *Boston Review*, May 25, 2020.

INTRODUCTION

6 **In *Between the World and Me*:** Ta-Nehisi Coates, *Between the World and Me* (New York: Spiegel and Grau, 2015), 83–84.

7 **Charles Eliot wrote "The New Education":** Charles W. Eliot, "The New Education," *Atlantic Monthly*, February 1869, 203.

CHAPTER 1: QUARTER-LIFE CRISIS

18 **The Panic of 1857 rocked:** Charles W. Calomiris and Larry Schweikart, "The Panic of 1857," *Journal of Economic History* (1991): 809.

19 **Here is a typical exam question:** "Harvard Entrance Exam of 1869," http://graphics8.nytimes.com/packages/pdf/education/harvardexam.pdf.

20 **Typically, after these general studies:** Eugen Kuehnemann, *Charles W. Eliot, President of Harvard University (May 19, 1869–May 19, 1909)* (Boston: Houghton Mifflin, 1909).

21 **Starting at the beginning of the nineteenth century:** William Cronon, *Nature's Metropolis: Chicago and the Great West* (New York: W. W. Norton, 1991).

23 **The great education project:** Roger L. Geiger, *The History of American Higher Education: Learning and Culture from the Founding to World War II* (Princeton, NJ: Princeton University Press, 2015); Frederick Rudolph, *The American College and University, a History* (New York: Knopf, 1962); John R. Thelin, *A History of American Higher Education* (Baltimore: Johns Hopkins University Press, 2004).

24 **For most of the nineteenth century:** Geiger, *History of American Higher Education*, 194.

25 **Congressman Justin Morrill proposed what:** William Belmont Parker, *The Life and Public Services of John Morrill* (Boston: Houghton Mifflin, 1925).

26 **statement of purpose from the Morrill Acts:** "Title 7, US Code 304, Investment of Proceeds of Sale of Land or Scrip," *Legal Information Institute*, https://www.law.cornell.edu/uscode/text/7/304.

27 **his tutor's income was all:** Henry James, *Charles W. Eliot, President of Harvard University, 1869–1909* (New York: Houghton Mifflin, 1930), 113. According to James, for a few weeks in 1863, Eliot seriously contemplated leaving higher education and going into business.

27 **Eliot was drawn to the University:** The University of Berlin was established in 1811 by Wilhelm von Humboldt, was renamed Friedrich-Wilhelms-Universität in 1828, and then, after other formal and informal name changes, was renamed the Humboldt University of Berlin in 1949, after both Wilhelm von Humboldt and his brother, the geographer Alexander von Humboldt.

28 **the curriculum at the University of Berlin:** R. D. Anderson, "Germany and the Humboldtian Model," in *European Universities from the Enlightenment to 1914* (New York: Oxford University Press, 2004).

28 **The Humboldtian university was cosmopolitan:** Robert Anderson, "The 'Idea of a University' Today," *History & Policy*, March 1, 2010, http:www.historyandpolicy.org/papers/policy-paper-98.html.

31 **He began his term with a bang:** Charles William Eliot, *Addresses at the Inauguration of Charles William Eliot as President of Harvard College, Tuesday, October 19, 1869* (Cambridge, MA: Sever and Francis, 1869).

32 **He believed vocationalism:** Charles W. Eliot, "The New 32,"

Atlantic Monthly, February 27, 1869, www.theatlantic.com/magazine
/archive/1869/02/the-new-education/309049/.

32 **Eliot listed what he considered:** James, *Charles W. Eliot,* 170–171.

33 **In his 1869 inaugural address:** Eliot, *Addresses at the Inauguration,* 50.

34 **Arthur Gilman, came to him:** Charles Eliot, quoted in Liva Baker,
*I'm Radcliffe! Fly Me! The Seven Sisters and the Failure of Women's
Education* (New York: Macmillan, 1976), 21.

34 **She would become the first president:** Dorothy Elia Howells, *A
Century to Celebrate: Radcliffe College, 1879–1979* (Cambridge, MA:
Radcliffe College, 1978), 1.

35 **Eugen Kuehnemann, a visiting professor:** Kuehnemann, *Charles
W. Eliot, President,* 9.

35 **The features of the modern American:** "Records of the President of
Harvard University, Charles W. Eliot, 1869–1930: An Inventory," Harvard University Archives, President's Office, http://oasis.lib.harvard
.edu//oasis/deliver/deepLink?_collection=oasis&uniqueId=hua05006.

39 **The new field of "human resources":** The first use of the term
"human resources" is thought to be in John R. Commons, *The Distribution of Wealth* (New York: Macmillan, 1893).

39 **the CEEB was charged with:** College Entrance Examination
Board of the Middle States and Maryland, *Plan of Organization for
the College Entrance Examination Board of the Middle States and
Maryland and a Statement of Subjects in Which Examinations Are
Proposed* (Ithaca, NY: Cornell University Library, 1900), https://
archive.org/details/cu31924031758109.

43 **The inventor of the single-best-answer:** Frederick J. Kelly, "The
Kansas Silent Reading Tests," *Journal of Educational Psychology* 7,
no. 2 (February 1916): 63–80.

CHAPTER 2: COLLEGE FOR EVERYONE

47 **As in all morality tales:** Special thanks to Danica Savonick for
recommending "Community."

52 **"You have to tell him":** As with other student comments in this
book, I have kept the identity of the individuals in this conversation
anonymous. This exchange took place at the CUNY Peer Mentoring
Workship sponsored by the Teagle Foundation at the Graduate Center, CUNY, on July 26, 2016.

53 **Before 1850, only a handful:** Arthur M. Cohen and Florence B. Brawer, *The American Community College,* 4th ed. (San Francisco: John Wiley & Sons, 2003); Stephen Brint and Jerome Karabel, *The Diverted Dream: Community Colleges and the Promise of Educational Opportunity in America, 1900–1985* (New York: Oxford University Press, 1989).

54 **community colleges had several distinctive:** "Historical Information," American Association of Community Colleges, www.aacc .nche.edu/AboutCC/history/Pages/default.aspx.

55 **there are 1,166 community colleges:** "Community Colleges Past to Present," American Association of Community Colleges, www .aacc.nche.edu/AboutCC/history/Pages/pasttopresent.aspx.

55 **For many of society's poorest:** Christopher Newfield, "The End of the American Funding Model: What Comes Next?" *American Literature* 82, no. 3 (2010): 611–635.

55 **Approximately 44 percent of students:** "Affordability and Transfer: Critical to Increasing Baccalaureate Degree Completion," National Center for Public Policy and Higher Education, June 2011, www .highereducation.org/reports/pa_at/index.shtml; Jennifer Ma and Sandy Baum, *Trends in Community Colleges: Enrollment, Prices, Student Debt, and Completion,* Research Brief (New York: College Board Research, April 2016), http://trends.collegeboard.org/sites/default /files/trends-in-community-colleges-research-brief.pdf.

55 **Average community college students:** Thomas R. Bailey and Clive R. Belfield, "Is College Worth It? For Whom?" (slide show, Center for Analysis of Postsecondary Education and Employment, September 11, 2015), http://capseecenter.org/wp-content/uploads/2016/01 /capsee-belfield-bailey-pi-meeting.pdf; "What Is an Associate's Degree?" GetEducated.com, accessed November 12, 2016, https://www .geteducated.com/career-center/detail/what-is-an-associate-degree.

56 **"social mobility index," a measure:** "2016 Social Mobility Index," CollegeNET, accessed January 2, 2017, www.socialmobilityindex .org.

57 **Educator Carol Dweck calls this:** Carol S. Dweck, *Mindset: The New Psychology of Success* (New York: Random House, 2006).

57 **When Professor Joshua Belknap teaches:** Joshua Belknap, "Our Students: Learning to Listen to Multilingual Student Voices," in *Structuring Equality: A Handbook for Student-Centered Learning and Teaching Practices,* ed. Graduate Center Learning Collective, https://

www.hastac.org/blogs/jbelknap/2016/12/05/chapter-1-our-students
-learning-listen-multilingual-student-voices. Special thanks to Joshua
Belknap for excellent conversations and insights on translingual
teaching during my course "American Literature, American Learning," in which students decided, in lieu of a term paper, to write a
book (*Structuring Equality*) together.

59 **We know student evaluations track:** Danica Savonick and Cathy
N. Davidson, "Gender Bias in Academe: An Annotated Bibliography
of Important Recent Studies," *HASTAC* (blog), January 26, 2015,
https://www.hastac.org/blogs/superadmin/2015/01/26/gender-bias
-academe-annotated-bibliography-important-recent-studies.

59 **"It's not just the periphery":** Special thanks to President Gail
Mellow for a series of conversations that took place beginning over
lunch in May 2015 and continuing throughout 2016, in person and
by email. I have also learned enormously from her book, coauthored
with Cynthia M. Heelan, *Minding the Dream: The Process and Practice of the American Community College* (New York: Rowman and
Littlefield, 2014).

62 **"tyranny of meritocracy":** Lani Guinier, *The Tyranny of Meritocracy:
Democratizing Higher Education in America* (Boston: Beacon Press,
2015).

62 **The Delta Cost Project:** Donna Desrochers and Rita Kirshtein,
*College Spending in a Turbulent Decade: Findings from the Delta Cost
Project. A Delta Data Update, 2000–2010* (Washington, DC: Amer-
ican Institutes for Research, 2012). See also Michael Fabricant and
Stephen Brier, *Austerity Blues: Fighting for the Soul of Public Higher
Education* (Baltimore: Johns Hopkins University Press, 2016),
128–130.

63 **taught by adjunct or contingent:** Tony Guerra, "The Average Adjunct Pay at Community Colleges," *Houston Chronicle,* http://work
.chron.com/average-adjunct-pay-community-colleges-18310.html.

63 **Those who achieve their associate's:** Lynn O'Shaughnessy, "Transfer Students: 8 Things You Need to Know," *US News & World Report,*
www.usnews.com/education/blogs/the-college-solution/2010/11/16
/transfer-students-8-things-you-need-to-know.

63 **"The students are not high risk":** Special thanks to Dr. Jade Davis, who kindly allowed me to interview her on August 11, 2015, and
in several subsequent conversations on topics of higher education
equity and innovation.

63 **John Mogulescu, dean of the School:** My thanks to Dean John Mogulescu for making time to speak with me on May 16, 2016, and with whom I continued to develop ideas in correspondence over the course of 2016.

69 **having a student drop out:** Jordan Weissmann, "America's Awful College Dropout Rates, in Four Charts," *Slate,* November 19, 2014, www.slate.com/blogs/moneybox/2014/11/19/u_s_college_dropouts _rates_explained_in_4_charts.html.

71 **where transfer of course credits:** David Jenkins and John Fink, *Tracking Transfer: New Measures of Institutional and State Effectiveness in Helping Community College Students Attain Bachelor's Degrees* (New York: Community College Research Center, January 2016), http://ccrc.tc.columbia.edu/media/k2/attachments/tracking-transfer -institutional-state-effectiveness.pdf.

CHAPTER 3: AGAINST TECHNOPHOBIA

76 **"prove" that college students:** Nicholas Carr, *The Shallows: What the Internet Is Doing to Our Brains* (New York: W. W. Norton, 2010); Sherry Turkle, *Alone Together: Why We Expect More from Technology and Less from Each Other* (New York: Basic Books, 2011). For overviews of several studies (pro and con) of computers in education, see Douglas Rushkoff and Leland Purvis, *Program or Be Programmed: Ten Commands for a Digital Age* (Berkeley, CA: Soft Skull Press, 2011); Howard Rheingold, *Net Smart: How to Thrive Online* (Cambridge, MA: MIT Press, 2012).

76 **the last information age in human history:** Historian Robert Darnton has argued that there are four great "information ages" in human history: the invention of writing in ancient Mesopotamia, the age of movable type, the age of mass printing, and our own Internet age.

77 **"Novel Reading, a Cause of Female Depravity":** Cathy N. Davidson, *Revolution and the Word: The Rise of the Novel in America* (New York: Oxford University Press, 1986; expanded edition, 2004).

77 **have not only banned devices:** Dan Rockmore, "The Case for Banning Laptops in the Classroom," *The New Yorker,* June 6, 2014, www.newyorker.com/tech/elements/the-case-for-banning-laptops -in-the-classroom. See also Darren Rosenblum, "Leave Your Laptops at the Door to My Classroom," *New York Times,* January 2, 2017,

www.nytimes.com/2017/01/02/opinion/leave-your-laptops-at-the
-door-to-my-classroom.html.

81 **renowned educator Benjamin S. Bloom:** Benjamin S. Bloom,
*All Our Children Learning: A Primer for Parents, Teachers, and Other
Educators* (New York: McGraw-Hill, 1981).

82 **Most lecturers scoff at clickers:** Craig Lambert, "Twilight of
the Lecture," *Harvard Magazine,* February 6, 2012, http://harvard
magazine.com/2012/03/twilight-of-the-lecture.

82 **"Generate pairs of three-digit":** Derek Bruff discusses this exercise in detail on his superb blog *Agile Learning,* http://derekbruff
.org/. I am grateful for permission to reprint this here. See September 9, 2015, "Thinking about Think-Pair-Share," http://derekbruff
.org/?p=3117. Other quotations come from an interview with Professor Bruff on July 1, 2016, and several prior and subsequent email
exchanges.

87 **In a 2014 analysis:** Scott Freeman, Sarah L. Eddya, Miles Mc-
Donough, Michelle K. Smith, Nnadozie Okoroafor, Hannah Jordt,
and Mary Pat Wenderoth, "Active Learning Increases Student Performance in Science, Engineering, and Mathematics," *Proceedings of
the National Academy of Sciences of the United States of America* 111,
no. 23 (2014): 8410–8415.

88 **in 1837 when a geometry professor:** Stephen E. Ambrose, *Duty,
Honor, Country: A History of West Point* (Baltimore: Johns Hopkins
University Press, 1999), 19.

89 **Whereas research confirms:** John Raven, "The Raven's Progressive Matrices: Change and Stability over Culture and Time," *Cognitive Psychology* 41 (2000): 1–48; James R. Flynn, "Massive IQ Gains
in 14 Nations: What IQ Tests Really Measure," *Psychological Bul-
letin* 101 (1987): 171–191; James R. Flynn, *What Is Intelligence:
Beyond the Flynn Effect* (Cambridge: Cambridge University Press,
2009), 1–2; James Flynn, "Why Our IQ Levels Are Higher Than Our
Grandparents'," filmed March 2013, TED video, 18:40, https://www
.ted.com/talks/james_flynn_why_our_iq_levels_are_higher_than_our
_grandparents?language=en.

89 **second decade of testing:** David R. Owen and T. W. Teasdale,
"Now the Good News on Declining S.A.T. Scores," *New York Times,*
October 14, 1987, www.nytimes.com/1987/10/14/opinionl-now
-the-good-news-on-declining-sat-scores-961687.html; Betsy Sparrow,
Jenny Liu, and Daniel M. Wegner, "Google Effects on Memory: Cog-

nitive Consequences of Information at Our Finger Tips," *Science* 333 (2011): 776–778, http://science.sciencemag.org/content/333 /6043/776.

89 **To summarize dozens of recent studies:** For an extensive discussion of the role of the Internet in cognition, see Cathy N. Davidson, *Now You See It: How the Brain Science of Attention Will Transform the Way We Live, Work, and Learn* (New York: Viking Penguin, 2010).

91 **Stanford University Professor Emerita Andrea:** "Andrea Lunsford on the Myths of Digital Literacy," YouTube video, 11:08, from *The Agenda with Steven Paikin*, October 2, 2009, https://www .youtube.com/watch?v=sIKu_hZT2BM, and follow-up interview with the author on June 27, 2016.

91 **The Stanford Study of Writing:** "Stanford Study of Writing," Stanford University, https://ssw.stanford.edu/.

92 **That students were willing to grant:** Andrea A. Lunsford, Jenn Fishman, and Warren M. Liew, "College Writing, Identification, and the Production of Intellectual Property: Voices from the Stanford Study of Writing," *College English* 75, no. 5 (May 2013): 470–492; Paul Rogers, "The Contributions of North American Longitudinal Studies of Writing in Higher Education to Our Understanding of Writing Development," in *Traditions of Writing Research*, ed. Charles Bazerman (Oxford: Routledge, 2010), 365–377.

92 **"On social media, audiences":** Andrea Lunsford, Lisa Ede, Beverly Moss, Carole Clark Papper, and Keith Walters, *Everyone's an Author* (New York: W. W. Norton, 2012).

93 **She encourages her students:** "Stanford Study of Writing," quoted in Carolyn Lengel, "How We Write Now," *News at Macmillan Learning* (blog), February 24, 2016, https://community.macmillan.com /groups/macmillan-news/blog/2016/02/24/the-literacy-revolution.

94 **Millennials read more than:** Kathryn Zickuhr and Lee Rainie, "Younger Americans and Public Libraries," Pew Research Center: Internet, Science & Tech, September 10, 2014, www.pewinternet.org /2014/09/10/younger-americans-and-public-libraries/.

95 **universities were still "banning" the use:** Noam Cohen, "A History Department Bans Citing Wikipedia as a Research Source," *New York Times*, February 21, 2007, www.nytimes.com/2007/02/21/education /21wikipedia.html.

95 **In LGBT 146:** Quoted in Cathy N. Davidson, "How to Go from Standard-Issue Term Paper to Social Change: Here's One Model"

HASTAC (blog), https://www.hastac.org/blogs/cathy-davidson/2016
/05/20/how-go-standard-issue-term-paper-social-change-heres-one
-model.

98 **New York City even maintains:** "NY Hackathons," http://nyhack
athons.com/.

99 **The open-source hackathon:** Alex Williams, "Two Harvard University Alum Win Disputed Salesforce $1M Hackathon Prize at
Dreamforce [Updated]," TechCrunch, November 21, 2013, https://
techcrunch.com/2013/11/21/two-harvard-university-alum-win
-salesforce-1m-hackathon-prize-at-dreamforce-for-mobile-service
-to-create-reports/.

99 **The purse for the Women:** Evan Misshula, "So What Does a Hackathon Have to Do with the Humanities?" *HASTAC* (blog), September 23, 2015, https://www.hastac.org/blogs/emisshulajjaycunyedu
/2015/09/23/so-what-does-hackathon-have-do-humanities. Special
thanks to Evan Misshula, who was a student in my course "Mapping
the Futures of Higher Education," for many conversations and an
email exchange over the course of 2015 and 2016.

CHAPTER 4: AGAINST TECHNOPHILIA

101 **"The Year of the MOOC":** Thomas L. Friedman, "Revolution Hits
the Universities," *New York Times,* January 26, 2013, www.nytimes
.com/2013/01/27/opinion/sunday/friedman-revolution-hits-the
-universities.html.

103 **Ownership activists Aaron Perzanowski:** Aaron Perzanowski and
Jason M. Schultz, *The End of Ownership: Personal Property in the
Digital Economy* (Cambridge, MA: MIT Press, 2016).

103 **Seymour Papert, a pioneer:** Seymour Papert, *The Children's Machine: Rethinking School in the Age of the Computer* (New York: Basic
Books, 2000), 149.

104 **I assemble a small team:** Special thanks to Kaysi Holman, the
chief producer of the MOOC, plus Demos Orphanides, Mandy
Barry, Sheryl Grant, Jade Davis, and Kristen Swago.

107 **"Let the revolution begin!":** Thomas L. Friedman, "Come the
Revolution," *New York Times,* May 15, 2012, www.nytimes.com
/2012/05/16/opinion/friedman-come-the-revolution.html.

108 **cyberattack on the New Hampshire:** Samuel Burke, "Massive
Cyberattack Turned Ordinary Devices into Weapons," CNN Tech,

October 22, 2016, http://money.cnn.com/2016/10/22/technology /cyberattack-dyn-ddos/.

108 **We subject the average American:** Council of the Great City Schools, *Student Testing in America's Great City Schools: An Inventory and Preliminary Analysis* (Washington, DC: Council of the Great City Schools, October 2015), www.cgcs.org/cms/lib/DC00001581 /Centricity/Domain/87/Testing%20Report.pdf. Council of the Great City Schools found that from pre-K to twelfth grade, students took about 112 mandatory standardized exams. See also "Study Reveals How Many Required Tests Students Take," CBS News, October 26, 2015, www.cbsnews.com/news/study-reveals-how-many -required-tests-students-take/.

109 **MOOC mania so engulfed:** Scott Jaschik, "U. of Virginia President to Leave over 'Philosophical Differences,'" *Inside Higher Education,* June 11, 2012, https://www.insidehighered.com/news/2012 /06/11/u-virginia-president-leave-over-philosophical-differences.

111 **"We Generation":** Ian Daly, "The We Generation," *New York Times T Magazine,* August 23, 2016, www.nytimes.com/2016/08/23 /t-magazine/we-generation.html.

112 **Wikipedia offered us all:** See Cathy N. Davidson, "The Calculus of Wikipedia," *HASTAC* (blog), https://www.hastac.org/blogs /cathy-davidson/2007/09/18/calculus-wikipedia. In September 2007, when the president of Middlebury College announced he was planning to ban Wikipedia from campus, I wrote to him arguing that, although by no means a final source, Wikipedia is useful in countering Western bias. The example I used was the Wikipedia entry on "calculus," which, in contrast to standard scholarly encyclopedias and even scholarly books in 2007, included Egyptian, Chinese, and Indian contributions to the field hundreds of years before the famous dispute between Newton and Leibniz over who "invented" calculus. A reference librarian at Duke University kindly emailed her colleagues around the world for me and was able to verify the accuracy of information that she was not able to confirm in any English-language source available at the time.

113 **Linnaeus also divided humanity:** C. Loring Brace, *"Race" Is a Four Letter Word: The Genesis of the Concept* (Oxford: Oxford University Press, 2005), 27.

113 **culturally biased classification hierarchies:** Tara McPherson, "US Operating Systems at Mid-Century: The Intertwining of Race

and UNIX," *Race After the Internet,* ed. Lisa Nakamura and Peter Chow-White (New York: Routledge, 2012), 21–37.

114 **"Wikipedia is a free online":** "Wikipedia," Wikipedia, December 18, 2016, https://en.wikipedia.org/w/index.php?title=Wikipedia &oldid=755547231.

115 **When I challenged the onsite students:** Cathy N. Davidson, "Changing Higher Education to Change the World," *#FutureEd* (blog), *Chronicle of Higher Education,* March 14, 2014, www.chronicle.com /blogs/future/2014/03/14/changing-higher-education-to-change-the -world/. Two members of our #FutureEd class contributed each week to the *Chronicle of Higher Education* blog, *#FutureEd: Thoughts from a MOOC on Higher Education,* from January 23, 2014, to March 14, 2014. I thank Brenda Burmeister, Malina Chavez, Matthew Clark, Christina Davidson, Jade Davis, David Dulceany, Kaysi Holman, Leslie Niiro, William Osborn, Barry Peddycord III, Elizabeth Pitts, Claire Antone Payton, Max Ramseyer, Clifford A. Robinson, and Jennifer Stratton for their tireless creativity and rigor. All conversations in the text occurred during the spring of 2014.

116 **"Knowledge is a public resource":** Cathy N. Davidson, "Is it Possible to Go from MOOC to Community? Some Guidelines in the Making," *HASTAC* (blog), January 24, 2014, https://www.hastac.org /blogs/cathy-davidson/2014/01/24/it-possible-go-mooc-community -some-guidelines-making.

117 **The second #FutureEd hackathon:** Kaysi Holman, "International Timeline of Higher Education," *HASTAC* (blog), December 17, 2013, https://www.hastac.org/wiki/international-timeline-higher -education.

117 **"Sometime between 3500 BC":** The authors of the time line cite Nicholas Grimal, *A History of Ancient Egypt* (Oxford, UK: Blackwell Publishing, 1992), 79.

120 **over 95 percent of colleges:** Clay Shirky, "The Digital Revolution in Higher Education Has Already Happened. No One Noticed," *Medium,* November 6, 2015, https://medium.com/@cshirky/the-digital -revolution-in-higher-education-has-already-happened-no-one -noticed-78ec0fec16c7#.5u2gq8q3h.

120 **When Starbucks surveyed its workers:** Ben Rooney, "Starbucks to Give Workers a Full Ride for College," CNN Money, April 6, 2015, http://money.cnn.com/2015/04/06/pf/college/starbucks-college -tuition-arizona-state/index.html. The secondary literature on MOOCs

is extensive. For an overview, see Elizabeth Losh, *The War on Learning: Gaining Ground in the Digital University* (Cambridge, MA: MIT Press, 2014), chap. 5.

120 **colleges and universities spent:** International Data Corporation, "US Higher Education Institutions Expected to Spend $6.6 Billion on IT in 2015, According to IDC Government Insights," in *Pivot Table: US Education IT Spending Guide, Version 1, 2013–2018,* Doc. no. GI255747, May 11, 2015, www.idc.com/getdoc.jsp ?containerId=GI255747.

121 **MOOCs are an example:** Richard Pérez-Peña, "Top Universities Test the Online Appeal of Free," *New York Times,* July 17, 2012, www.nytimes.com/2012/07/18/education/top-universities-test-the -online-appeal-of-free.html?_r=0.

121 **the National Science Foundation:** For a full discussion, see Christopher Newfield, *The Great Mistake: How We Wrecked Public Universities and How We Can Fix Them* (Baltimore: Johns Hopkins University Press, 2016), 252.

122 **Thrun was notably candid:** Max Chafkin, "Udacity's Sebastian Thrun, Godfather of Free Online Education, Changes Course," *Fast Company,* November 14, 2013, https://www.fastcompany.com /3021473/udacity-sebastian-thrun-uphill-climb.

122 **MOOCs aren't over:** Pérez-Peña, "Top Universities Test the Online Appeal."

122 **On Coursera's Signature Tracks:** Andrew Dean Ho, Justin Reich, Sergiy O. Nesterko, Daniel Thomas Seaton, Tommy Mullaney, Jim Waldo, and Isaac Chuang, "HarvardX and MITx: The First Year of Open Online Courses, Fall 2012–Summer 2013" (HarvardX and MITx Working Paper No. 1, January 21, 2014).

122 **MOOCs clearly offer benefits:** Chen Zhenghao, Brandon Alcorn, Gayle Christensen, Nicholas Eriksson, Daphne Koller, and Ezekiel J. Emanuel, "Who's Benefiting from MOOCs, and Why," *Harvard Business Review,* September 22, 2015, https://hbr.org/2015/09/whos -benefiting-from-moocs-and-why.

122 **"Online education isn't succeeding":** Shirky, "Digital Revolution in Higher Education Has Already Happened."

123 **After the MOOC hype has passed:** Tamar Lewin, "After Setbacks, Online Courses Are Rethought," *New York Times,* December 10, 2013, www.nytimes.com/2013/12/11/us/after-setbacks-online-courses -are-rethought.html.

125 **Google searches could be and had:** See, for example, Carole Cadwalladr, "Google, Democracy and the Truth about Internet Search," *The Guardian* Technology section, December 4, 2016, https://www.theguardian.com/technology/2016/dec/04/google-democracy-truth-internet-search-facebook.

126 **"The Ferguson Syllabus":** Lydia Lum, "Georgetown University Professor's Ferguson Syllabus Growing Nationwide," *Diverse Issues in Higher Education,* October 6, 2016, http://diverseeducation.com/article/87856/.

130 **We know from multiple studies:** See, for example, E. Bettinger and R. Baker, "The Effects of Student Coaching in College: An Evaluation of a Randomized Experiment in Student Mentoring" (NBER Working Paper No. 16881, National Bureau of Economic Research, 2011); S. C. Ender and F. B. Newton, *Students Helping Students: A Guide for Peer Educators on College Campuses* (San Francisco: Jossey-Bass, 2010); and George D. Kuh, Jillian Kinzie, Ty Cruce, Rick Shoup, and Robert M. Gonyea, *Connecting the Dots: Multifaceted Analyses of the Relationships between Student Engagement Results from the NSSE and the Institutional Policies and Conditions That Foster Student Success* (Bloomington: Center for Postsecondary Research, Indiana University Bloomington, 2006), http://nsse.iub.edu/pdf/Connecting_the_Dots_Report.pdf.

CHAPTER 5: PALPABLE IMPACT

135 **This grim story of education:** Yuzo Ueda, "The Life and Times of Tetsuya Ishida: Confession and Spirit," in *Tetsuya Ishida* (Hong Kong: Gagosian Gallery, 2014), 73. See also "Painting with the Entire Body and Saving the World One Brushstroke at a Time," Ansham For Me, March 4, 2015, http://anshamforme.com/2015/03/04/painting-with-the-entire-body-and-saving-the-world-one-brushstroke-at-a-time/.

137 **the Japanese Ministry of Education issued:** "Japan's Education Ministry Says to Axe Social Science and Humanities," Social Science Space, August 25, 2015, www.socialsciencespace.com/2015/08/japans-education-ministry-says-to-axe-social-science-and-humanities/.

138 **US Census Bureau report for 2014:** "Census Bureau Reports Majority of STEM College Graduates Do Not Work in STEM

Occupations," United States Census Bureau, July 10, 2014, www .census.gov/newsroom/press-releases/2014/cb14-130.html. It should be noted that the US Census Bureau has a wide, rather than a narrow, definition of a STEM occupation and includes in that definition sales and managerial occupations as well as social science.

138 **Most graduates working in STEM:** See Susan Adams, "The 10 Skills Employers Most Want in 2015 Graduates," *Forbes,* November 12, 2014, www.forbes.com/sites/susanadams/2014/11/12/the-10 -skills-employers-most-want-in-2015-graduates/.

138 **A 2007 National Academies' report:** Committee on Prospering in the Global Economy of the 21st Century, National Academy of Sciences, National Academy of Engineering, and Institute of Medicine, *Rising Above the Gathering Storm: Energizing and Employing America for a Brighter Economic Future* (Washington, DC: National Academies Press, 2007). See also Yi Xue and Richard C. Larson, "STEM Crisis or STEM Surplus? Yes and Yes," *Monthly Labor Review,* May 2015, www.bls.gov/opub/mlr/2015/article/stem-crisis-or -stem-surplus-yes-and-yes.htm.

139 **There are other problems:** "Computer Programmer: Overview," *US News & World Report,* http://money.usnews.com/careers/best -jobs/computer-programmer. See also Elizabeth Kolbert, "Our Automated Future," *The New Yorker,* December 19 and 26, 2016, www .newyorker.com/magazine/2016/12/19/our-automated-future.

140 **evidence suggests that over time:** Norman Matloff, "Software Engineers Will One Day Work for English Majors," *Bloomberg View,* April 22, 2012, http://www.bloomberg.com/view/articles/2012-04-22 /software-engineers-will-work-one-day-for-english-majors.

140 **Both Mark Zuckerberg:** Quoted in Matloff, "Software Engineers Will One Day Work."

140 **The research unambiguously reveals:** "6 Skills That Will Make You Indispensable," American Management Association, www.amanet .org/training/promotions/six-skills-for-managers-and-leaders.aspx.

140 **then we have to understand:** According to the American Management Association, these are the top skills required for promotion— and it is happy to provide online training in each of these vital areas.

141 **factors bearing on actual promotion:** David A. Garvin, "How Google Sold Its Engineers on Management," *Harvard Business Review,* December 2013, https://hbr.org/2013/12/how-google-sold-its -engineers-on-management.

141 **When Sha Xin Wei speaks:** Special thanks to Sha Xin Wei for allowing me to interview him and to take a tour of his new program on May 12, 2016, and to continue the conversation in numerous subsequent email and in-person exchanges throughout 2016 and early 2017.

142 **Sha Xin Wei's research:** Sha Xin Wei, "Topology and Morphogenesis," *Theory, Culture & Society* 29 (2012): 220–246.

144 **"The practical spirit":** Charles W. Eliot, "The New Education," 215.

148 **ASU president Michael Crow has dubbed:** Special thanks to President Michael Crow for an in-person interview on May 12, 2016, and to him and William B. Dabars for answering numerous questions by email over the course of 2016–2017.

149 **The first principle undergirding:** Michael M. Crow and William B. Dabars, *Designing the New American University* (Baltimore: Johns Hopkins University Press, 2015), 243.

153 **The new curriculum was designed:** General Education Committee, *Proposed Components of Revised General Education Curriculum* (Charlottesville: University of Virginia, College and Graduate School of Arts and Sciences, April 2016), http://as.virginia.edu/sites/as.virginia.edu/files/proposed_components_of_revised_general_education_curriculum_cepc_web3.pdf.

153 **Writing and speaking requirements:** See, for example, Cynthia Roberts, "Developing Future Leaders: The Role of Reflection in the Classroom," *Journal of Leadership Education* 7, no. 1 (Summer 2008): 116–130.

156 **Professor Ortiz considers her ideal:** William Navarre, "Dean for Graduate Education to Take Leave, Start New University," *The Tech,* January 28, 2016, http://tech.mit.edu/V135/N38/ortiz.html.

156 **If Professor Ortiz is successful:** My first in-person interview with Sara Hendren took place on December 1, 2015. Special thanks to Professor Hendren for making the time on numerous subsequent occasions to address my questions and describe her work and pedagogy.

157 **in collaborating with Chris Hinojosa:** "Socket and Limb with Chris Hinojosa," Adaptation + Ability Group, January 2015, http://aplusa.org/projects/limb-chris-hinojosa/.

160 **this traditional symbol replaced:** "The Accessible Icon Project," Accessible Icon Project, http://accessibleicon.org.

CHAPTER 6: WHY COLLEGE COSTS SO MUCH

163 **Dr. Cho, the attending ER surgeon:** All physician names have been changed for privacy, with the exception of my friend Eric Manheimer, who discusses the issues of cost and medical training in his beautiful and insightful book *Twelve Patients: Life and Death at Bellevue Hospital* (New York: Grand Central Publishing, 2013).

166 **High tuition costs not only:** Robert A. Scott, "Revealing the Truth About Student Loan Debt," *Times Weekly.com,* November 17, 2016; Grace Kena, Lauren Musu-Gillette, Jennifer Robinson, Xiaolei Wang, Amy Rathbun, Jijun Zhang, Sidney Wilkinson-Flicker, Amy Barmer, and Erin Dunlop Velez, *The Condition of Education 2015,* NCES 2015-144 (Washington, DC: US Department of Education, May 2015), http://nces.ed.gov/pubs2015/2015144.pdf.

167 **faculty are experiencing extreme cutbacks:** "Background Facts on Contingent Faculty," AAUP, https://www.aaup.org/issues /contingency/background-facts.

168 **Currently, 42 million Americans:** "Who Is Getting Rich Off the $1.3 Trillion Student Debt Crisis?" Democracy Now! June 29, 2016, www.democracynow.org/2016/6/29/who_is_getting_rich_off_the.

169 **For in-state residents:** "What's the Price Tag for a College Education?" CollegeData, www.collegedata.com/cs/content/content _payarticle_tmpl.jhtml?articleId=10064.

170 **The situation is most egregious:** Timothy Pratt, "Poor and Uneducated: The South's Cycle of Failing Higher Education," *The Atlantic,* August 25, 2016, https://www.theatlantic.com/education/archive /2016/08/the-failures-of-southern-universities/497102/; "State Funding for Higher Education Remains Far Below Pre-Recession Levels in Most States," Center on Budget and Policy Priorities, www.cbpp.org /state-funding-for-higher-education-remains-far-below-pre-recession -levels-in-most-states-1; and State Higher Education Executive Officers Association, *SHEF: FY 2015: State Higher Education Finance* (Boulder, CO: State Higher Education Executive Officers, 2016), www .sheeo.org/sites/default/files/SHEEO_SHEF_FY2015.pdf.

170 **In inflation-adjusted dollars:** Benjamin Ginsberg, "Administrators Ate My Tuition," *Washington Monthly,* September/October 2011, http://washingtonmonthly.com/magazine/septoct-2011/administrators -ate-my-tuition/.

170 **In her exhaustive study:** Sara Goldrick-Rab, *Paying the Price: College*

Costs, Financial Aid, and the Betrayal of the American Dream (Chicago: University of Chicago Press, 2016), 1, 15. All figures are adjusted for inflation.

171 **Here is a sobering example:** Jeff Muskus, "Ballooning Tuition Presents Challenges," *Yale Daily News*, April 13, 2005, http://yaledailynews.com/blog/2005/04/13/ballooning-tuition-presents-challenges/.

171 **dubbed "Generation Debt":** Anya Kamanetz, *Generation Debt: Why Now Is a Terrible Time to Be Young* (New York: Riverhead Books/Penguin, 2006).

171 **those with student debt are currently:** Ibid.

172 **Congress passed laws that:** James B. Steele and Lance Williams, "Who Got Rich Off the Student Debt Crisis," Reveal, June 28, 2016, www.revealnews.org/article/who-got-rich-off-the-student-debt-crisis/.

172 **And the government:** Ibid.

173 **Patriotism and support:** Lawrence E. Gladieux and Thomas R. Wolanin, *Congress and the Colleges* (Lexington, MA: Lexington Books, 1976), 1–14; Todd Gitlin, *The Sixties: Years of Hope, Days of Rage* (New York: Bantam, 1993).

173 **the slope of the trend line:** Scott Carlson, "A Public Good Then, a Private Good Now: Why Has State Support for Higher Education Dwindled as Enrollments Have Grown More Diverse?" *Chronicle of Higher Education*, December 2, 2016, A16–A17.

173 **There remains a racial component:** Carlson, "A Public Good Then," A16.

174 **Fall 2014 became a benchmark:** "Digest of Education Statistics, 2015," Institute of Education Sciences, National Center for Education Statistics, https://nces.ed.gov/programs/digest/d15/.

174 **Students of color are:** Michelle Goldberg, "This Is What Happens When You Slash Funding for Public Universities," *The Nation*, May 19, 2015, https://www.thenation.com/article/gentrification-higher-ed/.

174 **Ideology clearly plays a role:** Zoe Carpenter, "How a Right-Wing Political Machine Is Dismantling Higher Education in North Carolina," *The Nation*, June 8, 2015, https://www.thenation.com/article/how-right-wing-political-machine-dismantling-higher-education-north-carolina/.

174 **The example of North Carolina:** Quoted in Carpenter, "How a Right-Wing Political Machine."

175 **the Bureau of Labor Statistics:** "Nonprofits Account for 11.4 Million Jobs, 10.3 Percent of All Private Sector Employment," TED:

The Economics Daily, US Bureau of Labor Statistics, October 21, 2014, https://www.bls.gov/opub/ted/2014/ted_20141021.htm.

175 **North Carolina has cut per:** Michael Mitchell, Vincent Palacios, and Michael Leachman, "States Are Still Funding Higher Education Below Pre-Recession Levels," Center on Budget and Policy Priorities, May 1, 2014, www.cbpp.org/research/states-are-still-funding-higher-education-below-pre-recession-levels?fa=view&id=4135.

175 **even as tuitions rise to compensate:** Michael Mitchell, Michael Leachman, and Kathleen Masterson, "Funding Down, Tuition Up," Center on Budget and Policy Priorities, updated August 15, 2016, accessed May 26, 2016, www.cbpp.org/research/state-budget-and-tax/funding-down-tuition-up; Laura Devaney, "State Funding Slashes Boosting Tuition Significantly," *eCampusNews*, June 6, 2016, www.ecampusnews.com/campus-administration/state-funding-tuition/.

176 **"Dreams Stall as CUNY":** Chen, "Dreams Stall."

176 **"Why We Need Your Support":** "Why We Need Your Support," University of Texas at Austin, https://giving.utexas.edu/why-give/why-we-need-your-support/.

176 **education analyst Christopher Newfield:** Christopher Newfield, *The Great Mistake: How We Wrecked Public Universities and How We Can Fix Them* (Baltimore: Johns Hopkins University Press, 2016), 55.

177 **"administrative bloat":** Ginsberg, "Administrators Ate My Tuition." The comparison here is between full-time, nonfaculty administrative staff and full-time equivalent (FTE) faculty (a designation that acknowledges that a faculty position might now be filled by two or more part-time faculty members).

177 **According to a 2012 survey:** Casey Quinlan, "Universities Run into Problems When They Hire Presidents from the Business World," *ThinkProgress,* March 7, 2016, https://thinkprogress.org/universities-run-into-problems-when-they-hire-presidents-from-the-business-world-a66b2739c1a.

177 **Bringing in executives:** Ginsberg, "Administrators Ate My Tuition."

178 **When they're not faulting:** Dan Bauman and Brian O'Leary, "Executive Compensation at Public and Private Colleges," *Chronicle of Higher Education,* July 17, 2016, http://chronicle.com/interactives/executive-compensation; Stephanie Saul, "Salaries of Private College Presidents Continue to Rise, Chronicle Survey Finds," *New York Times,* December 6, 2015, www.nytimes.com/2015/12/07/us/salaries-of-private-college-presidents-continue-to-rise-survey-finds.html.

178 **The average faculty salary:** "2015–16 Tenured/Tenure-Track Faculty Salaries Survey," HigherEd Jobs, 2016, https://www.higheredjobs .com/salary/salaryDisplay.cfm?SurveyID=37.

178 **see the university in crisis:** One of the most prescient books to analyze the crisis in the increasingly corporate university is Bill Readings, *The University in Ruins* (Cambridge, MA: Harvard University Press, 1999).

178 **Recently, Governor Scott Walker:** Steven Salzberg, "Scott Walker Takes $250 Million from U. Wisconsin, Gives $250M to Billionaire Sports Team Owners," *Forbes*, August 14, 2015, www.forbes.com /sites/stevensalzberg/2015/08/14/scott-walker-takes-250-million -from-u-wisconsin-gives-250m-to-billionaire-sports-team-owners/.

178 **UW faculty became fair game:** Nico Savidge, "UW-Madison Spent $23.6M to Keep Faculty After Recruitment Offers Surged," *Wisconsin State Journal*, October 14, 2016, http://host.madison.com /wsj/news/local/education/university/uw-madison-spent-m-to-keep -faculty-after-recruitment-offers/article_fa573122-b639-5685-87dd -da66c9b96f25.html.

179 **2017 *Equality of Opportunity Study:*** The Equality of Opportunity Project, "Highest Upward Mobility Rate Colleges," www.equality -of-opportunity.org/; "Some Colleges Have More Students from the Top 1 Percent Than the Bottom 60. Find Yours," *New York Times*, January 18, 2017, https://www.nytimes.com/interactive/2017/01/18 /upshot/some-colleges-have-more-students-from-the-top-1-percent -than-the-bottom-60.html.

180 **The media loves to dote:** Kellie Woodhouse, "Lazy Rivers and Student Debt," *Inside Higher Ed,* June 15, 2015, https://www.inside highered.com/news/2015/06/15/are-lazy-rivers-and-climbing-walls -driving-cost-college.

180 **a spike in price increases:** Siva Vaidyanathan, "A Study in Total Depravity," *The Baffler*, no. 20, 2015, http://thebaffler.com/salvos/study -total-depravity.

182 **cognitive neuroscientist Steven Pinker:** Steven Pinker, "The Trouble with Harvard," *New Republic*, https://newrepublic.com/article /119321/harvard-ivy-league-should-judge-students-standardized-tests.

182 **The wealth of Harvard:** Wendy Brown, *Undoing the Demos: Neoliberalism's Stealth Revolution* (New York: Zone Books, 2015), 199.

183 **Anderson School went private:** Jon Wiener, "UCLA Business School to Go Private; a Blow to the Public University," *The Nation,*

June 8, 2012, www.thenation.com/article/ucla-business-school-go -private-blow-public-university/.

185 **new money-saving methods:** "Reshaping Arizona State, and the Public Model," *New York Times,* April 10, 2015, www.nytimes.com /2015/04/12/education/edlife/12edl-12talk.html.

186 **Community colleges emphasize:** Center for College Affordability and Productivity, *A Summary of 25 Ways to Reduce the Cost of College* (Washington, DC: Center for College Affordability and Productivity, September 2010), http://centerforcollegeaffordability.org/uploads/25 _Ways_Summary.pdf. See also Brad Wolverton, Ben Hallman, Shane Shifflett, and Sandhya Kambhampati, "Sports at Any Cost," *Huffington Post,* November 15, 2015, http://projects.huffingtonpost.com/ncaa /sports-at-any-cost.

186 **Other ways of lowering expenses:** Vanderbilt University, *The Cost of Federal Regulatory Compliance in Higher Education: A Multi-Institutional Study* (Nashville, TN: Vanderbilt University, October 2015), https://news.vanderbilt.edu/files/Cost-of-Federal-Regulatory -Compliance-2015.pdf.

188 **students pay differential tuitions:** Helaine Olen, "Australia Gets Student Loans Right: And Why It Should Make Americans Very, Very Jealous," *Slate Magazine,* November 12, 2015, www.slate.com/articles /business/the_bills/2015/11/australia_s_student_loan_system_should _make_americans_jealous.html.

188 **A college degree confers:** Eduardo Porter, "Dropping Out of College, and Paying the Price," *New York Times,* June 25, 2013, www.nytimes.com/2013/06/26/business/economy/dropping-out-of -college-and-paying-the-price.html. See also Cathy Davidson, "Why Does College Cost So Much—and Why Do So Many Pundits Get It Wrong?" *HASTAC* (blog), August 24, 2013, www.hastac.org/blogs /cathy-davidson/2013/08/24/why-does-college-cost-so-much-and -why-do-so-many-pundits-get-it.

189 **City College of San Francisco:** Dave Berndtson, "San Francisco Becomes First City to Offer Free Community College Tuition to All Residents," *PBS NewsHour,* February 8, 2017, www.pbs.org/newshour /rundown/san-francisco-becomes-first-city-offer-free-community -college-tuition-residents/.

190 **six schools in the CUNY system:** CollegeNET, "2016 Social Mobility Index," www.socialmobilityindex.org.

190 **"Here's my prediction":** Jesse McKinley, "Cuomo Proposes Free

Tuition at New York State Colleges for Eligible Students," *New York Times,* January 3, 2017, www.nytimes.com/2017/01/03/nyregion/free-tuition-new-york-colleges-plan.html.

190 **California voters reversed:** Teresa Harrington, John Fensterwald, and Ashley Hopkinson, "Voters Back All Three Education Initiatives on California Ballot," *EdSource,* https://edsource.org/2016/voters-backing-three-california-education-initiatives-in-early-returns/572394.

191 **cost of ensuring excellence:** Christopher Newfield, "What Is New About the New American University?" *Los Angeles Review of Books,* April 5, 2015, https://lareviewofbooks.org/article/new-new-american-university/.

CHAPTER 7: THE MEASURE OF A STUDENT

193 **"You give a dog a treat":** Special thanks to Alexander Coward for generously sharing his time in a first interview, on June 30, 2016, followed subsequently by email correspondence, phone calls, and further interviews throughout 2016–2017.

195 **Butler investigated how over:** Ruth Butler, "Enhancing and Undermining Intrinsic Motivation: The Effects of Task-Involving and Ego-Involving Evaluation on Interest and Performance," *British Journal of Educational Psychology* 58 (1988): 1–14.

198 **"If you don't, we'll fire you":** Josh Logue, "Losing His Job for Teaching Too Well?" *Inside Higher Ed,* October 13, 2015, www.insidehighered.com/news/2015/10/13/popular-lecturer-berkeley-will-lose-job-despite-strong-record-promoting-student.

199 **United States has a STEM crisis:** Xianglei Chen and Matthew Soldner, *STEM Attrition: College Students' Paths Into and Out of STEM Fields* (Washington, DC: National Center for Education Statistics, Institute of Education Sciences, US Department of Education, November 2013), https://nces.ed.gov/pubs2014/2014001rev.pdf.

203 **The term *grade* seems:** Neil Postman, *Technopology: The Surrender of Culture to Technology* (New York: Knopf, 1992).

203 **Others give the credit to:** George Wilson Pierson, "Undergraduate Studies: Yale College," *A Yale Book of Numbers: Historical Statistics of the College and University 1701–1976* (New Haven, CT: Yale Office of Institutional Research, 1983), 310; Jack Schneider and Ethan Hutt, "Making the Grade: A History of the A–F

Marking Scheme," *Journal of Curriculum Studies* 46, no. 2 (2014): 201–224.

203 **The term *grade* had another:** Mary Lovett Smallwood, *An Historical Study of Examinations and Grading Systems in Early American Universities* (Cambridge, MA: Harvard University Press, 1935); "Grade," *Online Etymology Dictionary,* www.etymonline.com/index .php?term=grade.

204 **began experimenting with letter grades:** "Grade Creation," Mount Holyoke College, www.mtholyoke.edu/offices/comm/news /grade_creation.shtml.

205 **to yield an "intelligence quotient":** For a fuller account of IQ and standardized aptitude tests, see "How We Measure," in Cathy N. Davidson, *Now You See It: How the Brain Science of Attention Will Transform the Way We Live, Work, and Learn* (New York: Viking Penguin, 2011), 105–131.

206 **I. E. Finkelstein grew alarmed:** I. E. Finkelstein, *The Marking System in Theory and Practice* (Baltimore: Warwick & York, 1913).

206 **As a young chemistry teacher:** Mary Lovett Smallwood, *An Historical Study of Examinations and Grading Systems in Early American Universities* (Cambridge, MA: Harvard University Press, 1935); "Grade," *Online Etymology Dictionary.*

207 **he advocated standardized achievement:** For excellent discussions of standardized testing, see, for example: Franz Samelson, "Was Early Mental Testing: (a) Racist Inspired, (b) Objective Science, (c) A Technology for Democracy, (d) The Origin of Multiple-Choice Exams, (e) None of the Above? (Mark the RIGHT Answer)," in *Psychological Testing and American Society, 1890–1930,* ed. Michael M. Sokal (New Brunswick, NJ: Rutgers University Press, 1987), 113–127; Theodore M. Porter, *Trust in Numbers: The Pursuit of Objectivity in Science and Public Life* (Princeton, NJ: Princeton University Press, 1995); Peter Sacks, *Standardized Minds: The High Price of America's Testing Culture and What We Can Do to Change It* (New York: Da Capo Press, 2011); and Anya Kamenetz, *The Test: Why Our Schools Are Obsessed with Standardized Testing—But You Don't Have to Be* (New York: PublicAffairs, 2015).

209 **"If you had a job at McDonald's":** Alexander Coward, "Blowing the Whistle on the UC Berkeley Mathematics Department," October 11, 2015, http://alexandercoward.com/BlowingTheWhistleOnUC BerkeleyMathematics.html.

211 **in *Research in Higher Education*:** Shari L. Gnolek, Vincenzo T. Falciano, and Ralph W. Kuncl, "Modeling Change and Variation in *US News & World Report* College Rankings: What Would It Really Take to Be in the Top 20?" *Research in Higher Education* 55, no. 8 (December 1, 2014): 761–779, doi:10.1007/s11162-014-9336-9.

211 **trying to crawl back:** Nick Anderson, "Berkeley Is Facing Big Budget Trouble, 'Painful' Measures Ahead for Nation's Top Public College," *Washington Post,* February 10, 2016, https://www.washingtonpost.com/news/grade-point/wp/2016/02/10/berkeley-is-facing-big-budget-trouble-painful-measures-ahead-for-nations-top-public-college/.

212 **And it's a solitary profession:** John Ziker, "The Long, Lonely Job of Homo academicus," *Blue Review,* March 31, 2014, https://thebluereview.org/faculty-time-allocation/; Colleen Flaherty, "So Much to Do, So Little Time," *Inside Higher Ed,* April 9, 2014, https://www.insidehighered.com/news/2014/04/09/research-shows-professors-work-long-hours-and-spend-much-day-meetings; "What Do Faculty Do?" American Association of University Professors, https://www.aaup.org/issues/faculty-work-workload/what-do-faculty-do.

213 **Carnegie Classification of Institutions:** The Carnegie Classification of Institutions of Higher Education, http://carnegieclassifications.iu.edu/.

215 **Opting out of SAT/ACT:** Jonathan Lash, "Results of Removing Standardized Test Scores from College Admissions," Hampshire College, September 21, 2015, https://www.hampshire.edu/news/2015/09/21/results-of-removing-standardized-test-scores-from-college-admissions.

216 **Hampshire remains "deeply committed":** Jonathan Lash, personal correspondence with author, October 19, 2016.

217 **That is the question being:** These interviews took place in Manhattan, Kansas, on April 7–8, 2015. Student names and personal details have been changed. Special thanks to Meadowlark director of Health Services Annie Peace, the residents of Meadowlark Retirement Community, Professor Michael Wesch, and his class (past and present) for allowing me and my research assistant, Danica Savonick, to interview them and to be part of their class.

218 **"A Vision of Students Today":** Michael Wesch, "A Vision of Students Today," uploaded October 12, 2007, YouTube video, 4:44, https://www.youtube.com/watch?v=dGCJ46vyR9o.

220 **When he returned home:** Jordan Thomas, "Getting Real: Jour-
neys from a College Gap Year: Jordan Thomas: TEDxMHK," April
14, 2016, YouTube video, 15:35, https://www.youtube.com/watch?v
=ZUMMFXaM140.

220 **He went to live in Taos:** "Kansas State University Anthropology
Student Receives Marshall Scholarship to Study Food Systems, Social Sustainability," *K-State News,* November 24, 2015, www.k-state
.edu/media/newsreleases/nov15/marshallscholar112415.html.

221 **"Household" movement:** Steve Shields and LaVrene Norton, *In
Pursuit of the Sunbeam: A Practical Guide to Transformation from
Institution to Household* (Manhattan, KS: Manhattan Retirement
Foundation, 2006), back cover; change matrix, 54–55.

224 **assault against all of public:** "Ten States with Biggest Higher Education Cuts," Center on Budget and Policy Priorities, www.cbpp
.org/ten-states-with-biggest-higher-education-cuts; Michael Mitchell, "Mapping State Funding Cuts for Higher Education," Center
on Budget and Policy Priorities, March 6, 2015, www.cbpp.org/blog
/mapping-state-funding-cuts-for-higher-education.

225 **governor and legislators aggressively cut:** "Cuts to Kansas'
Higher Education System Jeopardize Our Economic Future," Center on Budget and Policy Priorities, www.cbpp.org/sites/default/files
/atoms/files/sfp_highered_ks.pdf; AP Wire and Matt Stewart, "Kansas
Legislators Approve Budget Plan," fox4kc.com, May 2, 2016, http://
fox4kc.com/2016/05/02/kansas-legislators-approve-budget-plan/.

CHAPTER 8: THE FUTURE OF LEARNING

227 **The Red House is exactly:** Special thanks to Randy Bass, Ann
Pendleton-Jullian, and all of their students and colleagues at Georgetown who allowed me to interview them on May 6, July 13, and July
24, 2016, and in multiple follow-up email and phone conversations.

229 **Jack DeGioia wants:** John DeGioia, "Advance Our Work," Designing the Future(s) of the University, Georgetown University, https://
futures.georgetown.edu/advance-our-work/.

229 **The American Enterprise Institute:** Michael B. Horn and Andrew
P. Kelly, *Moving Beyond College* (Washington, DC: Center on Higher
Education Reform, American Enterprise Institute, August 2015),
https://www.aei.org/wp-content/uploads/2015/08/Moving-Beyond
-College.pdf.

230 **US universities now contribute:** "About University Research," Association of American Universities, https://www.aau.edu/research /article.aspx?id=12010

231 **Partnerships work in all:** One of Randy Bass's closest research colleagues for innovation is Bret Eynon, a historian and the associate dean for academic affairs and founder of the Center for Teaching and Learning at LaGuardia Community College (CUNY). See Randy Bass and Bret Eynon, *Open and Integrative: Designing Liberal Education for the New Digital Ecosystem* (Washington, DC: Association of American Colleges and Universities, 2016), https://secure .aacu.org/store/detail.aspx?id=GMSDIG.

231 **human jobs will be automated:** Bryan Dean Wright, "Robots Are Coming for Your Job," *Los Angeles Times,* March 28, 2016, www .latimes.com/opinion/op-ed/la-oe-wright-robots-jobs-data-mining -20160328-story.html.

232 **"Principles and Challenges of Childhood":** Provost Robert Groves, "Pedagogical Innovation Made Real," *Designing the Future(s) of the University* (blog), March 18, 2016, https://futures.georgetown .edu/pedagocial-innovation-made-real/.

234 **"Designers don't *think* their":** Bill Burnett and Dave Evans, *Designing Your Life: How to Build a Well-Lived, Joyful Life* (New York: Knopf, 2016), xxv.

234 **Pendleton-Jullian is somewhat skeptical:** Ann Pendleton-Jullian and John Seely Brown, *Pragmatic Imagination: Single from Design Unbound* (Blurb, 2016).

235 **the legendary former chief scientist:** "About John Seely Brown," www.johnseelybrown.com/bio.html.

235 **generation as "excellent sheep":** William Deresiewicz, *Excellent Sheep: The Miseducation of the American Elite and the Way to a Meaningful Life* (New York: Free Press, 2014).

237 **perhaps the most shameful event:** Scott Jaschik, "What the Protests Mean," *Inside Higher Ed,* November 16, 2015, https:// www.insidehighered.com/news/2015/11/16/experts-consider-what -protests-over-racial-tensions-mean.

241 **Patrick Awuah, returned home:** Special thanks to Patrick Awuah for an interview on August 24, 2016, and numerous email exchanges over the course of 2016.

245 **was named a MacArthur Fellow:** "MacArthur Fellows Program:

Patrick Awuah," MacArthur Foundation, September 28, 2015, https://www.macfound.org/fellows/929/#sthash.IfoUzZOU.dpuf.

246 **American Association of University Professors:** "The Status of Non-Tenure-Track Faculty," American Association of University Professors, June 1993, https://www.aaup.org/report/status-non-tenure-track-faculty; "Background Facts on Contingent Faculty," American Association of University Professors, https://www.aaup.org/issues/contingency/background-facts.

250 **moving seven-minute video:** Estefany1987, "I Am Going to College," uploaded May 25, 2016, Vimeo video, 7:25, https://vimeo.com/168101620.

250 **The videographer posing these:** Special thanks to all of the remarkably talented, dedicated, and serious students who shared their ideas with me for the conclusion to this book during the summer and fall of 2016. Although I refer to them only by first name for reasons of privacy, I wish I could honor them more. They give me hope for the future.

TEN TIPS FOR TRANSFORMING YOUR INSTITUTION

271 **do not come from white-collar backgrounds:** Philip W. Jackson, *Life in Classrooms* (New York: Holt, Rinehart and Winston, 1968). See also Buffy Smith, *Mentoring At-Risk Students Through the Hidden Curriculum of Higher Education* (Lanham, MD: Lexington Books, 2015).

INDEX

CATHY N. DAVIDSON has taught at a range of institutions, from community college to the Ivy League. She was at Duke for twenty-five years, where she became the university's (and the nation's) first vice provost for interdisciplinary studies. In 2014, Davidson moved to the City University of New York, where she is founding director of the Futures Initiative and a distinguished professor at the Graduate Center. She is cofounder and codirector of the world's first and oldest academic social network, the Humanities, Arts, Science, and Technology Alliance and Collaboratory (HASTAC.org, known as "Haystack").

Davidson has published more than twenty books, including *Revolution and the Word: The Rise of the Novel in America* and *Now You See It: How the Brain Science of Attention Will Transform the Way We Live, Work, and Learn*. She is the 2016 recipient of the Ernest L. Boyer Award for "significant contributions to higher education." In 2019, *The New Education* was awarded the annual Frederic W. Ness Book Award by the Association of American Colleges and Universities, and, in 2021, the Council of Colleges of Arts and Sciences presented Davidson with its annual Arts and Sciences Advocacy Award. She served on the board of directors of Mozilla, was appointed by President Barack Obama to the National Council on the Humanities, and has twice keynoted the Nobel Prize Committee's Forum on the Future of Higher Education.